The Pursuit of Power in Popular Music

NEW YORK   LONDON   TORONTO   SYDNEY   TOKYO   SINGAPORE

Moguls

and

Madmen

Jory Farr

SIMON & SCHUSTER

HOUSTON PUBLIC LIBRARY

SIMON & SCHUSTER
Rockefeller Center
1230 Avenue of the Americas
New York, New York 10020

Copyright © 1994 by Jory Farr

SIMON & SCHUSTER and colophon are registered
trademarks of Simon & Schuster Inc.

Designed by Hyun Joo Kim

Manufactured in the United States of America

10   9   8   7   6   5   4   3   2   1

Library of Congress Cataloging-in-Publication Data

Farr, Jory.
   Moguls and madmen : the pursuit of power in popular music / Jory
Farr.
      p.   cm.
    1. Sound recording industry—United States.   2. Popular music—
United States—History and criticism.   I. Title.
ML3790.F37   1994
781.64'0973'09045—dc20   94-11357
                                                   CIP
                                                    MN

ISBN 0-671-73946-8

Acknowledgments

My thanks go out first to all the people whose love and encouragement made it possible for me to write this book. They include above all my wife, Jane, who's always believed in me, helped transcribe interviews when she should've been in bed, read over chapters, jacked into Lexis, shared her legal expertise and commonsense wisdom and gave me many a wonderful back and neck rub that sent me into sleep; and my son, Zachary, who, at age two, already reminds me each day why I am here.

Deep thanks must go to my parents, Marshall and Beatrice Farr, who helped shape my moral values and gave me my first taste of love's sweetness and the beauty of language; and my brother, Evan, who reached out to be friends amid all our obvious differences.

And I send special love and thanks to my aunt Louise, whose radiant love and deep understanding of life have fed me down the years, and my uncle Gerry, a wise elder.

Friendships nourish talents and opposition is the secret

6

Acknowledgments

strength of friendship. So were it not for Robb Fulcher, Berkley Hudson, Pascal Nabet-Meyer, Jim Kammerud, David Bloom, Steve Pokin, Ken Symington, Scott Klar, Chuck Bauerlein, Hector Aristizabal, and my friends in the Rolling Earth Men's Council, my life would be diminished.

And I never could've remained as centered as I did were it not for drumming with my friend Ernesto Salcedo, who knows the ancient rhythms and shared them with me. The music fed my soul and the talks that followed deepened my understanding of all music.

My thanks also go to Paulo Mattioli, master drummer, teacher, friend and instrument maker, who built my djembe and started me on another musical journey.

This book would not have been possible if Mel Opotowsky hadn't believed in my talents and submitted my work for the Pulitzers, giving me the space and time to be in two worlds. And I thank Richard De Atley and Sally Ann Maas for their patience and understanding through the last three jangly years.

My vision of life was recently deepened by a number of great teachers—Malidoma Somé, Michael Meade, Jack Kornfield, Luis Rodriguez, Onaje Benjamin, Dadisi Sanyika and Miguel Rivera, who shared their wisdom with me and ninety-three other men up in the Malibu Mountains.

I must thank Jim Griffin, who eight years ago helped plant the seed of an idea that became the book. Also, I am grateful to people like Bruce Raeburn, Michael P. Smith, Dick Shurman, Bill Bentley, Bob Koester, George Massenburg and Bill Ivey, who know the history of the music; and writers like Tom Moon, Greil Marcus, Greg Kot and Rick Mitchell, who've talked music and shared their insights with me down the years.

I am grateful to my agent, Sandra Choron, who helped shape the ultimate direction of the book and gave me hope even as I considered giving up; Eric Steel, for a new start; Lydia Buechler and Steve Messina, who carefully and thoughtfully copyedited the manuscript; Eric Rayman, for legal help; and David Shipley, who believed in my talent from the beginning.

Naturally, I thank all the people who let me use their voices in this book, though they may not have fully understood just what they were getting into.

Great musicians and storytellers, in this world and the other world, made me take up music and inspire me always. So let some of them be praised: the Neville Brothers, Van Morrison, Bob Dylan, Muddy Waters, James Brown, Tom Waits, Howlin' Wolf, Otis Rush, Johann Sebastian Bach, Robert Johnson, Richard Thompson, Thelonious Monk, D'Gary, Charles Brown, Los Muñequitos de Matanzas, Huun-Huur-Tu, the Meters, Bruce Springsteen, Joni Mitchell, Charlie Parker, Sonny Rollins, Burning Spear, Bessie Smith, Joe Henderson, R.E.M., Hank Williams, the Wild Tchoupitoulas, Otis Redding, Duke Ellington, Miles Davis, Professor Longhair, Prince, the Holmes Brothers, Billie Holiday, Sweet Honey in the Rock, Shirley Horn, Miriam Makeba, Jimi Hendrix, Buddy Guy, Bill Evans, Clifton Chenier, Jimmie Dale Gilmore, Boozoo Chavis, Bob Marley, Ray Charles, Joe Higgs, Aretha Franklin, John Hiatt, Rickie Lee Jones, Lightnin' Hopkins, Irma Thomas, Arthur Alexander, Etta James, Fela Kuti, Jerry Lee Lewis, Pasty Cline, Big Joe Turner, Jimmie Rodgers and Ma Rainey.

Beyond all this, I thank the Creator, who gave me whatever talent and wisdom I have.

To Janie and Zachary,

who kept me sane and
got me through it all

*The elders say depression is
the absence of rhythm.*

—Malidoma Patrice Somé

*Where love rules, there is no will to power; and
where power predominates, there love is lacking.
The one is the shadow of the other.*

—Carl Jung

Contents

14

Contents

Prologue

Rock and roll started as a jubilant shout: a promise of freedom hidden in the mongrel melding of black blues and white hillbilly music. But underneath that explosion of ecstasy was a deep well of sorrow. For the blues of the Delta, the literal and metaphorical river that had given rock life, was the cry of African-Americans oppressed—a lament of the human soul as profound as anything this country has ever produced.

It was hard to conceive of American popular music at all without that cry. And rock, the dominant music for the past two generations, was impossible to imagine without the intermarriage of black and white culture: the terrifying howl of Robert Johnson mingled with the ghostly wail of Hank Williams and Jimmie Rodgers; the butt-shaking, juke-joint boogie of Big Joe Turner and Wynonie Harris crossed with the hellfire rockabilly of Merrill Moore and Jerry Lee Lewis. Each culture that had shaped American music—and you had to add the Latin and Caribbean cultures coming up through the generations—was born of joy and sorrow. Each had contributed to the wild dance that was our national music.

Yet by the mid-1970s rock and R&B had veered far from their original roots. Great musicians had always sprung from regional soil, and music itself sounded different from one area of the country to the next; but record companies, intent on creating the illusion of a homogeneous pop culture—on making people assimilate—had calculatedly sought to erase cultural differences.

Listening to the synthetic, monotonous beat of most modern R&B and rock, it was hard to imagine that it had descended from the ancient, fluid African clave and call and response, which always triggered the interaction between musicians. But then the mechanical frequencies of popular music reflected the sped-up, dehumanizing rhythms of modern machine culture, which has fouled the Earth, poisoned the waters and robbed us of our very spirit.

Even now, this musical desensitization is still very much alive. Explaining to me in 1992 how he'd carefully removed the soulful, nasal quality of the vocals that were traditionally part of country and bluegrass music, thereby making the singing "acceptable" to a mass audience, Nashville music mogul Jimmy Bowen put it simply: "We took the honk out of it." Yet vapid as most of it was, country music was still connected, albeit tenuously, to a culture and a people with a shared set of values and meanings.

Rock had once had a common set of meanings; it signified rage and rebellion—even political resistance. But the culture had fragmented a thousand different ways and the reference points—the deep meanings—had unraveled. The mass pop audience still consumed the music, but only because the audience, music critic Greil Marcus observed, had been carefully "organized into market segments—complex and recombined segments of age, race, class and gender—efficiently predictable, containable markets that can be sold identity, or anyway, self-recognition, packaged as music."

Forty years ago it had been different. In the 1950s, hundreds of independent labels in the United States recorded an astonishing array of music that had authentic origins in the culture—from the ferocious Delta-inflected blues of Chicago's Chess Records to the protoplasmic soul of Memphis's Stax/Volt Records to the influential postwar R&B and jazz of Los Angeles's Aladdin Records. But in 1994, six major conglomerates—Time Warner, Sony, Thorn-EMI, Matsushita, PolyGram and Bertelsmann—accounted for 96 percent of the business. And the conglomerates thought of music in global terms, fretting that rap and country, now in ascendance, didn't export well.

Traditionally, it was independent record companies that nurtured much of the greatest music. But now the indie that managed to produce a hit or two was almost sure to get swallowed up by one of the majors. That process was already occurring in endless joint distribution deals; the fear of not being the first to exploit a regional phenomenon seemed to fuel the whole industry. As corporations, not individuals, took responsibility for making records, the music inevitably suffered.

If you loved music it was hard not to be cynical. The people who had brought the great geniuses of American regional music into the emerging pop culture had mainly loved music. Men like Ahmet Ertegun, who worked with everyone from Ray Charles to Big Joe Turner; John Hammond, the A&R scout who had discovered Billie Holiday and Count Basie; and Sam Phillips, the Memphis DJ turned producer who had given the world Elvis Presley and Jerry Lee Lewis—they weren't lured to their life's work by money, power and fame. They were driven by the beauty of the music, the simple poetry of the lyrics and the blazing intensity of the artists, certain they had found something wholly amazing even if the rest of the country dismissed it all as so much "nigger" music. They immersed themselves in African-American culture and schooled themselves in musical history. They helped produce some of the most astonishing music ever recorded.

But in the 1990s few visionaries were left. The most powerful people in the field—men like EMI Music CEO Jim Fifield, who came from General Mills, and Warner Music Group chairman Robert Morgado, a former chief of staff to New York governor Hugh Carey—were essentially bean counters with little knowledge of music. And most of the new generation of A&R[1] people, drawn from radio, advertising and promotion, were attracted to the power and glitter of celebrity, not the radiant soul of the music. Invariably, they knew little or nothing about blues and jazz, much less the music of Africa, Asia, Europe and Latin America. Many lacked even the most fundamental grasp of songwriting, harmony and arranging.

The music business still had smart, dedicated people. The trouble was, they were forced to operate in a ruthless world where short-term profits were the only goal. Music, which had once connected all of us to a spirit world, was now nothing more than a commodity. It had become inextricably entwined with the media-entertainment business: a many-tentacled, agglomerated monster that competed fiercely for international leverage and quick return on investment. And even the most powerful record men weren't immune to being crushed in the new environment.

But who were these record men? The movie business had a long-standing mythology. Americans showed interest in the film moguls' lives just as sports fans did in the personal fortunes of the powerful people who owned franchises. Comparatively speaking, though, most of the music industry was faceless. A relative handful of figures—the Ahmet Erteguns, Sam Phillipses and David Geffens—had captured the national imagination; but the rest, with rare exceptions, mostly insulated themselves from the prying eyes of the media.

None of which was surprising. Rocked by scandals—from the sexual harassment charges that led to shameful exits by top executives at Geffen and Island Records to stories of mobsters controlling the industry laid out in books like *Hit Men* and *Stiffed: A True Story of MCA, the Music Business and the Ma-*

---

[1] The letters stand for "artist and repertoire." A&R people are responsible for the music that goes out on a label's records.

Prologue

fia—pop music's power brokers were legitimately scared of the press. It took me nearly a year to get anyone of power to consent to be part of this book. And first meetings tended to elicit cynical responses. "This isn't another *Hit Men?*" Elektra Entertainment chairman Bob Krasnow[2] asked me before I could pull out a tape recorder. And when I said it wasn't, he blew out a cumulus cloud of cigar smoke and eyed me skeptically.

In choosing whom to profile, I didn't go purely by clout; such a book would be boring. Besides, who has the most "juice," as power is commonly known, changes from year to year. That being the case, I looked for a mix of archetypes and a variety of musical settings. Liberty Records president Jimmy Bowen, Nashville's grand pooh-bah, lives in a culture altogether different from the world of Eazy-E, the gangsta-rap impresario, president and founder of Ruthless Records. But both men nonetheless embody the style and substance of the cultures that spawned them. And both enjoy wielding power.

This book is *about* power and personality—and the interplay between those two forces. But it's also about the enchantment and danger that lie therein. Presuming themselves almighty, knowing they could treat people rudely and get away with it, most of the music moguls I dealt with loved to test the limits of their power. They made you phone twenty times before answering a call, scheduled meetings only to break them off at the last minute (without explanation) and whenever possible sought to put you off balance. They made their own rules only to break them and make new ones.

At times I felt like Odysseus, caught up in a bizarre new land, encountering people with their own strange rituals, initiations and ruling mythology. I sensed how easy it would be, under the soulless spell of this kind of power, to be corrupted. But then I would realize the marginal, isolated existence of these people. For the power they possessed was the same power

---

[2] Krasnow and Sire Records president Seymour Stein initially agreed to be profiled in the book, but later failed to cooperate.

that made their lives empty, the same power that would devour some of them.

There are women in this book, but not powerful executives. Though many talented women work in the field, the inner circle I encountered is a virtually all-male club, where sexism is rampant. The stories women have told about surviving in the business are harrowing—but they are stories for another, different book that deserves to be written soon.

By the same token, bigotry runs deep in this world. The most powerful record men are mostly white and many of them live in denial and ignorance. When I told the arrogant president of a major label that he knew little about African-American music and might not even recognize a great young artist coming up, he scowled at me and told me to turn off my tape recorder. "I'm glad we stole their music," he said with disgust. "I *hate* blues and jazz."

The record industry came of age during a tumultuous time, a period in history when America fought two world wars, gave birth to jazz, founded a recording industry, sent men and women into outer space, unraveled many of the mysteries of the atomic universe and built itself into the richest, most powerful nation in the world. The people who ran the business were able to use music to carve out a national identity from what was once a bouillabaisse of regional cultures. And maybe more important, the best of them relied on their instincts—not the voice of faceless committees—to make records.

That many of my subjects are Jewish is no accident. Like the first film moguls, who were all Jewish and just a step away from the shtetls of Eastern Europe, many of the dominant figures in pop music are also Jews, drawn into a field that anti-Semites long considered beneath their dignity.

The seismic shifts that have changed the music business have all occurred swiftly. In the more than three years it took to write this book, Virgin Records and Motown Records, the last two major independent record companies left, were sold to PolyGram for nine hundred million and three hundred million dollars, respectively. In 1991, SoundScan, the first accurate way of measuring sales, was introduced, forever changing the way record companies did business. By providing weekly sales figures that are the music industry equivalent of the Nielsen ratings, SoundScan allowed record companies to open their big releases the way movie studios open films—amid expensive barrages of hype.

In some respects, artists appeared to be gaining power. Between March 1991 and September 1992, five of the biggest stars in pop music—Janet Jackson, Michael Jackson, the Rolling Stones, Madonna and Prince—signed contracts valued at between forty-five and sixty-five million dollars each. And most of these superstars have their own labels. But young musicians are still easy marks for unscrupulous managers, lawyers and labels.

As for the entertainment conglomerates, they are gearing up for the biggest revolution of all, which is coming quickly due to the feverish pace of technology: the direct sale of music over fiber-optic lines or via cable and/or satellite. Such a revolution is going to place record labels and entertainment monoliths in head-on competition with phone companies, cable giants, electronics conglomerates and other corporations with access to digital transmission.

This isn't some futurist's fantasy either. Already, the technology is available. Right now fiber-optic lines allow for CDs to be manufactured anywhere. And armed with a smart TV-computer and modem setup, you could pull CD selections off a menu and have them digitally downloaded to a blank CD— even as the album jacket and art come in over the laser printer in the spare bedroom. What is holding such a system back are the complex and controversial corporate alliances that are necessary, which pose threats to the very structure and existence of record/distribution companies and retailers, not to mention performers' royalty compensation. How real are these threats?

In May 1993, Blockbuster Entertainment, the country's largest video retailer and owner of some four hundred record stores and a rapidly growing number of amphitheaters, teamed up with IBM and announced a joint venture geared to manufacturing laser discs in stores. They had merely to announce the venture before the major labels raised a howl of protest. But no one disagreed with the estimate that soon, perhaps by the end of the century, such a system would be available, raising the next obvious question: Why, with a computer, would stores, much less record companies, be needed at all?

Yet for all the technological and corporate shock waves coming down the pike, the business is still filled with colorful people: rebels, loners, egomaniacs and operators. The son of a dirt-poor Baptist preacher who went on to play with Elvis Presley, Tony Brown rose from rural North Carolina to the top of Nashville's power elite. And Eazy-E used the vulgar poetry and jackhammer beats of gangsta rap to found an empire that took him from the mean streets of Compton to the gated palazzos of white wealth north of Malibu.

Benny Medina escaped L.A.'s black, gang-infested streets to become a record, film and TV producer. And Tom Zutaut has gone from being a high school radio freak with a passion for hard rock to being a multimillionaire superscout and vice-president for David Geffen.

This book is not for them, however. It's for all the musicians—and the musicians to come—who want to know what they're up against.

CHAPTER 1

Tom Zutaut and the Nymphs

The Sad, Strange
Ballad of Inger
Lorre

Tom Zutaut was sitting in his Geffen Records office one afternoon in March 1991 when Inger Lorre of the Nymphs stormed in. Zutaut, the A&R man who'd signed her to the label, had seen her do all sorts of strange and outrageous things since he'd known her. But he would never forget what happened moments later.

Enraged that he had allowed her record producer to be pulled away just weeks before her own album would be completed—to mix Guns N' Roses' long overdue *Use Your Illusion* CDs—and enraged that her band hadn't been allowed to play live for some two years, the Nymphs' lead singer decided she'd had enough. She climbed atop Zutaut's desk, pulled down her shorts and proceeded to piss, invoking the name of each band member she felt he'd betrayed. Always dramatic, Lorre had brought flowers along and let one flutter down in each of their memories: guitarists Sam Merrick and Jet, drummer Alex Kirst and bassist Cliff D.

"This is for me," the red-haired rock diva finally hissed, throwing the last flower down for herself as Zutaut stared into her crotch, watching in amazement. "And don't ever *piss* on my fucking band again!" With that, she hiked up her shorts and stalked out of his office.

"Can you imagine having a woman standing on your desk doing that?" Zutaut asked me a few weeks after the incident, as we sat in his office and listened to songs, played at molar-twisting intensity, from the Nymphs' forthcoming album. "It had me wondering, next time she was upset or angry, what would she do? Would she drive her car through the front door of Geffen Records? Inger used to call me in the middle of the night, mad about this or that. It's been grueling getting this music out of her. But I just deal with it because she's a genius."

With long blond hair, a reddish beard and a thick, massive head set atop a bearish body, Zutaut looked like some rock and roll version of Falstaff. His soft, doughy voice and his baby face made him look androgynous. But he had a cunning smile, steely blue eyes and a swaggering arrogance. And his cherubic countenance belied a ferocious competitiveness.

In a secretive business in which scenes combust and self-destruct in the relative wink of an eye and batting zero for twenty is no failure if the next band sells a few million CDs, Zutaut was the closest thing to a Ted Williams. Seven of the bands he'd signed, from hard-rock icons Guns N' Roses and Mötley Crüe to folk-rocker Edie Brickell and Japanese New Age synthesist Kitaro, had become stars, with platinum and multi-platinum records. Guns N' Roses' first two records alone sold some twenty million copies, generating as much as $150 million in profit for Geffen Records.

All this had made Zutaut a rock and roll player. But Guns N' Roses was established and Zutaut couldn't afford to rest on his laurels. What made David Geffen pay his enormous salary, more than a million dollars a year plus even larger bonuses, were new bands that came out of nowhere and sold millions of records. And that's why Zutaut, or Zoot, as he was known by his bands and friends, was willing to put up with Inger Lorre's strange, sometimes disturbing behavior.

It was nothing new. For years he had witnessed the crazy, unpredictable, frequently self-destructive behavior of Axl Rose, leader of Guns N' Roses, a wild, druggy tribe of Hollywood headbangers Zutaut had signed after hearing the band perform at Hollywood's Troubadour. Zutaut had seen police subdue Rose with taser guns, after the singer had taken an overdose of

PCP and worked himself into a rage. He'd stayed up through the night when Rose, who'd overdosed more than once, was at death's door, doctors pumping his stomach.

All this was normal. As an A&R scout, Zutaut circulated in a subterranean world filled with misfits, scenesters, hustlers and drug-addicted musicians. Nirvana, also signed to Geffen,[1] was the perfect example. One of the acclaimed rock bands of the nineties, it was fronted by Kurt Cobain, an admitted junkie who, with his drug-addicted wife, Courtney Love, had just sired a child.[2] Zutaut hated drugs. Only occasionally did he even drink. But who could say that an artist's creativity wasn't somehow entwined with the strange visions drugs or madness brought? Van Gogh cut his ear off, Coleridge smoked opium and many of the biggest rock stars, from Jim Morrison to Lou Reed, experimented with hard drugs.

In that sense, Zutaut was different from many of his peers. Most A&R people preferred to work with established artists— bands who were proven entities and could deliver records on time. Yet new bands were what always drove the music business. And new bands, especially rock and roll bands likely to create ferociously unsettling music, were invariably composed of troubled souls. The best A&R men had to be comfortable with that or they wouldn't last a week.

Zutaut had first run into Lorre at a Chrysalis Records party in December 1989. It was a typical industry affair, a buzzing hive of promotion and marketing executives and A&R men mixed in with mailroom clerks, musicians and scenesters. A pretty boring party, Zutaut thought, until he noticed a thin, beautiful red-haired sylph dressed in a black leotard, combat boots, a brown velvet jacket and a Russian cap with colored feathers exploding out of her hair.

---

[1] Nirvana was signed by Gary Gersh, then one of Zutaut's two A&R rivals at Geffen, now president of Capitol Records.

[2] Cobain and Love underwent drug rehabilitation and were in and out of substance-abuse clinics. Cobain committed suicide in the early spring of 1994.

"She was this shining light in a room of dullards," Zutaut told me one night late in the summer of 1991, when we were sitting in the living room of his Malibu Canyon house. "So I went up to her and said, 'Who are you?' And she said, 'I'm Inger Lorre. Who the hell are you?' I said, 'What are you—a rock and roll singer?' And she said, 'Yeah, how did you know?'

" 'I have a funny feeling about you, and I can't tell you why,' " Zutaut remembered telling Lorre, " 'but I think we're going to sell millions of records one day. When you get a tape, send it to me.' "

Four months later, Zutaut got a Nymphs demo from Lorre. He couldn't believe the bestial roar on the cassette came from the waif of a woman he'd met. The songs were raw, the recording quality primitive. But the sound was volcanic—the most aggressive singing he'd ever heard coming from a female. One of Zutaut's assistants warned him Lorre would be trouble, noting that she was unstable, given to strange behavior. But Zutaut couldn't resist the challenge.

Lorre oozed charisma, and charisma, Zutaut knew from experience, was half the game in rock and roll. Charisma was what set apart most successful rock groups from the hordes of wanna-bes. Lorre might be trouble, but Zutaut prided himself on being able to handle tantrums, threats, rants and frantic calls at three in the morning—as long as there was the promise of a payoff. And the Nymphs, whose sound prefigured the nineties girl grunge to come, could be huge. All he had to do, Zutaut figured, was keep Lorre from self-destructing.

To hear Zutaut tell it, Lorre was a raving lunatic when she wasn't a genius: a witchy trickster who shot heroin and scattered chaos in her wake. Early on, he said, he got a taste of what the singer was about when she invited him back to her Hollywood apartment.

"She showed me all these naked pictures of herself and her boyfriend—the two of them fucking," Zutaut recalled. "And she told me she had a ring through her clitoris."

The ring had an allegory to it. When she and her boyfriend[3] had split up, Lorre marked the occasion by having her engagement ring melted down and pierced through her vagina—a reminder that lust should never rule her life. That was what Zutaut claimed Lorre had told him. But Lorre had a very different story to tell.

"He asked to see pictures of me," she said. "Me and my boyfriend had done this nude photo shoot with a photographer named Greg Norman, who was really famous, and I showed them to Tom. But I don't have any ring through my vagina. Tom Zutaut's a liar. He's a pig."

In fact, Lorre's account of her budding relationship with her new A&R man is shockingly different from Zutaut's. According to Lorre, Zutaut started acting odd right after he signed the Nymphs[4] and commenced taking her to the Ivy, his favorite restaurant in Beverly Hills and a place known for attracting Hollywood's stars and power brokers.

"That first night he started putting his hands all over me," Lorre said. "And each time he did it more and more. And I felt, 'Oh, Jesus, I'm in this really deep. I let him touch my knee last time, so I have to let him touch my thigh this time.' And then he'd touch my arm and my shoulder. I felt, 'This is what I have to do as a woman, because women can't get ahead. So I'll play this stupid game. . . .' I was just a Jersey girl who was definitely starstruck. I'd never seen that part of Hollywood. Tom would tell me what I had to order, and eat like a Roman and order three desserts. But I would just order a salad and stare at all these luminaries around us."

Lorre said she accompanied Zutaut many times to the Ivy. On each occasion, she said, he would come on to her. "He'd

---

[3] Lorre's boyfriend in question was the late Chris Schlosshardt, who was in a group called the Sea Hags.
[4] The Nymphs were signed for more than eight hundred thousand dollars, according to Lorre. Geffen wouldn't comment on the amount of the advance.

say, 'You could have this all the time. I could make life really easy for you. You're really beautiful. I have a place in Hawaii.' In elevators, he'd try to put his mouth on me. And when he was hugging me he would always try to cop a feel. He was disgusting, he was sleazy. . . . He sexually abused me in many ways. He touched me, he said horrible things. He'd bring me on trips and buy me all these clothes and then be all over me."

When Zutaut invited Lorre over to his Hollywood Hills house, a week or so after meeting her, he cooked her dinner. Conversation, according to Lorre, was anything but normal.

"Tom said when he signed me that he knew me from before, from ancient Egypt—because I was 'the keeper of the cats' and he was the Pharaoh two thousand or three thousand years ago. He also told me that a UFO landed in his backyard and Jesus Christ came out and told him to sign Axl Rose and that's why he knew to sign Guns N' Roses. I mean, I didn't know if he was mad or he was playing at trying to be mad or if he thought that stuff impressed me or what. I still don't know to this day."

"I'm not going to answer the accusations of a madwoman. It's all lies. Why print lies?" Zutaut said when I told him of Inger's charges. "This is an insane person that's been locked up in a nuthouse. I'm not interested in the slightest. It's all horseshit. She's been doing this ever since she got dropped. She's bitter."

But later, when he'd calmed down, he talked about their history together. At no time, Zutaut said, did he ever make any sexual overtures to Lorre. And while he remembered taking her to the Ivy "a couple of times," he said it was at her initiation.

"She would call and ask if I could take her and one of her boyfriends, maybe Johnny Depp or whoever she was dating, to the Ivy. And she would meet me there. But I never touched her. Nothing ever happened."

As for talk of ancient Egypt and reincarnation, Zutaut claimed their discussions had a completely different tenor.

"Inger was taking vocal lessons from some guy at the time. And she said, 'He [the voice teacher] claimed he knew you in another life and that he knew me too. And we were all together in ancient Egypt.' And I said to Inger, 'It's possible. That could in fact be true.' But *she* was the one who told *me* that she lived in ancient Egypt and was 'the keeper of the cats.' She insisted that she knew me in this other lifetime and all I said was that it was possible. I *do* believe in reincarnation, by the way. I believe in intertwining lives down the aeons. I believe that as a matter of course."

But Zutaut denied that he and Lorre ever discussed how he signed Guns N' Roses. "I never told her that a UFO landed in my backyard, although I might've talked to her about UFOs."

In any event, Lorre claims that Zutaut invited her over again, a week later, and this time she asked if she could bring her guitarist, Sam Merrick. "I wanted to see if he'd say the same things. And he did. He filleted some swordfish out on his porch and . . . pointed out where the UFO landed in his backyard. He said, 'That's where it landed. It was a beam of enormous white light.' Sam was looking down at the floor, about to crack up laughing. But even Sam could tell he was creepy."

If Lorre offered little resistance, she said it was because she was scared. Zutaut, after all, controlled the band's fate. Moreover, in the world of rock and roll, he was a major player—an executive at one of the most powerful labels in the world and a person who could make or break a music career.

"I felt like I had to let him put his hands all over me. I felt he was my ticket to success. . . . A lot of feminists would say, 'Hey, you should've never let him touch your knee in the first place.' But if this guy's gonna meet with me next week and give me eight hundred thousand dollars, I'm gonna let him touch my knee."

Lorre's accusations of sexual advances by Zutaut[5] wouldn't be the first time charges of improper sexual behavior were leveled against an executive working at Geffen Records. Marko J. Babineau, the onetime manager of David Geffen's DGC label

---

[5] Lorre first told me of Zutaut's alleged sexual advances in December 1993, well after she'd parted company with Geffen Records.

and head of promotion for Geffen Records, resigned September 4, 1991, after his twenty-eight-year-old secretary, Penny Muck, charged that he'd masturbated in front of her in her office, ejaculating "onto a magazine she was reading."[6] And Babineau wasn't the only pop music bigwig accused of sexual misconduct. In a story that would appear on the front page of the *Los Angeles Times* November 3, 1991, two other power industry executives—Jeff Aldrich, a former vice-president of A&R for RCA, and Mike Bone, a promotion hotshot who had been president of three major labels—were implicated in sexual-harassment complaints. RCA fired Aldrich, and Bone left Island Records in December 1990, not long after the alleged incident of harassment occurred.[7]

Beyond the sexual overtures, Lorre claimed, Zutaut also meddled in her personal life, telling her she couldn't have a boyfriend because it was going to ruin her career. "That's the reason I broke up with Josh Richman, who was my boyfriend. Tom would call me at Josh's house. Every single night. Every night and every morning. Not only just to check on me, but to bother us if anything was going on. Finally we would just turn the answering machine off. We would have like ten messages on there from Tom."

"He struck me as the fat kid who never got any pussy," said Richman, an actor, writer and Hollywood scenester who dated Lorre for a time and was friends with Guns N' Roses[8] and other

---

[6] Sources at Geffen told the *Los Angeles Times* that Babineau had sexually harassed other female employees at the label as early as 1984, when he was appointed to head up promotion at Geffen Records. Benjamin Schonbrun, Muck's attorney, also alleged that Geffen Records "had knowledge of the deviant behavior of one of its executives and did not take appropriate measures to ensure a safe and sexual-harassment-free environment at Geffen for years."

[7] Bone was accused by Lori Harris, a former administrative assistant at Island, of making sexual advances at an industry party and firing her for refusing to give in to his demands. Bone went on to became copresident of Mercury Records.

[8] Richman appeared in such films as *River's Edge* and *Heathers*. He also worked on some of Guns N' Roses' videos.

famous actors and musicians in Hollywood. "He definitely meddled in her life. . . . He wanted her, he definitely wanted her. Any guy that gets to a really charismatic girl and makes her have a huge career doesn't want anyone else to have the benefits of this girl's career while fucking her. He wants them. If it's not a given in the A&R world, it's a given with Tom Zutaut. And I can tell you this right now, he *wanted* Inger Lorre. I don't know what he did. She was so nuts that he could always say that he was just coddling her; he could always say that she led him on. But the reality is that he fucking bullshitted me and tried to get me out of the picture all the time. . . . But what happened to him—this is the scary thing. He really wanted to be with her and realized he wasn't going to be able to. And he also realized that it backfired . . . the more unhappy [Inger] got, the further she got into dope."

When I brought up Richman's account of those days, Zutaut bristled.

"Josh likes to attach himself to people of fame or notoriety. It's a pretty sad role at the end of the day. But I never meddled in their life. Seeing him was actually a good thing. He used to help Inger get to gigs at times. But their relationship split apart. Towards the end of their relationship, they got fairly abusive towards each other. I remember him calling me up and saying, 'I can't take any more shit from this bitch. I'm bailing.'"

No matter who was telling the truth, no one would dispute that, long before Zutaut met her, Inger Lorre was living the sort of archetypal life that spawned rock's troubled souls.

"I've had a really screwed-up life," Lorre said the first time I ever talked to her. "My parents didn't really understand me. They sent me to many, many shrinks. But I had an uncle, an orthodontist, who took me around. He turned me onto the Who, Black Sabbath, Led Zeppelin. Then he killed himself. He told me I was going to be a star; at least he fed my dreams. But my parents used to buy me chemistry sets and microscopes.

They bought me a metal detector. They didn't understand me at all."

Though her parents seemed normal enough—both her mother and father were computer scientists—Lorre hardly had a typical childhood growing up in upper-middle-class Old Bridge, New Jersey. At five, she was an unusual kid, into her own world, not all that interested in playing with other children. She recalled playing her mother's only two rock albums— the Rolling Stones' *Through the Past Darkly* and the Beatles' *Revolver*—"until they had that 'melty' smell.

"The beginning of '2000 Light Years from Home' just really scared me. And I thought, 'If this could scare me, I want to scare other people.' I lived very much in a dream world. The Nymphs is a space I created where I can be this singer. My reality is different from other people's. Some people think I'm insane."

For a while, in grade school, Lorre wanted to be an anthropologist, and a class trip that took her to the Metropolitan Museum, where she saw exhibits on Egypt, left a deep impression on her. "We saw the Pharaoh's tombs and I remember I didn't want to leave. It was something beyond words. I cried when they took me away."

In high school, Lorre had dozens of boyfriends, most of them musicians or what she called "degenerates"—guys who were hanging out in front of the nearby 7-Eleven. By the time she was sixteen, she was in New York, playing bars with the Undead, a punk group. But that era was in its death throes.

For a while she went to Pratt Institute, where she studied art. Then she went on to study cartooning at a school in Dover, New Jersey.

"I was going to be this great artist—the new Salvador Dalí. Then, I went to cartooning school for a year. I was the only female cartoonist there."

But at nineteen she gave up cartooning. Music beckoned. In the mideighties, Lorre decided to move to L.A. and start a band. There, in 1987, she formed the Nymphs. But the first incarnation of the band was laughable.

"I couldn't find people to play with me. I had blond hair and was real thin, and people immediately thought: Blondie or 'Til Tuesday. But I was into the Stooges, Patti Smith and Captain Beefheart and the Velvet Underground. All I could get was this really fat Mexican drummer from a mariachi band. And I had this guitarist who thought he was a guitar god but was totally bald, with a beer belly and glasses. I had all these total misfits, because no one who I thought was cool would play with me."

The Nymphs played wherever they could but were getting nowhere until Zutaut met Lorre at the Chrysalis party. "I had this really bad attitude," Lorre says of their encounter. "But I guess Tom saw through all that."

But from the moment she was signed, Lorre said, Zutaut was always undermining her relationship with the band, heightening the built-in tension between them and creating new divisions.

"When we were in England he always wanted it to be 'me and Tom.' The band would do all this work but then Tom would fly me first class on MGM Grand airlines. It really created so much tension between me and the band.

"He saw the way the band was broken up. I got my own bedroom and the guys had to sleep in the bunks. Meanwhile, Tom would say, 'You're a star. You deserve this.' "

At other times, Lorre said, Zutaut would call and tantalize her with things he knew she wanted.

"Zutaut bought my favorite pinball machine—because I really like the Elvira pinball machine—and installed it in his basement and would call me up and say, 'I have it now. Why don't you come over? We can play pinball.'

"I used to really hate myself for a while. I thought, 'I'm not really talented. It's just because he wanted to fuck me.' But then I thought, no, there were a million other models [he could've] recorded. Obviously there was the music."

Musicians need to perform. With practice comes proficiency and confidence, and artists crave attention. Playing live is both self-gratifying and self-validating. But the Nymphs weren't allowed to perform, according to Lorre.

Living on a fixed income, partying with the fast crowd in Hollywood, some of the band members started experimenting with hard drugs. More than once Zutaut told Lorre she had to straighten up if she wanted to make a record at all. But Lorre insists she wasn't doing heroin in the beginning.

"I'd say, 'Why?' I didn't have the problem. I had never even tried heroin until two years into my record deal when I was sitting around my apartment and had nothing to do. All this time on my hands, and heroin's the best time killer in the world.

"It's almost like Zutaut turned me into this monster. He fed into all my psychoses. He'd give me money, he'd give me cars. He was letting me become this completely uncontrollable monster, and watching it happen. He lives vicariously through his artists. He did that with Axl Rose until Axl realized it and got a new shrink. Tom likes the whole drama—the young, beautiful loser."

I ran this by Zutaut and he shook his head as if he'd heard it all before.

"The band could play live whenever they wanted or wherever they wanted," he said. "[But] people don't understand how difficult it was to get Inger to show up for a gig. They were afraid to book shows. You never knew whether she would show up or not."

As for pushing her into heroin addiction, Zutaut said Lorre was lying about that. From all outward appearances, Zutaut was convinced Lorre was a junkie from the moment he met her because of her strange and erratic behavior and because her fiancé—Chris Schlosshardt—had died of a heroin overdose.

"She'd always not show up for important recording sessions or miss important dates. And when you confronted her one of two things would happen: She'd get better for a while or she would tell you to fuck off and she'd disappear and get better for a while. The Nymphs unraveled because Inger got junked out and walked off in the middle of a tour—just before the single was going to be promoted."

Was Lorre lying? Was there some truth in what she said?

That was hard to say. She swore up and down that what she was saying was true. Yet Zutaut had said something prophetic about Lorre a few months before the Nymphs' debut came out.

"Inger has the face of an angel and the heart of a demon. You never know when she'll turn on you."

What was certain was that Lorre's life was spinning out of control. Depressed, lonely, angry, addicted to drugs, cut off from her friends and family, she became more and more unstable. The songs she wrote for her album reflected her mood. On "Wasting My Days" she sang about dropping out of the human race entirely, and on "Sad and Damned" she sang of a living hell she'd painted herself into: a place with no chance of an exit. And if you listened to "Cold," Lorre's ghostly words made you fear for her sanity: "When people smile at me it turns my blood to ice."

Typically, her manager should've dealt with her crises. But dapper, middle-aged Arnold Stiefel, who along with partner Randy Phillips guided the careers of rock heavyweights like Rod Stewart, was a mismatch from the start. Zutaut had directed the Nymphs to Stiefel-Phillips because it had clout and was one of the few management companies known to spend its own nickel—money beyond what the record label gave—to promote its artists. But Lorre loathed the man who was ostensibly in charge of her budding career.

"Whenever I would freak out, Arnold would have me come over, but he wouldn't want to deal with me. He was so used to managing Rod Stewart. So he would just say, 'It'll be OK, darling,' and have one of his assistants run over. He would spend time picking out dresses for Rod Stewart's wife, Rachel Hunter. And I'd say, 'If you're picking out clothes for Rod Stewart that's one thing. But does Rachel Stewart have a fucking contract with you? I do.' "

Stiefel was tempted more than once to drop Lorre. But he had once done that with another band Zutaut had signed and sent his way and regretted the decision ever since. That was when he and Phillips had managed Guns N' Roses,[9] who Zutaut had boasted would be superstars. Back then, Axl, Slash and company were a bunch of down-and-out pissant street rats who wrought havoc just about wherever they went. When Stiefel made the mistake of letting the band stay in a famous Hollywood mansion one weekend, Guns N' Roses promptly trashed the place. Outraged, Stiefel soon dropped the band, probably glad to be rid of them, figuring he'd watch them self-destruct. But of course Guns N' Roses became huge and Stiefel spent many an hour—how many untold millions was 20 percent of Guns N' Roses' net worth?—ruing his decision, according to Zutaut.

Who could say that Lorre wouldn't be the next Guns N' Roses? That's why Stiefel endured Inger's screaming and ranting, delegating day-to-day dealings with her to assistants. Yet one afternoon in April when I accompanied Zutaut to a rehearsal, Stiefel called in a panic: Lorre had fired him and was acting really insane.

"Arnold, she's crazy—she's in the middle of an insane nervous breakdown," Zutaut said, trying to calm Stiefel over the car phone as we headed to a Guns N' Roses mix. "She accuses people of trying to rape her. She'll find out what your weaknesses are and try to attack you. Hey, she's calling everyone in the business and trying to ruin *my* reputation. Arnold, she's accused me of having an affair with you. So do we want to buy her a plane ticket back here so she can scream in our faces? I'm all ears. Whatever you think we need to do, I'm ready."

Seeing the singer come undone, fearing that all his hard work was unraveling—that Inger would self-destruct before the band's album even came out—Zutaut consulted with her family and quickly arranged for Lorre to get drug rehabilita-

---

[9] Stiefel-Phillips briefly managed Guns N' Roses, but after the split the band was managed by Alan Niven. Now the band's manager is Doug Goldstein.

tion. It was decided that she should be sent to Hazelden, a private hospital in Minnesota where rich people recover from nervous breakdowns.[10] But once there, Lorre started acting berserk.

"She was pulling nurses' hair, spitting at them and trying to hit them over the head with chairs," Zutaut recalled.

And after that, her mood only blackened. She called up everyone she knew, spinning wild stories. She dialed *Rolling Stone* correspondent David Wild, who'd just moved to Los Angeles, and asked him for airfare back to L.A. And she called Stiefel, screaming hysterically, telling him he was fired, accusing him of having a homosexual affair with Zutaut.

"They sent me away to Minnesota to this rich-boy nuthouse," Lorre would say later. "Tom Zutaut said, 'If you cooperate and get well, we'll let you record.' But I got transferred to this cheesy state facility. I get to this place and there were all these crazy people staring at the TV. . . . I finally escaped. I was trying to get back to New Jersey and my parents' house, but I couldn't raise the fare and no one would send me the money. This one dude at the airport said he'd give me the money if I gave him head, but I said no way."

Nor was it the first time Lorre was committed. Lorre would later claim that Zutaut had her committed to mental hospitals three separate times.[11] "I would say, 'What's wrong with me?' And Tom would say, 'You're not stable enough.' And I'd say, 'Do you know any artist that is?' He would put me in these places in L.A. . . . so he could have an alibi and anything I would say about him he could say was crazy. I felt like Frances Farmer. No one would believe me. They would say, 'Oh, yeah, she's

---

[10] David Geffen paid for Lorre's treatment.

[11] Zutaut says he never committed Lorre to any hospitals. "Her parents committed her. I remember from the early days her mother calling me on the phone and pleading with me to get her to a hospital. I wouldn't have the authority to do that alone. But at certain times, when Inger was so whacked out on heroin, everyone around her—band, management, record company and parents—helped. It was pretty much a joint effort."

nuts.' I *did* do outrageous antics onstage. But I always went all out."

With Lorre out of commission and the album only weeks away from completion, Zutaut and Stiefel decided to finish the record without the singer. Already, the mixes sounded great. And when Zutaut played the record, completed in late summer, for David Geffen and label president Eddie Rosenblatt, both liked it.

The Nymphs' eponymous debut was released in October of 1991, and Geffen's marketing department gave it a major push, with full-page ads in key rock publications. But two months later, sales were dismal. MTV didn't like "Sad and Damned," the surreal video to the first single, which featured perhaps the most grotesque and memorable moment in music-video history: Lorre downing a teacup full of real maggots. There was no real buzz on the Nymphs here or abroad, and the band hadn't played in a long time. Figuring the Nymphs needed to build fan support, Zutaut arranged for the group to make its New York debut at the Limelight, Manhattan's trendy cathedral turned nightclub, in mid-December during the Christmas break. Even Lorre's spirits seemed to brighten at the prospect of finally playing.

"This is our homecoming gig. You've got to come out. It's going to be awesome," Lorre said a few days before the show. We were eating lunch at Lucy's El Adobe, a Mexican joint on Melrose Avenue, near the Paramount studio. Dressed in black pants and a black angora sweater, Lorre looked beautiful. But her skin—an eerie porcelain white—and her cunning eyes made me think of vampires.

"It's going to be like Martha Graham if she were fronted by Black Sabbath. I'll be dancing barefoot like Martha did."

But a few moments later, her mood turned corrosive. She pushed her food around the plate, but didn't touch it. "I eat like a fly," she said, "but not what flies eat."

Lorre said that Zutaut was the one who caused her to have a nervous breakdown. She charged him with trying to break up her band and replace them with session men. She'd stopped using smack, she insisted, though most of her band was still strung out. However, Zutaut, who talked to her a day before the New York show, merely laughed at her accusations and confessions.

"That's the story she tells everyone. But she's a junkie. The other day, when I talked to her, she said her goal was to get enough money to score smack. That's why she looks so young. People who take smack carefully stay youthful. If it doesn't kill you, you end up temporarily looking younger, like the vampire who thrives on blood. But if you quit, you age horribly."

As for ruining her band or undermining her relationship with them, Zutaut said she was exaggerating.

"When I first saw the band they couldn't play; they hadn't rehearsed. I suggested we use session guys for certain things. But then the band practiced and sounded great. I have to give them credit; they got really good. Now, we just have to make sure she gets on that plane."

Lorre got on the plane and both Zutaut and Geffen marketing vice-president Robert Smith flew out to be with the Nymphs for the crucial Limelight gig, along with two members of the Stiefel-Phillips management team. At the sound check everything was going well. Lorre sounded like a she-demon as the band roared through songs like "Wasting My Days" and "Supersonic."

"She's gonna blow people away," Zutaut confidently predicted.

But a few songs later Lorre came undone. Someone had turned off the monitors, and all of a sudden she couldn't hear her vocals. Furious, the singer hurled curses at her guitarist Jet, accusing him of playing too loud.

Worried now, Zutaut decided to take Lorre back to his hotel, where he could keep a watch on her until the band was scheduled to go on, around 11:00 P.M. The time was important because at 12:30 sharp the Limelight became a disco.

"The show's going to go great," Zutaut told Lorre as the

limo sped uptown to the Ritz-Carlton. "There's going to be a big crowd." But Lorre seemed unaccountably desolate. Her life, she said, was a mess: a series of wrong turns.

"This is going to be a tough album to put over because radio doesn't want to play it and MTV doesn't want to touch it," Zutaut said. "We're going to have to take it to the streets. You're going to have to play clubs everywhere."

This pep talk had the opposite effect. Lorre seemed to grow more despondent with each passing minute. And that wasn't surprising. Earlier, she'd taken five vials of buprenorphine, an opioid.[12]

"I'm not afraid of death, but all of my friends are gone. Five of my high-school friends killed themselves before I was eighteen," she announced. She was sitting now in Zutaut's plush room at the Ritz-Carlton, and as she talked she sewed a snow-white veil—it would transform her into a "virgin feminist"—and stuffed a "magic" black pillow with snow-white feathers.

Zutaut ordered room service, but Lorre passed up dinner for two scoops of ice cream and a cup of tea. She talked in disjointed sentences, jumping from cancer, which a family member was battling, to drug addiction and AIDS. By now, Robert Smith had arrived and a limo was waiting. Smith paced up and down Zutaut's room. But Inger Lorre, lost in a narcotic depression, wasn't in any shape to perform.

"When I tested negative for AIDS I was disappointed," she said in a faraway voice. "I've never felt so close to suicide."

This wasn't the kind of talk that Zutaut or Smith wanted to hear—not after flying across the country. Inger Lorre, whom the Geffen company would spend over a million dollars on, was unraveling before their eyes.

"Inger, we've got to go. We're late as it is," Zutaut said finally, exasperated. And without looking at anyone, Lorre

---

[12] Late in 1993, remembering the Limelight night, Lorre said she was "wasted" and in no mood to perform. She said that Perry Farrell, the lead singer for Jane's Addiction, had introduced her to the doctor who gave her the drug.

wordlessly gathered together her things, stuffing her outfit, her pillow, her knife and other props into an old leather suitcase.

As the limo sped downtown, Lorre complained that she wasn't getting the money she was owed from her managers.[13] Then she mentioned Nirvana and her eyes went cold. Signed to Geffen, the Seattle grunge band's major-label debut, *Nevermind*, was just then exploding, selling, without need of any marketing blitz or imaging campaign, tens of thousands of records a day.[14]

"Why's Nirvana selling so many records?" Lorre whined.

"We've spent way more money on you than we did on Nirvana, Inger," Smith said. "That album just sold itself. It's a fluke."

The Nymphs were waiting when Lorre arrived, an hour late; they glared at her when she offered no explanation for her lateness. They would've liked to slowly strangle her, their murderous expressions said. But first they would do the show. Yet just as they got the signal to go on, Lorre went white with panic: She'd forgotten her white veil.

"I can't go on without the veil!" she screamed.

"Inger, you have to go on," Zutaut said, his face going white. "You don't need the veil." But Lorre gave him a vicious look. "No! I won't go on without the veil!" she howled, stomping around the room, lost in a raging tantrum.

This was the last straw. Lorre's bandmates—Merrick, Jet, Kirst and Cliff D.—hurled curses at her, stomped out, played one song and stormed off the stage.

"There's not enough money to put up with this," Geffen flack Lisa Gladfelter muttered under her breath.

Someone was sent to retrieve the veil, eating into the al-

---

[13] Stiefel had advanced each of the musicians some money to live on, but Lorre had used the cash, according to Zutaut, to buy heroin and rent an expensive apartment.

[14] *Nevermind* eventually sold more than ten million copies, catapulting Nirvana to the top of the grunge heap and lead singer Kurt Cobain into near-overnight celebrity.

ready shortened time the band would have to perform. Meanwhile, Zutaut, who'd been frantically looking for Neville, the Limelight's manager, finally found him and convinced him not to pull the plug on the show. Lorre would be back, Zutaut promised. A little before 12:30, an hour and a half after the band was supposed to go on, Inger finally emerged with her white veil.

Half the crowd had left by now, but the Nymphs managed to get off a half-dozen songs in the next thirty minutes. Lorre sang "Wasting My Days," a song inspired by heroin, "Imitating Angels," a kind of dirge about how far from grace all we humans are, and a few other songs off the album.

It was the Nymphs' first gig in almost three years and it was horrible. Zutaut was in shock, his face drained of all color. When Lorre finished the set, she cut the "magic" pillow open, hurling white feathers into the air, which fell like winter snowflakes on the crowd. Glassy-eyed, dressed in black tights and tunic, framed against a stained-glass window illuminated with seraphim and cherubim, Lorre herself looked like some mad, fallen angel.

A few months later, in Santa Monica, she took off her top at the L.A. Music Awards, revealing blackened nipples. She told a Playboy Channel interviewer there that her record included backward masking that said she'd fornicated with Jesus. And on February 28, Lorre caused her first riot: at Anaheim's Marquis, before four hundred or so people, she performed fellatio on her boyfriend, actor Rodney Eastman, onstage—midway through the group's set.

"We had to take her out of there in a limousine," said Lisa Gladfelter, who was there. "It got ugly. The police came. Guys were punching each other."

"Inger has more passion than any female rock singer I've heard," Zutaut had said eight months earlier. But after Lorre's exploits, the label had almost dropped her. And even Zutaut's clout—he got the album released in Great Britain and convinced Geffen to pump more money into breaking the band—couldn't make up for the perception that the Nymphs, for all their talent, weren't going anywhere, that they were likely to crash and burn.

In retrospect, the Geffen publicity/marketing machine, which fanned windstorms of hype for its bands, couldn't create stars overnight. Had the Nymphs played more and released an independent record quickly to capitalize on their uniquely grungy sound; had the band built up a following the normal way before putting out a major-label debut, the album might've actually gone somewhere. But then Lorre was her own worst enemy.

Zutaut said he tried to get a CD out quickly, to capitalize on the band's unique sound. And Geffen talked about putting out an independent EP.

"We cut five or six tracks at a studio up in Marin. But Inger went berserk and started throwing things. She basically walked out of the sessions and refused to finish them."

The Nymphs were bombing, but Zutaut tried to appear optimistic. "It ain't over 'til it's over," he told me a few months after the album had been released and was seemingly dead in the water. He was convinced the Nymphs still had a chance if the British press would just get behind the band. But that never happened. Despite some favorable reviews and a costly overseas marketing blitz, Great Britain never warmed up to the Nymphs. Six months after the album was released, it had gone nowhere. Geffen would spend a fortune trying to break the band, but the CD ended up selling only about seventy-five thousand copies.

I'd first met Zutaut five years before, when he'd just signed Guns N' Roses. Like an inventor who held in his hands some secret that would shake up the world, he played a tape for me from one of the band's live shows. The singer, whom I would meet later that night for drinks, was Axl Rose, a wild, tormented kid from Indiana. And the song, called "Welcome to the Jungle," about arriving in the smog-and-stucco shithole that was Southern California, was four minutes of seething rage.

"Critics don't like this kind of music, but they're going to sell millions and millions of records," Zutaut told me after playing a few more songs off the tape. The comment was a test, the prediction, a boast: the cocky prophecy of a twenty-six-year-old hotshot. Guns N' Roses hadn't even begun recording its Geffen debut. But Zutaut's judgment couldn't be easily dismissed.

When Zutaut was all of twenty-two and scouting bands for Elektra Records, he'd signed Mötley Crüe, one of the most successful metal bands in history. While at Elektra he guided Dokken, a heavy-metal band, to huge sales. And he brought Kitaro and Enya, both New Age artists, to Geffen, where their records went platinum. He also claimed that when he was in the midst of leaving Elektra he was planning to sign Metallica to Geffen.[15]

It was Guns N' Roses, though, that made Zutaut's reputation. When many of his other records stiffed, when Lorre drove him crazy, Zutaut could still count on the satisfaction and financial rewards that came from discovering Guns N' Roses. And he never tired of telling the story of how he discovered the band at West Hollywood's Troubadour.

"Everyone had talked about finding the next Jim Morrison—I'd heard these stories for years in L.A.—but in my mind this was as close as anyone had come. Axl was the most charismatic, electrifying performer that I'd ever seen in my life. Not only that, but the musicians were amazing. Slash was the best guitar player I'd ever seen. The two of them were like Mick [Jagger] and Keith [Richards]."

Fearful that other scouts might sign the band first, Zutaut did something unusual that night. "Even though the band was only on its fourth song," he said, "I decided to walk out. There were all these other A&R people, and I'd rather have them

---

[15] Zutaut claimed Metallica wouldn't wait for his deal to be finalized with Geffen, and so he reluctantly handed over the signing to an Elektra A&R man. Elektra chairman Bob Krasnow hotly denied that Zutaut had anything to do with signing Metallica.

think I left because I didn't like it than stay to the end and let them think I was interested in the band. As I left the club, one A&R guy asked, 'Don't you like the band?' And I said, 'No, man, I'm going home because it's too loud.'

"When I got home I couldn't sleep, but the next day I called Axl. And he said, 'You didn't even see the whole show. We thought you didn't like it.' But I said, 'I had to leave because there were too many other A&R people watching me. You've got yourself a record deal. I don't need to hear or see anything else. I just want to be the guy to help you take this out to the rest of the world.'

"Could anyone ever capture this on tape? Would the band ever get focused enough to make a record? You never really knew," Zutaut said. "When they came around Geffen Records, people would walk the other way, afraid they might bite. And when I'd go visit the house where they were staying, they'd be living knee-deep in old hamburger wrappers. Once I walked into the house and the toilet was ripped from the floor and the kitchen sink had become the toilet. There were turds floating in the sink—because someone in a fit of rage had destroyed the toilet."

Guns N' Roses would squander its six-figure advance, try to overrule Zutaut's decisions, not show up for expensive recording sessions and live in a state of chaos that had Geffen brass wondering if they'd poured all their money down a rat hole.[16] Everyone in the group was doing drugs—heroin, cocaine—or booze. And Axl Rose was already subject to the sudden fits of depression and rage that still fuel outbursts that make headlines almost everywhere the band turns up.

"Tom was the only guy behind the Guns N' Roses vision besides the guys in the band," said Slash. "When we were

---

[16] When Guns N' Roses squandered its initial living expense money— some $150,000—before even setting foot in a recording studio, it was Zutaut who begged and got the band more money each time. The band got some $350,000 as its original advance, according to Zutaut, which was one of the largest advances at that time for a new rock band.

struggling in Hollywood to try to get gigs, he was the only guy that showed up at our show and saw through the Hollywood glitz. He fought hard for us at the record company, because as far as the industry was concerned we were vermin. Even now he's behind whatever it is we want to do when other individuals at the record company aren't. Guns was always on the verge of disintegrating—we're extremists. We were always getting busted and getting in fights. And there'd be an occasional overdose."

Appetite for Destruction seemed as if it was always destined to be a best-seller, but when Zutaut signed Guns N' Roses, its noisy, aggressive music was anathema to radio. No station in the country would play "Welcome to the Jungle," the first single of the album, and MTV wouldn't touch it. But the band was kept on a grueling touring regime. And then, about three months after it was released, something happened: *Appetite for Destruction* suddenly started selling like mad, two to three thousand records a day, without any airplay. For months, says Zutaut, David Geffen himself had begged MTV to play the video, and when the network finally did—at 3:00 A.M.—it became MTV's most requested clip. A year after its release, the album had gone gold. By 1989, the band had rocketed to stardom. *Appetite for Destruction* would eventually sell more than fourteen million copies worldwide.

But there was a cruel irony. Rose, the rock singer Zutaut would become famous for discovering, ended up despising him. Why? According to speculation within Geffen and on the part of other people close to the band, Rose came under the influence of psychics and healers, one of whom was a woman from Arizona who served as his past-life regression therapist. That woman convinced the rock star to sever ties with all negative people, or "users," in his life. To this day, Rose supposedly believes Zutaut is one such "user."

"If his psychic told him that I wasn't any good for him," Zutaut said, acknowledging their ruptured relationship, "perhaps that's why he doesn't speak to me anymore. But I do speak to him through his management. I'm still the A&R person.

"Axl was the last angry man when he was signed. From what I understand, Axl went through a lot of sexual abuse as a small child. He's said he was sodomized by his father.[17] And I remember sitting with Axl one night during the time we were recording the *Use Your Illusion* albums, and he broke down and cried and talked about how he was abused as a kid and how he found out his sister was abused. . . . Axl's in his late twenties physically, but emotionally is probably only four or five years old."

But Zutaut wouldn't say anything else about their relationship or the circumstances that drove a wedge between them.

"That's the sad thing. Tom helped make Axl famous," someone at Geffen told me, "but Axl Rose hates Tom's guts."

Zutaut's family roots went back to the coal-mining regions of West Virginia, where the large extended clan still gathers every year. But his rock and roll instincts developed precociously in Park Forest, Illinois, twice an all-American town. A tuba player, he might've ended up with a career in the symphony if he hadn't gotten bitten by the rock and roll bug. By the time he was ten, he was buying every new pop and rock record that came out.

"After a couple of years of doing that I started noticing that I had this ability to pick the ones that became hits," Zutaut said. "And I was almost always right."

At his high school's ten-watt FM station, he became a DJ and convinced major labels to send him records. Instead of gong to college, he took a mailroom job with Warner-Elektra-Atlantic's Chicago distribution center, where he quickly rose through the ranks doing field inventories with unprecedented speed. But it was Zutaut's uncanny ability to spot hit singles and get them added to the playlist of a major Midwestern radio

---

[17] Rose made his charges of sexual abuse in a *Rolling Stone* article.

station that got Elektra's vice-president of sales to take notice and hire him. Zutaut was now based in L.A., and he hit the clubs almost very night. He kept a log of bands he thought were great, which he passed to Elektra's A&R department. When nothing happened, he got frustrated. Eventually Joe Smith, then head of Elektra, gave him a shot at A&R.

The first band he signed was Mötley Crüe, whose high-heeled shoes and vampy makeup had made them the butt of endless jokes. But nobody laughed when the group's first album sold millions of copies. When I asked him about those early days, Zutaut smiled.

"I had no money then. I didn't like my job. I just had this dream, this vision, that I would help all these musicians bring their music to the world. And it came true, like a prophecy."

By the time he was in his midtwenties, Zutaut had a house in the Hollywood Hills, a BMW and a fast, fast life. A few years later, with Guns N' Roses' success, he was one of the highest-paid people in the record business, a millionaire with homes in Malibu, the Hollywood Hills and the Hawaiian island of Kauai.

He ate in the most expensive restaurants, traveled the world first-class, dated models and eventually married a young Australian he met on vacation, a beautiful woman named Bronwyn Rudge. Bronwyn and Zutaut had a child named Claire. But nuptial life after that was anything but sweet. Soon, the marriage broke up and a nasty divorce ensued, which left Zutaut bitter and chastened.

For a while Zutaut retreated into himself, nursing his wounds. He cut back on the long hours he'd been putting in and holed himself up at one or another of his houses. But by the summer of 1991 he was working hard, signing lots of new groups.

Though he saw himself doing bigger things soon, he was happy for the time being working at Geffen. Zutaut had had a few offers to become president of a new label, but such an opportunity also came with risks. Recently eight new labels had started, each with huge financing behind it. But who knew how long any of them would last in the cutthroat world of entertainment? The label that had a hundred million dollars behind it one year could be out of business two years later. And the president who didn't produce hits wouldn't last long.

With four monstrous mortgages and a millionaire's sybaritic lifestyle, Zutaut knew he was safer at Geffen. There he had a huge, guaranteed salary, and his past successes still carried cachet. He was one of the few A&R men with the clout to sign a band for almost any amount of money. Hiring and firing producers, conceiving marketing strategies, negotiating advances, overseeing every detail of recording and breaking a record, Zutaut wielded enormous power. He saw himself as heir to the tradition set by people like John Hammond.

Back in the thirties, Hammond, Columbia Records' legendary A&R man, roamed America by car, looking for the geniuses of American music. Hammond found Kansas City legend Count Basie while tooling around the Midwest with his radio on, and he discovered Billie Holiday playing in the smoky dives of Harlem. Things were different then. A&R men tended to know and love music; many had musical training. And popular music was a regional phenomenon, not a global market to exploit.

But everything had changed and changed quickly. Now there were multimillion-dollar advances and two-million-dollar recording budgets.

Nine out of ten A&R men were flakes or charlatans, people who knew next to nothing about music and were lured to the field by glamour, quick money and celebrity. They chased trends and signed bands that churned out records imitating the musical genre of the season. And if they signed two dozen bands and one hit it would make up for the other twenty-three mistakes. With hindsight, they could look brilliant—to the gullible. But the truth was, an original artistic vision that surfaced was almost an accident.

Pop music had become the darling of Wall Street, a global growth industry and one of America's biggest exports. And the A&R men, who once had desks facing each other and pulled down a couple hundred dollars a week, were now big shots who attached auras to themselves. Those who found stars—whether by luck or skill or both—were soon courted *like* stars, paid enormous sums of money for their supposed prescience. Never mind that most of them were flying by the seat of their pants and didn't know what they were doing.

By the late seventies, the best A&R men were making a hundred thousand dollars or more a year. Fifteen years later, the top salaries, with bonuses or points (profit sharing tied to sales of a record), could add up to a million dollars or more annually.

"Who wouldn't want the job? People would do it for free," said Steve Moir, a onetime A&R man who now owned an L.A.-based company that manages record producers. "But the pressure is intense. If you're getting four hundred thousand dollars a year and you don't produce a hit in the first few years, you're looked at as a failure."

Zutaut, who handled the fate of more than two dozen bands, wasn't immune to the pressures. For all his past glories, he hadn't broken a new band in years. And his misses had cost Geffen a small fortune. To see how he was doing in the winter of 1992, Zutaut merely had to look at his colleague and rival, Gary Gersh, who'd brought David Geffen Nirvana. A year after Nirvana's rise to stardom, Gersh, thirty-eight, was named president of Capitol Records. Zutaut had to be envious.

"I want to have my own label—a sort of rebel outpost," he'd told me a few months earlier. "I know it will happen. It's just a matter of when."

But by 1994, Zutaut was still an A&R executive working for David Geffen. And none of his new bands were going anywhere, much less putting up the kind of numbers that made David Geffen smile.

"My experience has never been that an A&R person sets out to change someone by force," John Doe, one of the founders of the acclaimed L.A. punk band X, once told me. "The change is always encouraged by stimulating greed and the impulse for fame and fortune. The danger is that if you listen to them and write their kind of songs and your record doesn't do well, then you doubt their wisdom."

Certainly, Inger Lorre doubted some of Zutaut's wisdom. But she couldn't hold him or Geffen responsible for her demise. After the Limelight fiasco, things had gone downhill for her in a hurry. During the summer, Lorre had gotten in a fight with her boyfriend, Rodney Eastman.

"We got in this huge fight in my apartment, about a day after shooting my 'Imitating Angels' video. We were both wired, really tense. We fought and screamed; the cops came once, then left. But me and Rodney got in another screaming match. And this time I was taunting him, daring him to hit me. So he hit me. Then I hit him and we were rolling around on the floor. We were fighting over the keys and I was so mad that I jabbed him with the key and it punctured the area above his knee."

Neighbors called the police again, and this time the two were tossed in the slammer—Eastman in a men's prison in L.A. County and Lorre in a women's prison.

"I was there for four days, and the only reason I made it out alive was because I have an Egyptian Eye of Horus tattoo on my back. All the Mexican women were afraid of it and all the black women thought it was voodoo. They asked me if it was voodoo and I said yes. My hair was dyed black with white streaks at the time, so they were calling me Beetlejuice."

Lorre's father, who was on vacation, came and bailed her out. By then, Lorre had lost a lot of weight from nervous exhaustion. She hadn't slept during the whole time she was in prison.

"You couldn't sleep there," she said. "People would come up and steal your shoes and blankets."

Not long after being bailed out, Lorre was on tour with Peter Murphy. She had another chance to restore some credibility with her label and put her musical career on track. Yet Lorre managed to sabotage things again.

"She was selling backstage passes to fans in exchange for

money to buy drugs," Zutaut said, describing the tour as a total fiasco.

Then one night, opening for Murphy in Miami, Lorre refused to go out on stage at all. The Nymphs, having reached their limit, went on without her and then promptly fired her.

For a while Lorre rumors circulated. Someone told me she was having a lesbian affair with the singer in some New York band, which turned out to be false. Actually Lorre was back in New Jersey, living with her parents, getting therapy and trying to put her life back together.

"She was just too insane," Zutaut said at the beginning of 1993, when I spent a day with him at his 150-acre farm near Monticello in Virginia. "I couldn't handle it. Every few weeks, Inger would leave a message on my machine, filled with obscenities. I dropped her."

But Lorre had a different story to tell when I called her just before Christmas 1993.

"[Tom] told me, 'I'm gonna keep you forever. You're never gonna make records again unless it's for me.' And when he knew I was really poor he called me up and offered to buy my publishing for ten thousand dollars.[18] And I told him, 'Fuck you.' Because I'd been offered five hundred thousand dollars at one point and didn't sell it then, though I should've.

"There was a huge buzz on us when Geffen signed us, but they kept us on ice until it all died down. Tom was going to do it his way. But you have to hit something while it's hot—that's the way the business is. Even the Hole record came out before ours. People were calling me a Courtney Love wanna-be,[19] which was ridiculous."

For a long time, Lorre was bitter. But she says she's over that now. "I don't live with hate anymore. Because it eats you up."

---

[18] Zutaut denied he ever sought to buy her publishing, although he conceded the topic may have been broached when the Nymphs came asking for more money from Geffen.

[19] Hole, fronted by Courtney Love, was signed after the Nymphs by Zutaut's rival, Gary Gersh.

And she says she doesn't act crazy anymore. Moving back to New Jersey, away from Hollywood, helped. And so did seeing a therapist.

"My shrinks tell me that I'm really talented but I have low self-esteem, that I let people goad me into things. I'm just gullible. I was diagnosed for severe depression. The shrink would tell me I was schizophrenic—that some people are born without arms and legs but I was born without certain chemicals.

"I *was* crazy. I did oral sex onstage. That's when I was really disturbed. At the Limelight I was going insane. I was supposed to be onstage in fifteen minutes but I was sewing a veil. I hated being there and everything about it. I wished I was dead."

I asked her about her new band. Lorre's voice came alive.

"It's called Black Sheep Heaven. Our record is going to be made for half the price the Nymphs' [record] cost and it's going to be on Atlantic or Elektra. They're both interested. I just have to make my choice. And my next album is going to make Tom Zutaut sick."

CHAPTER 2

Ruthless Records

Guns, Gangstas
and Lawsuits

"**S**ee this?" Jerry Heller said, pulling a .380-caliber pistol out of the lightweight jacket he'd just put on. "We gotta carry guns around here."

It was the sort of comment I might expect to hear from a Colombian judge appointed to try a Medellín drug-smuggling case, or a detective threatened by a crazed killer he'd put away years ago who was now getting out of jail. But Heller wasn't a judge or a detective. A fifty-two-year-old former booking agent, he was the cohead of Ruthless Records, the L.A.-based rap label founded by N.W.A (Niggaz with Attitude) member Eric (Eazy-E) Wright. And he wasn't carrying heat just because it was fashionable in L.A.'s gangsta-rap community.

No, Heller packed a gat for the same reason that everyone at Ruthless Records carried guns in the spring of 1993: He believed he had reason to be constantly scared for his life, ever since a huge black man known as Suge (pronounced "Shug," short for "sugar") Knight, accompanied by a menacing posse, had taken to dropping by Ruthless's Canoga Park offices. All you had to do was walk into Ruthless Records to feel the paranoia. It hung in the air like a thick, poisonous cloud and it existed well before Ruthless filed its $250 million lawsuit in 1992. Filed under the RICO (Racketeer Influenced and Corrupt Organizations) Act, which was meant to protect small businesses from extortion and blackmail, the lawsuit charged Knight and Andre Young—the ex-N.W.A producer/rapper known as Dr. Dre—along with platinum-selling rapper Tracy Curry (the D.O.C.), platinum-selling singer Michelle Toussant (Michel'le), Sony Records and the independent L.A.-based Solar Records, with participating in an extortion scheme that robbed Ruthless of three of its major stars and nearly destroyed the company.[1] Like life imitating art, the lawsuit replicated the violent world of gangsta rap. Told in legal jargon was a story of guns and thugs, greed and revenge and allegations of criminality at the highest levels of the entertainment business. But what was going on at Ruthless Records showed something else: that if you made music with and about violence, you could expect to be thrown into a violent world. And that would be nothing like the world of normal society.

"We've lived in constant fear. Suge would just walk into our office and say, 'You know who I am? I'm Dre's manager. We're taking over.' He'd look around and tell his gangbangers to go and get the guns from the car," Heller said, referring to an incident in February 1991 when Knight demanded royalty payments for Dre, D.O.C. and Michel'le, all of whom had been signed to Ruthless but were now managed by him. "Then Suge would bend over and there'd be a huge gun sticking out of his ass pocket."

Heller paused, his eyes darkening. Tall and potbellied, he had prematurely pure white hair, a large nose and a jowly face that gave him a look that fell halfway between an alligator and a hunting dog. He spoke in dramatic tones with an accent that still had traces of his Midwestern roots back in Shaker Heights, a suburb of Cleveland, Ohio.

"And you know what? He did a good job of scaring us. There was a guy who came in here one day and put his finger up to my head and said, 'I could've blown you away right now. But if you had a real bodyguard I couldn't have come in here.'"

---

[1] The judge dismissed the RICO causes of action contained in Ruthless's third amended complaint. But Ruthless's lawyers have left open the possibility of bringing claims against defendants other than Sony in California state court.

Everyone at Ruthless had stories like that. Ira Selsky, the corporate attorney for Ruthless, claimed Suge had barged into his office one afternoon and stolen documents from him. And after repeatedly calling Heller's assistant, Gary Ballen, and threatening him on the phone, Knight came over one day with five of his cohorts. According to Ballen's sworn affidavit, Knight forced him to write an apology to the singer Michel'le for "disrespecting" her. Ballen counted himself lucky. Not long afterward, he bought a 120,000-volt stun gun, enrolled in martial-arts classes and talked about getting a gun for himself until his wife talked him out of it.

"I still have trouble sleeping at night. And my wife and I got into arguments over the gun," Ballen said in his affidavit.

"We had to move our offices," said Heller. "I used to stay at the Four Seasons or I'd go to Newport Beach all day. For a while we were afraid to come to the office and worked out of a house in Sherman Oaks. One of my assistants wrote me a letter at one point saying he couldn't work here because he was afraid they'd kill him and his wife and child. It was ugly."

Along the way, Heller said he had paid out thousands of dollars in what he called extortion money to Dre's manager, so it wasn't as if he and Eazy weren't prepared for the worst. In fact, they had anticipated the dark night somewhere down the line when one or both of them would be confronted by Knight and asked to sign over releases that would terminate all existing production and recording agreements between Ruthless and Dre, D.O.C. and Michel'le. It was clear to them that Knight was building up to that. That's why Heller paid a fortune for surveillance and protection. Two massive bodyguards, Animal and Michael, patrolled the Ruthless offices at all times. They kept a shotgun behind the desk in the front room—just in case. And wherever Heller went, Michael, an enormous black man with the bulging build of Arnold Schwarzenegger and the towering height of an NBA forward, went also. Because who knew when or where Knight or someone else who hated Heller might show up at his house with a gun?

Each night, before Heller could even walk into the front door of his two-million-dollar Mountainview Estates mansion in Cal-

Jory Farr

abasas, a bodyguard searched the house, looking under the beds and in closets for bombs or intruders. Heller tried to make his house a refuge from the fear he lived with, but it was hard. The security company he used had installed elaborate and expensive alarm systems that had to be constantly set and deactivated. And one gun wasn't nearly enough in a house as big as Heller's.

"I have a minimum of a dozen guns around the house in places where I could get caught—coming out of the Jacuzzi, coming out of the swimming pool, watching television downstairs, going to the bathroom upstairs, in the gym," Heller said one afternoon in July, the day after FBI agents had arrested a group of white supremacists who were planning to blow up the First African Methodist Episcopal Church in Los Angeles in the hopes of igniting a race war. "Every night that I go to sleep, I have a .380 under my pillow and I have a .25 automatic hidden nearby. We have pepper-gas canisters all over the house. My girlfriend carries a gun and Mace wherever she goes."

Heller leaned in close. Talking about guns, Mace, alarms and all his elaborate rituals these past few years only intensified the howling fear that sat in his gut. His jaw tightened. His eyes bulged, terrified by their own vision.

"I haven't had a whole night's sleep since November of 1990," he said in a bitter, dark voice. "I come home a different way every day, always looking in my rearview mirror. Every time a car drives slowly by my house, or the dogs bark, I have to get up with my gun and check it out. Every time I hear something in my attic I have to call a bodyguard to come back. My life has been absolute hell. This business to me used to be so much fun that I didn't care to play golf or anything—until I met these scum thugs."

Eazy had come of age in the era of the Crips and Bloods.[2] Growing up in South Central Los Angeles, he'd lived with

---

[2] The Crips and Bloods, the two major gangs in L.A. during the 1980s and 1990s, derived their lifestyle from the Mexican pachuco gangs of the 1930s and 1940s. In 1991, police estimated there were eight hundred gangs and one hundred thousand gang members.

shootings, drugs, beatings and arrests. Life in the hood, with its daily meanness and random violence, had inured him to the violence of the world. Like all gangsta rappers, Eazy talked tough, and a reckless bravado made him ignore signals that others might've heeded. Which is why when Dre invited him to talk over "differences" at a studio at Solar Records one night in April 1991, Eazy took him up on the offer and showed up alone. It turned out Dre wasn't there when he arrived. Instead, Eazy said, he found himself alone with Suge Knight and two armed thugs.

"I went over there and Suge said that some of my groups— Above the Law, Michel'le, Kokane, D.O.C. and Dre—wanted to leave me. I knew that they wanted me to sign releases. I was told before, if it came down to that, not to sign them. But Suge said he was holding Jerry hostage in a van. Then he told me he knew where my mother lived," Eazy said, as Heller and Michael Klein, a lean, Israeli-born businessman and security specialist Heller had brought in for help, sat in the rap mogul's black-walled office listening to a story they'd heard many times.

"I figured he *did* know where my mother lived. I listened to him for a while. And then Suge called in his boys, who were carrying lead pipes, and brought out the contracts. And Suge said, 'I heard you was trying to get me killed, blood.' I figured either I'd sign the papers, get my ass kicked or fight them. So I signed the papers."

"Did you ever see Suge?" Klein asked, fixing me with his deep-set eyes.

"The guy is six foot two and weighs three hundred twenty pounds," Heller said.

"You have to understand Suge's reputation," said Klein.

"There were stories that he went around scaring Vanilla Ice," said Eazy, referring to the mysterious way in which Knight had secured ownership of seven songs on the white rapper's album *To the Extreme*, which had sold fifteen million copies.

"Suge's going through a trial right now, here in Hollywood, for beating up these two brothers," Klein said, referring to a lawsuit filed by two rappers, George and Lynwood Stanley, in

L.A.'s Superior Court, charging Dre's manager with battery and assault.[3]

"For pulling a gun on two brothers that Dre knew for years," said Eazy. Up until now, Eazy had a cocky grin on his face that said he was a match for anyone who fucked with him. But as he told the story, his mood gradually changed. "Suge hit the guy in the head with a gun, made him take off all his clothes, robbed him," Eazy said, and his eyes showed real fear.

"Eazy knew he was kicking the shit out of people," Klein said, his eyes registering some nameless fear. "So when he walked in that room that night it wasn't just some guy saying, 'Sign some papers.'"

No one could doubt that Marion "Suge" Knight, who had once played semipro football, had a knack for violence. Long before he became Dre's manager, back in November of 1987, when he was living in Las Vegas, Knight had been arrested for grand larceny auto, carrying a concealed weapon, use of a deadly weapon, attempted murder and battery with a deadly weapon. The charges were all dismissed, but Knight was again arrested December 14, 1990, for battery with a deadly weapon. Court records showed that on February 22, 1993, Knight was given a two-year sentence with probation for assault and ordered to pay restitution. Five months later, in mid-July, George and Lynwood Stanley had filed a lawsuit against Knight, claiming that at a meeting in Hollywood Knight had ordered them to lie on the floor and take off their clothes, threatened their lives, fired a shot at them and then beaten them severely before robbing them.

As for Dre, he had his own dark past. At twenty-eight he was known as much for his rap sheet as his rap records. The DJ turned producer turned rap star had beaten up on Fox TV talk show host Dee Barnes in 1991, prompting a twenty-million-dollar lawsuit.

---

[3] Knight declined to be interviewed for this book but denies the Stanley brothers' allegations and has denied in depositions Eazy and Heller's account of his obtaining the releases.

"I was in the wrong, but it's not like I broke the bitch's arm," Dre later said.[4]

Eventually he pleaded no contest to criminal battery charges in the case and settled out of court. But his troubles with the law were just beginning. In October 1992, Dre attacked a police officer in New Orleans during a hotel-lobby brawl in which he allegedly pummeled two other men. As part of his sentence for that offense he was forced to wear an electronic beeper that told police his whereabouts at all times. Meanwhile, in February 1992, Dre appeared in court in Van Nuys to face charges that he had busted the jaw of Woodland Hills producer Damon Thomas. Four months later, on June 2, the rap star pleaded guilty to a count of battery and was fined ten thousand dollars and sentenced to ninety days' house arrest.

Dre was no angel—that much was certain—and it was no secret that he despised Heller and Eazy. Anyone who wanted to know how deep that hatred went simply had to check out his smash-hit album, *The Chronic*, whose single "Dre Day," with his rapping partner, Snoop Doggy Dogg, contained his take on the Ruthless story.

The song's video, in heavy rotation on MTV all through the summer of 1993, featured an Eazy-E look-alike jumping up and down like a clown as a fat, white, bespectacled actor—an obvious stand-in for Heller—ordered a group of grinning black rappers around as if they were so many ignorant darkies. It was a chilling video: a gangsta-rap fable that served as both a vicious insult, complete with anti-Semitic underpinnings, and a fierce warning.

---

[4] Dre was quoted saying this in Jonathan Gold's September 1993 *Rolling Stone* cover story on him and Snoop Doggy Dogg, the Long Beach–based rapper whose debut, *Doggystyle*, was briefly the number one pop album in the country. Snoop, whose real name was Calvin Broadus, was wanted by police in connection with a murder, which happened shortly before his record was released. The violence in his personal life together with the violence in his lyrics and his overnight fame put him on the cover of major magazines across the country.

"I work for Sleazy-E—I wouldn't have it any other way," the fat white executive told the grinning Eazy look-alike. And with all the rappers gathered around him, he flashed a cunning smile: "Just sign your life—I mean your name—on the contract."

When Dre started rapping his message could hardly have been clearer. After scattering rhymes about how N.W.A used to be one happy family of homies, Dre talked about being *ganked*. "Now I'm *gankin'* you, little ho . . . So strap on your Compton hat and . . . watch your back/'Cause you might get smoked," the rap star said, using the street slang word *gank*, which meant "swindle." Waving a gun, surrounded by dozens of scowling blacks dressed in gang apparel, Dre walked and talked like a gangster. The video concluded with a statement saying that everything in it was "fictitious." But Heller and Eazy got the message.

"The song's a threat against us," Heller said. "A violent threat against Eazy and me."

Heller hadn't started in the black-music business. His music career began when he worked as a booking agent in the mid-sixties for Chartwell Artists, Ltd., a talent agency that handled the first Ali-Frazier fight and the first Elton John tour in America. Then he went into business for himself.

At Heller-Fischel, a booking agency he founded with Don Fischel that specialized in music, Heller handled bands like Styx, Journey, the Electric Light Orchestra and Boz Scaggs. "We did the Crosby-Nash acoustic tour and worked with Van Morrison—lots of big acts. I was a superstar when I was twenty-seven," Heller said, his voice puffed up with the memory of being around the big shots who shaped the rock and roll business. "We were always more than an agency and less than a management firm. But the booking business is not a fun business. I knew everyone who was important. I'd represented lots of stars and made tons of money."

Sometime in the late sixties, Heller got a letter from a kid who was a senior at the University of Illinois. He was doing some concerts there and wanted to be an agent.

"So I hired him and brought him to my house. His name was Irving Azoff and he lived at my place. Phil Casey, who heads the black-music department at MCA, worked with Heller-Fischel. I hired him when he got back from Vietnam."

Heller left the agency in 1976 and worked on tours for various artists. In 1978, with new wave starting to happen, Heller represented L.A. groups like 20/20 and the Zippers as both a booking agent and the person who put together their record deals. At some point he bought out Fischel and ran the agency, hiring other people to work for him. He did booking for Joan Armatrading and freelanced for other companies until about 1985, when he met Eazy-E.

Heller had heard about a scene that was happening at a pressing plant in Hollywood called Macola. It intrigued him: Black youths with little or no musical education were getting their rap recordings pressed on the cheap.

"I heard this scene was going to change the focus of the music business. It used to be that the music business was centered around the studio, with top producers getting so many thousands of dollars per track. Now we had kids who were making records in their garages with little machines that they'd bought at the Guitar Center. Now the focus was paying the money to get the records pressed. And this little Macola pressing plant was granting entrepreneurs and musicians credit to press their records."

Heller liked rap music and especially liked how it was made. It didn't require lots of pricey producers because much of the music was sampled from the rubble of seventies funk—James Brown, George Clinton and P-Funk. By the mideighties, when N.W.A came along, an unknown rap group could, for a pittance, make a record that would sell five hundred thousand or more copies. And the savvy record label that put it out didn't have to spend a fortune, as major labels did, imaging the group and paying off independent promoters to work radio. Almost no one played rap on radio; it was played on boom boxes and in jeeps and cars. And if the grooves were dope, people would line up to buy it.

At Macola, Heller met the World Class Wreckin' Cru, which included Dre and other future members of N.W. A. One of the rappers from the World Class Wreckin' Cru, Alonzo Williams, was working with a group called C.I.A., which became the Stereo Crew, which included Ice Cube and Sir Jinx.

"There was a group called Egyptian Lover and a group called Timex Social Club," Heller remembered. "Two Live Crew, M. C. Hammer, Ice Cube—all these people were doing rap records there."

Of all the B-boys hanging out at Macola, Dre would be the most important—not because of his rapping ability but because of his producing talents. His signature sound, a raw, sinuous funk with live drums and bass, was what propelled virtually all of the albums he produced for Ruthless into monster hits. Rap was a producer's medium and the Ruthless sound, which was the gangsta sound, was Dre's sound: a nasty, crazy slice of anarchy that was as identifiable as a Beach Boys chorus.

Of course, the lyrics, laced with talk of "bitches," "hoes" (whores) and "trix," weren't necessarily what parents wanted their kids reciting. Gangsta rap thrived on misogyny, as well as homophobia and race-baiting rage. By the time N.W.A came out with *Efil4zaggin*, its final album, gangsta rap seemed played out as a genre—a dead-end road offering nihilism and blank rage. But rap's roots went far deeper than the gang-ridden neighborhoods of South Central L.A.

Rap had surfaced in the South Bronx and part of its mythology, spread by critics and rappers themselves, was that it came from the boasting and toasting traditions in reggae. But anyone who remembered the New York blackout of 1977, and the looting and arson that followed, knew that rap music, which stood for the rage of African-Americans in that angry hot summer, had nothing to do with the "riddims" of Jamaica.

In fact, the first raps had probably come out of prison culture and were a form of oral storytelling with bragging rights:

prisoners reciting toasts that glorified the life of crime, fables that told how a man in jail had been cheated on by his girl-friend or set up by someone to take a fall. Two decades earlier, in the fifties, radio DJs had even done prison-style raps over the air. The best-known black DJ, Douglas "Jocko" Henderson, even had a show that prefigured the coming hip-hop obsession with sci-fi themes. No doubt he was later heard by New York club DJs, who refined the jivey patter.

But the true roots of rap were James Brown's hard funk and the music of a group of militant African-American ex-convicts called the Last Poets. Released in 1973, the Poets' album *Hustler's Convention*[5] contained radical raps, such as "Niggers Are Scared of Revolution," that anticipated the rage, politics and Afrocentric themes that would become a cornerstone of hip-hop more than a decade later.

Rap didn't start out being overtly political. Even Public Enemy, whose scathing rhymes about racism and black rage set to a rumble of scratches, split beats, loops and drop-outs, didn't begin as social commentators. Chuck D, who founded Public Enemy, started rapping for the fun of it. Yet rap changed fast. Inevitably, as it reached out to the disenfranchised black youth, the music became a forum for a newly revived black national-ism. The speeches of assassinated former Black Muslim leader Malcolm X, who had always been the model for angry young blacks, surfaced in the songs of New York rappers along with fiery snippets from minister Louis Farrakhan. And with all this came radical reinterpretations of history as well as anti-Semitic rants and ugly attitudes toward women and homosexuals. Blar-ing out over giant boom boxes carried by scowling black youths, rap music scared white people just the way they were scared

---

[5] The raps on *Hustler's Convention* were written and performed by Jalal Nuriddin, the leader of the Last Poets. The album reportedly sold eight hundred thousand copies. As for the true origins of rap discussed here, I am indebted to Steven Hager's landmark book on hip-hop culture, *Hip-Hop: The Illustrated History of Break Dancing, Rap Music and Graffiti.*

when they heard Stokely Carmichael and Malcolm X and the Black Panthers speak about "honkies" and "white devils" back in the sixties.

If Public Enemy was the leading New York rap group, then N.W.A was the epitome of Southern California rap. Its most famous song, "Fuck tha Police," was nowhere near as sophisticated or intelligent as any of the best New York rap, but the song embodied the vulgar, trigger-happy, we-don't-give-a-fuck rage of the black youths who lived in the stucco-and-smog jungles of South Central Los Angeles. It was a song that could only come out of a city like L.A., where gangs are a religion and vast, sprawling ghettos have produced a generation of virtual psychopaths. In L.A., joining a gang, knocking up a "bitch," killing your rivals and enduring some jail time were all rites of passage. The gangs themselves were death cults, complete with formal and elaborate rituals for initiating new members and saying goodbye to dead ones. And gangsta rap was the perfect music for that lifestyle, loaded down as it was with warnings of betrayal, murder, revenge and a short, violent life. Gangsta rap blared from jeeps and BMWs driven by drug dealers, the new capitalist warlords. But it also appealed to rebellious white kids who picked up on its raw machismo and shocking statements.

"When I met Eazy he played me 'Boyz-N-the-Hood,' and I knew I wanted to be involved with that," said Heller, referring to what would be the first gangsta single. After hearing the song, he handed over most of his responsibilities to a partner and focused on shaping N.W.A's career.

"I believed that rap would become the most important music of the nineties. And I thought that by 1990 it would be a major arena attraction—that the skateboarders and surfers and radical white youths of this country were going to espouse rap as they had the Rolling Stones and Guns N' Roses. I thought that this would be the next expression of rebellion among kids."

The media tended to either denounce gangsta rappers as dangerous monsters or glorify them as the new urban documentarians. Of course they were neither. They were simply satisfying the public's thirst for violence while scattering enough commentary to appear socially responsible. And some rappers were documentarians. Whether you agreed with them or not, groups like Public Enemy made ferociously powerful music that, at its best, carried a potent political message: a warning for whitey and a summons for black youth to hunt out their proud heritage. Some of the most profound, life-affirming music of the nineties was coming from rappers who embraced life and hope instead of death and despair—groups like Arrested Development, Disposable Heroes of Hiphoprisy and the Jungle Brothers. But gangsta rap, which is what Heller's label specialized in, had a far different message.

"In contrast to their New York Rap counterparts . . . who were tribunes of Black nationalism, Los Angeles gangster rappers disclaim all ideology except the primitive accumulation of wealth by any means necessary," Mike Davis wrote in *City of Quartz*, his book about L.A.'s shadowy history and dystopic subcultures. "In supposedly stripping bare the reality of the streets, 'telling it like it is,' they also offer an uncritical mirror to fantasy power-trips of violence, sexism and greed."

Violence seemed to be the top agenda: the racist violence L.A.P.D. cops leveled at blacks and the revenge fantasies the gangsta rappers spawned. Ice-T's song "Cop Killer," released a month before the Los Angeles riots by Sire Records, a Warner Bros. affiliate, was the prototype and got the most publicity, kicking off a national protest and boycott of Warner Bros. The rapper withdrew the record eventually—after police groups picketed the Time Warner shareholders' meeting in Beverly Hills. But there were plenty of other cop-killing dreams flowing out of hip-hop culture.

In the wake of the Los Angeles riots, gangsta rappers were elevated to the unofficial status of urban oracles: prophets of the coming racial Armageddon. But what they were saying wasn't necessarily about healing. In the winter of 1992, a rapper named Tupac Amaru Shakur, signed to the Time Warner–affiliated label Interscope Records, was facing a lawsuit by a Texas widow who said his album *2Pacalypse Now* led to the murder of her highway trooper husband. The music was vindicated when an Austin jury sentenced the actual cop killer to death. But like Dre, Shakur had a life that paralleled the violence in his music.

He'd been arrested in New York on November 18, 1993, for forcible sodomy and unlawful imprisonment of a twenty-year-old woman at a swank Manhattan hotel. And a month earlier he'd been charged with two counts of aggravated assault after allegedly shooting and wounding two off-duty police officers in Atlanta.[6]

Not all the West Coast rappers came off the streets. Paris, an Oakland-based gangsta rapper, was supposedly a university graduate with a degree in economics. When Time Warner executives warned him to change the lyrics to his single "Bush Killa," a song about assassinating then-president George Bush, Paris formed his own label, Scarface Records, and sold three hundred thousand copies of the offending album, *Sleeping with the Enemy.*

Cop-killing was a growth industry, and gangsta rappers were hard-core capitalists, adept at exploiting instant markets. Dre himself had written his own police revenge fantasy—"Mr. Officer," a song that depicted a cop in a casket and never appeared on his album *The Chronic.* But his other songs—"A Nigga witta Gun," "Rat-Tat-Tat-Tat," "Lyrical Gangbang"—were the perfect theme music for the lurid stories of drive-bys and murders that played out each week in the *Los Angeles Times.*

Jimmy Iovine, the coowner of Interscope Records, Dre's label, called Dre "a brilliant innovator. If this was a white art-

---

[6] The alleged sodomy occurred at New York's swank Hotel Parker Meridien, where Shakur was supposedly part of a four-man sex attack. As for Shakur's other violent propensities, in March of 1993 he was arrested for allegedly assaulting a limo driver outside the set of Fox TV's *In Living Color.* He also allegedly attacked director Allen Hughes last spring after being dismissed from Hughes's film *Menace II Society.* Shakur was arrested April 30, 1994, in Hollywood after police said they found a concealed handgun under his car seat. A week and a half later he began serving a fifteen-day jail term for the Hughes attack. Shakur also faces two assault cases in Atlanta.

ist," Iovine said, "I believe that these court cases would be a footnote in the story." Asked about Dre's violent reputation, James Bernard, the editor of the rap magazine *The Source*, told a *Los Angeles Times* reporter: "We've all heard stories about his troubles, but I don't think anybody in the hip-hop world holds that against him. Like Prince and Phil Spector, he has serious credentials and artistic integrity. And really, in the final analysis, this guy is not asking us to accept who he is as a person, but to listen to the music he makes."

But Dre's work, even judged purely as pop artifice, was dreadful. Though he was touted as a "genius" by many critics, his music was a throwback to a soulless period in black culture. Instead of ingenious sampling fused to a ferocious live performance, Dre served up lame raps over monotonous bass and drums. In seven years, gangsta rap had gone nowhere, and Dre was the embodiment of that stagnation.

Of course, white music critics, many of them past forty and afraid of being seen as dinosaurs, found ways to rationalize all the ugliness in the gangsta music. When rappers called black women "bitches" and depicted them as conniving whores, this was "street" reporting. As for violence, gangsterism, anti-Semitism, half-baked racial theories and the blind pursuit of wealth—that was all an inevitable part of growing up in the hood, the grim karmic payback for white oppression.

"You have a lot of people who are really afraid of being caught with their hip pants down. That's why you have major white critics calling an anti-Semitic Public Enemy lyric provocative—as if this were thought-provoking as opposed to repulsive bullshit," said writer and critic Greil Marcus. "When Ice Cube says, 'I don't really believe any of this stuff. I'm just saying what it's like out there on the mean streets,' that's bullshit. Ice Cube wants to blow up Korean grocery store owners because he doesn't like them. And to condescend to these people and say they're naive documentarians is like saying we're the anthropologists and they're the natives."

Greg Sandow, the music editor of *Entertainment Weekly*,

who was the first writer in L.A. to cover gangsta rap in depth as a critic with the now-defunct *Herald Examiner*, believed N.W.A were "important artists" in the history of rap.

"If they're taken as the founders of the gangsta genre, they have to be important," said Sandow, "though the misogyny has lately gone way out of bounds. That seemed less important back then because it was so new and you could shrug it off. I went to the first few live N.W.A shows and I would see women scream along to songs that I would think they would object to. So it was clear that a white person, not part of that culture—that it was rash to judge it." But Sandow conceded that most writers didn't look hard enough at the hateful messages contained in the visceral music.

"There was so much talk about violence and gangs in 1989 that you could not get a balanced view," Sandow said. "What made defending N.W.A seem so crucial were all the bullshit attacks pouring out from the police and the media saying that rap incited violence. But I think that [we] were too quick to embrace this whole thing without being critical. With everything that's come out since, it appears that N.W.A were in it more for money than anything else. But for a lot of blacks and hip-hoppers, money was a way to some kind of serious respect."

Heller would talk about the members of N.W.A as "major" artists making profound music. It was one of his set pieces when confronted with charges that his gangsta rappers exploited the homicidal rage, misogyny and nihilism in L.A.'s black ghettos.

"N.W.A are the most important documentarians of our generation," he told me. "Even though they rap in first person, it's a third-person point of view. They don't espouse any of the things they write about. What they say is that these are the things that exist—the reality they grew up with. If you don't like sexism or chauvinism, that doesn't mean it's not reality."

But more than anything else, Heller smelled big money in gangsta rap. Like early rock and roll, it was linked with rebellion and rage, its swaggering boasts and raw rhythms intimately tied up with sexuality. Besides, vicious attitudes toward women weren't restricted to black culture. Plenty of white, Latino and Asian youths, jilted by a girlfriend or working out some rage toward females, could relate to a gangsta rapper calling a woman a "bitch."

"You can't sell two million rap records to kids in the inner city. That's a way to sell two hundred thousand records," Heller said one afternoon as he was driving to lunch. "You have to market it to the white kids. And let's face it—no matter how old you are as a rock and roller, you still got to give twelve-year-old boys hard-ons." Heller smiled conspiratorially, looking at me sidewise. "And you still have to get twelve-year-old girls' pussies wet."

Neither Suge Knight nor Dre nor their attorney, David Kenner, a short, chunky man who wore his hair slicked back in a ponytail, would talk to me. But both the rapper and his manager had plenty to say in depositions. Asked about the releases, Dre said that Eazy willingly signed them because it was the right thing to do—right because Eazy and Dre had a contract from the very beginning, when Ruthless was founded, saying that the two were fifty-fifty partners. Dre denied that there were any threats or that there was any extortion or intimidation. And while he had a police record, he claimed he was never a gangster.

Neither Heller nor Eazy nor Michael Klein was surprised that Knight denied ever calling them with threats or coming there with gangbangers and guns. But in a deposition the ex–football player turned bodyguard turned manager floated out something that shocked everyone at Ruthless. Knight swore that in the late part of 1990 Heller had contacted him at a meeting outside Ruthless's new offices. There, Knight claimed, at their first get-together, Heller had given him a check for just under ten thousand dollars, asking him to consider murdering rap star Ice Cube, a onetime member of N.W.A who'd left the label for a solo deal with Priority Records. Later, Knight said,

Heller gave him another five thousand dollars to think about the same act.

"Never mind that Ruthless wasn't even at its new office then," said Michael Bourbeau, the Ruthless attorney who had deposed Knight. "But then everything Suge says is preposterous. Here's a convicted felon who goes around threatening people."

When I mentioned Knight's murder-for-hire accusation, Heller shrugged. "He's a liar. It's not even worth responding to."

Heller maintained all along that he was the innocent victim of a cold-blooded scam—a conspiracy that went to the highest levels of Sony Music Entertainment, to the offices of the label's chairman himself, Tommy Mottola. But Dre and Knight painted Heller as a greedy, scheming operator—the worst example of the "predatory, money-grubbing Jew" in the entertainment business—and Eazy as his willing dupe.

Hearing both sides was like entering two different realities. Asked in deposition about his understanding of the financial agreement concerning N.W.A, Dre said, ". . . the deal was I was going to do the work in the studio. He [Eazy] was going to put [up] the money. And we were gong to split everything fifty-fifty, the profits . . . everyone understood that me and Eric was trying to build something . . . build a record company."

Asked if he told any other members of N.W.A that he was going to be Eazy's partner, Dre said he "didn't remember," but he did recall mentioning the arrangement to Ice Cube, who didn't complain. Heller laughed a small, sour laugh that said he was not amused when I mentioned Dre's version of reality.

"N.W.A was set up a certain way. There *were* partners, but Eazy owned the company. Ruthless was the publisher. There was an equal split of the net, but Eazy founded N.W.A and Ruthless, so he owned the company. It would be like if Mick Jagger owned Atlantic Records."

"Since Ruthless was formed, Dre has never told anybody about his partnership. He told the new lawyer he has *now*, but not any of his lawyers in between. Why aren't there any letters to that effect?" Klein asked me. A self-made millionaire from the garment business—his company finished such products as Guess jeans—Klein spoke excellent English in a thick Israeli accent. He considered the music industry no different from any other business. "Wouldn't you tell your lawyers that you weren't getting the money due you and you had a fifty-percent contract?"

"To say he was a fifty-percent owner of Ruthless is preposterous," said Bourbeau. "He never had a single discussion from the time he was driving around with Eazy until December 1992, when he has discussions with his lawyer."

From the beginning, Heller said, he acted as N.W.A's manager—something Eazy confirmed. But in his deposition Dre denied that Heller ever managed him or N.W.A. Beyond that, Dre insisted that the group was formed in 1987 when Heller and Priority Records president Bryan Turner gave Dre a seventy-five-thousand-dollar check backstage at a concert in Phoenix and had him sign an exclusive artist's recording agreement. When I asked Heller about this, he shook his head.

"It's a lie. We have a signed contract to prove that I was N.W.A's manager," Heller said. "And N.W.A was formed sometime in 1989. So it's an absolute lie when Dre says that the group was formed in 1987."[7]

"Besides, in earlier depositions, in a Birmingham case that's going on right now, Dre said Jerry *was* his manager," Klein said, referring to a paternity suit against N.W.A rapper MC Ren pending in Alabama. "They asked him who owned Ruthless Records and he said Eazy did. And they asked him who his manager was and he said Jerry was."

To believe that Dre and Eazy were fifty-fifty partners, in Heller's view, you would have to believe that he had a contract with Eazy or Ruthless that entitled him to a half stake in the business. But Dre had no copy of such a contract.

On the other hand, Ruthless said it had plenty of signed, written contracts, including one that mentioned Eazy as the

---

[7] In fact, N.W.A had an album on *Billboard's* black LP chart in 1988, a year before Heller says the group was formed.

sole shareholder in Ruthless Records. Asked why he was un-happy at Ruthless, Dre was blunt.

"Because of Jerry Heller," Dre said in an April 1992 inter-view for *BRE*, a monthly black entertainment magazine. "He took advantage of everyone except Eazy. They conspired to fuck the artists on Ruthless. When Eazy and I first got together it was me doing the music and him putting up the money. Jerry comes in and talks him into fucking everybody. Suge, my man-ager, pulled my coat to the bad contracts. I was young and didn't know anything. The big numbers were coming in but they weren't the *right* numbers. Jerry's gonna leave Eazy broke. He grabbed the wrong nigga's coattail. He should've grabbed the one with the talent."

Knight also talked up his and Dre's case against Ruthless in the black press.

"Things weren't right at Ruthless," Knight told a reporter in the same issue of *BRE*. "People like D.O.C. weren't being properly paid for their services. Dre was as hot as any producer both in or out of the rap world but you'd never know it by the financial situation going on. I looked at Dre's contract and decided he could do better."

There were other members of N.W.A who didn't think they were getting the money they deserved from Heller or Eazy. Back in 1989, when N.W.A split up, Ice Cube, whose real name was O'Shea Jackson, left the rap group and the label complain-ing that Heller and Eazy were skimming off a lot of money that should've gone to the group. Signing with Priority Records, which was Ruthless's distributor, Ice Cube soon became a star on his own with hard-core gangsta albums like *AmeriKKKa's Most Wanted*, *Death Certificate* and *The Predator*. That he then despised Heller, N.W.A's manager, was obvious. His 1991 song "No Vaseline" advocated putting a bullet in the head of a "white Jew telling you what to do."[8]

---

[8] The song was off the album *Death Certificate*, which also contained "Black Korea," an attack on Korean grocery-store owners. Heller claims he and Ice Cube now get along.

"When Ice Cube split up he felt that he wasn't getting the kind of money that he believed he was worth," Heller told me, as if the bad blood between him and Ice Cube were a minor rift in a once wonderful relationship. "He decided he wanted to be Eazy-E. It's a determination that he made. Our publicist, Pat Sharbonay, wanted to be his manager, and the only way she could be his manager was if I wasn't his manager. So he attacked that relationship in the traditional way: 'Why are you fuckin' around with that white Jew?' The second way he attacked it was to suggest larceny: 'That guy is stealing from me.'"

Around the music industry and even on the streets, though, a different story was circulating. There was talk that Heller had been eagerly waiting for the kind of big score he got with N.W.A—that his specialty was exploiting young black artists while using Eazy as a front. Though no one could prove it, it was bruited about that N.W.A had released its first album without any contract.

And certainly by the time N.W.A's breakthrough album, *Straight Outta Compton*, came out, Heller could see he'd hit the jackpot. The album quickly sold 750,000 copies and set up a fifty-city tour. Yet during that tour, Ice Cube charged that Heller was instrumental in breaking up the group.

Ice Cube claimed that during a Phoenix stopover on that N.W.A tour Heller, serving as the group's manager, promised a $75,000 check for everyone who signed a contract he'd drawn up.[9] The quick payoff enticed everyone to sign but Ice Cube, who brought in an accountant and a lawyer. What they discovered was shocking, according to Ice Cube. Out of the $650,000 the tour grossed, Jerry Heller had kept $130,000. By contrast, Ice Cube took home only $23,000.

Thus, though he wrote half of the material on *Straight Outta Compton* and Eazy-E's *Eazy-Duz-It*, albums with combined sales of some three million, Ice Cube received only

---

[9] This claim appears in an interview with Ice Cube in the December 1993 issue of the hip-hop magazine *The Bomb*. However, he did not consent to be interviewed for this book.

$32,000. What's more, although he was signed to Ruthless Records, Ice Cube wasn't signed with N.W.A.

For Ice Cube, the only answer was to leave the group and get out of the predatory relationship with Heller, who he was convinced was swindling him.[10]

Heller dismissed all the accusations with a wave of his hand, as if to say anyone smart should know otherwise.

"No one has ever filed a suit against us or a cross-complaint. In Ice Cube's case he had a battery of lawyers and accountants come in and check the books and everyone was satisfied with the results. They've said we stole from them, but they haven't been able to prove one thing."

"No one's ever sued us," Eazy said when I asked him the same question. He flashed me a big-toothed smile. "If we took their money, how come they haven't sued us?"

"We hired two law firms," said Heller, his voice all patience. "They went in and looked at all the books. They made some recommendations to us as to accounting procedures. It cost each of us a little over twenty-seven thousand dollars to have them go in and look at the Ruthless books. Ice Cube had thirteen attorneys go through the books but not one of them was able to shake the foundations of their contracts based on what they said were the merits of their discontent. Even now, no one has filed a cross-complaint."

As for Dre's complaint that Heller and Eazy had been stealing him blind, Heller bristled.

"Here's a guy who made millions of dollars and was paid millions of dollars by Ruthless." We were driving up to Heller's Calabasas house and he took a detour and showed me Dre's house, almost exactly the same. "Does that look like the house of someone who isn't getting paid money? We send him big royalty checks all the time. Dre said he wasn't getting paid. In

---

[10] According to *The Bomb,* Ice Cube said at the time that Heller was spreading rumors that he left N.W.A because he was envious of Eazy's talent.

his deposition he said he got no money in 1991. Well, we have a 1099 for six hundred ninety thousand dollars."

A few weeks later, back at his office, Heller pulled out his 1099 federal tax forms, which showed payouts to Andre "Dr. Dre" Young from 1987 to 1992 of more than one and a half million dollars.

"And that doesn't include performances and other appearances," Heller said, shaking his head in disbelief. "Listen, the guys who did this ruined our company. We were the most successful young company of the nineties. Everything we put out was huge. *Supersonic* [an album by the female rap trio J.J. Fad] went platinum. Michel'le—platinum. D.O.C.—platinum. N.W.A—double platinum. Eazy-E—double platinum. But they took two years out of our lives. Dre never did another thing for us after that. Michel'le never did another thing for us. The meteoric ride that came from Eazy building this company— they ended that. Now we're starting all over."

Knight and Dre weren't the only enemies hatching conspiracies, according to the suit. Ruthless named Sony Music Entertainment and Solar Records, an independent record company based in Los Angeles and run by Dick Griffey, as defendants. All three companies had business relationships with one another: Solar had a deal with Sony whereby Sony made money available to Solar to sign new talent, whose records Sony and Solar would jointly distribute. Similarly, Ruthless had a production deal with Sony that dated back to 1989, which called for Dre to produce a number of rap records for Sony. According to Ruthless's subsequently dismissed complaint, Solar and Sony entered into a conspiracy when they saw a window of opportunity to permanently take Dre, one of the hottest rap producers in the country, away from Ruthless.

"It was just like *The Godfather*. Sony wanted Dre, who was a very hot producer, so they had releases drafted for Knight to bring to Eric Wright," said Bourbeau, who had drafted the complaints. "They wanted him to sign the papers. And if he didn't sign the papers, he knew the consequences. The very first thing Sony did was to give Dre a million bucks for the music publishing rights in the spring of 1991. This was before all of the intimidation. [Sony] said, 'We'll give you one million dollars and you get out of the contract. We'll help you—we'll draft the releases. You just get them signed and we'll put your records out.'"

"Sony's intention was to use Dre for the movie *Deep Cover*, and they got to Dre through Solar" is how Klein put it one afternoon. He'd been nervously pacing up and down, reading over police records on Suge that had been faxed over to him from Nevada, but now he sat down and hunched over. "That's who they really wanted. So how did they get him? Well, Solar and Suge had a relationship with him. And I'm sure Solar and Suge and Sony came up with this scam. How could Sony get releases? Well, I imagine Suge must've said, 'Don't worry, I'll take care of that. Just have one of your lawyers draw up the releases for me and I'll get them signed.' It was all a conspiracy. They never thought we were going to sue. They thought they'd be able to work something out, pay peanuts for what happened and they'd have Dre. Dre was going to go with Sony. They had it all planned out. They had his new album scheduled to be released. *The Chronic* was going to be a Sony release, but not until we sued did they take it off the release schedule. Then [Sony] said, 'This is too deep for us, and we're going to have problems if we go ahead.'"

When *The Chronic* was finally released it was on the Death Row/Interscope label. Every day when Heller looked at *Billboard*, where Dre's album was hovering near the top of the pop charts, he could recalculate how many millions of dollars he'd lost. (*The Chronic* would spend eight months in Billboard's Top Ten and become the top-selling hard-core rap album in history.)

"We licensed *The Chronic* just to mitigate our damages. That record would've been ours if it hadn't been stolen. It's sold three million units. You're talking millions and millions of dollars. But we had to make a deal with Interscope because Dre wouldn't deliver the record to us—because of what Sony did."

According to Ruthless's third amended complaint, David Glew, the president of Sony's Epic label, and Hank Caldwell, another Epic executive, had met repeatedly with Suge Knight to discuss Dre's contracts with Ruthless. Ruthless alleged it had repeatedly warned Sony about Knight's violent tendencies.

"We kept telling Sony that we were going to sue if they didn't stop," said Klein, "but they thought we would never sue them. Who were we, this puny little record company? They thought we would go away or take a small settlement. But they were wrong. When we sued they took *The Chronic* off the list of scheduled releases."

In deposition, Dre said that an attorney named Michael Frisbee had drafted the releases that Knight allegedly had forced Eazy to sign. This was a key point in Ruthless's supposed conspiracy, because Ruthless believed it had evidence that Frisbee was an outside counsel for Sony: The footer at the bottom of the release documents was the same as the one used by Scott Aronson, the attorney for Sony Music Publishing.

"What we saw was that twenty-four hours after the releases were signed by Eazy," Bourbeau said, "Suge sent a fax to Caldwell and Glew at Epic saying Dre was available for all production work. And it asked for a hundred twenty-five thousand dollars in advance."

"We had attorneys," said Klein. "If Sony was interested in having releases drawn up, why didn't they contact our attorneys? But they went ahead with their own plan. And right after they got the releases, Suge sends them a fax saying that Dre is ready to work on new projects—please send money. Where did they come off using someone like Suge to start with, knowing his reputation? Why would any Sony lawyer draw up releases?"

Even now, Sony's evil plan was bearing fruit, according to Ruthless, in the form of illegal profits from the Sony/Solar soundtrack to the film *Deep Cover*. Heller and Klein found it outrageous that the soundtrack, released in May 1992, conveyed the copyright to the Dre-produced material on the album to Sony and Solar. More galling yet, the hit title track, which described the murder of an undercover cop, was the debut of Snoop Doggy Dogg, soon to become a major rap star himself.

"The *Deep Cover* contract was illegal because Sony was using artists still signed to Ruthless," said Bourbeau. "Other than having gotten the extorted releases, they had no right to use them. We told them that the releases were invalid. But they then drew up a *Deep Cover* contract. We told Sony, 'Don't put it out,' but they did anyway. The whole goal was to raid Ruthless's assets. And while this may go on in the music business all the time, it doesn't make it lawful."

"Sony had a contract with Dre knowing that Dre was signed to Ruthless. They *knew* that," Klein said. "And our lawyer wrote everybody letters saying how these releases were obtained. But they used them anyway. Wouldn't any businessman in his right mind say, 'How is it possible?' Because there was no consideration."

"The releases didn't say, 'We release you for three million dollars and ten percent of the profits,'" said Heller. "It said nothing, which is the most ridiculous thing in the world. They're saying we just gave away everything out of the goodness of our hearts."

Of course, Wayne Smith, a partner at Gibson, Dunn & Crutcher, the California law firm defending Sony, had a very different tale to tell.

"They haven't filed a complaint yet that can withstand a motion to dismiss," Smith said when I asked him about all the charges leveled against his client. "And for all their wild ranting and raving, they haven't gotten past the simple litmus test of the judge saying, 'You've actually stated a legal claim here.' Just because their attorney is spouting these accusations doesn't mean it amounts to anything.

"What's really happening is a simple dispute between an artist and his label. Dre became unhappy with Ruthless—it's that simple. Dre decided he didn't want to work for Eazy-E; he wanted to do his own recording. And he set out to negotiate with some other companies. One of the companies he decided to negotiate with was Sony."

Smith didn't deny that Sony was interested in signing a publishing agreement, a recording agreement and a producing agreement with Dre. But in the end, he said, Sony didn't sign Dre to anything but a publishing deal because the company couldn't feel certain that he was free to sign.

"We knew that Ruthless was taking the position that the contract they had bound Dre to release solo material through Ruthless," Smith said. "But it's clear that Dre has the right to write, sell and publish music separate and apart from Ruthless; Ruthless only holds rights to his music if he performs it for Ruthless. So Sony signed Dre up to a publishing agreement for the rights he did not hold for Ruthless. It absolutely escapes me how Michael Bourbeau can make any federal case out of this. I know he screams about it. But I attribute it to his lack of knowledge of the music business.

"Companies that have publishing businesses sign artists who are under contract to other record companies all the time. Big record companies sign songwriters who haven't released *anything*—if they think they are promising. It is an ideal situation for a publishing company to go after someone who is a good enough performer, someone who already has a recording contract, because you know that if they're good enough to have a recording contract, the odds are that they're going to write some music that's going to get recorded. Ruthless says this is all part of some grand scheme to destroy their company. But Sony was very careful. They only signed Dre to the rights that Ruthless didn't have."

Ruthless claimed that Frisbee was an outside counsel for Sony, that the two were essentially in collusion. But Smith denied that Frisbee had ever represented Sony in any transaction. How did he get hold of releases with Sony's footers on them?

"Dre and Knight went to Michael Frisbee," said Smith, "and we understand that he was given copies of releases that

Sony had done for some publishing agreements that never got signed. He then used those as his forms to draft the releases that freed Dre, D.O.C. and Michel'le from their obligations as recording artists and producers.

"Next thing we know about the releases is we hear that Dre and Knight have them but they won't give them to us. They said, 'We can enter into the contracts because they have these releases.' But they won't show them to us. Knight told us, 'They were gotten legitimately, but the reason I can't give you a copy was because I promised Eazy when he signed them that I wouldn't give them to anybody without his approval.'"

Eventually, Knight did show copies of the releases to Sony. But by then, the company had decided not to sign Dre to any further deals.

"We never did anything that relied on the releases. We don't know whether they're valid or not. We only know that there's a dispute over them."

As for the *Deep Cover* brouhaha, Smith couldn't comprehend Ruthless's position. Sony didn't dispute the fact that it had contracted with Dre to do work on the soundtrack to the film. And it was neither uncommon nor illegal for an artist from one label to do a soundtrack for another.

"Since Dre was doing some work for other labels, it seemed reasonable that it was OK," said Smith. "Ruthless claimed that its contracts with Dre prohibited him from performing on the *Deep Cover* soundtrack. But the fact of the matter is, Sony utilized Dre's contracts at a time when he said he was free to do it. If he was not free to do it, Ruthless and Dre have a breach of contract. If it turns out Dre did not have the right to sell us what he sold us, then Ruthless has a breach of contract against Dre and Sony has a breach of warranty against Dre. But that's not a RICO suit or a conspiracy. And those aren't very sexy claims. If they're there, we'll litigate them."

If anything, Smith said, Ruthless was itself engaged in unscrupulous business practices. Why? Because Sony had a contract with Ruthless whereby Ruthless was to provide albums by new artists to Sony and those albums were to be produced by

Dre, "but when we got the first three albums, they weren't produced by Dre. The credits they gave didn't even represent that Dre had produced the required material on them, though later they said it was Dre. But the credits they gave us didn't show that. And when Dre was in negotiations with us, he told us he didn't produce those albums. We thought the albums weren't very good. The first two didn't perform very well. We got the third album, by Above the Law, and we listened to it." Sony didn't think much of it. In fact, its lawyers considered suing Ruthless for breach of contract. But instead, Sony came back to Ruthless with a proposal.

"We thought if we could get one really good song on the album we could salvage something," Smith said. "We asked if we could get Above the Law to do another song and have Dre produce it. Ruthless said, 'Great—but Dre won't work for us. Can you get him to do it for us?' So we asked Knight to get Dre to produce an Above the Law cut to go on the album. We had the absolute right to take one cut off the Above the Law album and put it on the *Deep Cover* album. And we had to pay over and above what we should have paid to Ruthless to get the song. We came within a hair's breadth of suing Ruthless over all this, but decided it wasn't worth it, because litigation is expensive. Forget it. They screwed us. We won't take any more albums from them."

I asked Smith about the allegations that Tommy Mottola, the feisty Italian fighter who had climbed to the top of Sony Entertainment, was involved in the alleged racketeering conspiracy. Smith laughed.

"Saying Tommy Mottola is engaged in a criminal conspiracy because Dre is recording a cut for a soundtrack album is so far-fetched as to be ludicrous. Tommy was dating Mariah Carey. Would you be worried about one cut on a *Deep Cover* album? Does Tommy Mottola sit back and covet Ruthless artists and say, 'Let's go figure out some way to get them'? It's garbage. Look, Sony had Aerosmith for a while. Aerosmith moved to Geffen. Aerosmith is unhappy with Geffen and wants to sign with Sony again. Sony signed them—subject to completion of their obligations to Geffen. Bourbeau worked this into one of his pleadings, saying that Sony was in this pattern of destroying their competitors' talent, but now it seems to have dropped out of their arguments.

"They said in one of their complaints that Tommy Mottola is a well-known wiseguy, that he's got connections to organized crime. They miscited some information from the book *Hit Men*. They said really, really scurrilous stuff."

Even if Sony had some culpability, proving that the entertainment conglomerate, much less Mottola, was involved in racketeering was not going to be easy. In order to prove a RICO conspiracy, you had to prove that one enterprise committed two or more serious crimes—like murder, extortion or blackmail—in connection with the operation of another enterprise. But in California, judges didn't particularly like the RICO statutes, which seemed to be invoked far too frequently. The act was originally intended to address racketeering and the power organized crime could exert over smaller businesses. But in practice, every court seemed to come up with its own interpretation of RICO.

Already, Smith had filed two successful motions to dismiss the case, forcing Ruthless to come back with a third amended complaint. If this one was dismissed, Bourbeau vowed the case would go to the appellate courts.

"If they don't get a RICO claim, the federal claim will be gone. But what's silly about all this is that Ruthless had a state court claim to determine whether the releases were valid or not. But they futzed around with that. Bourbeau was always whining that no one would show up for their depositions, but he never got a court order to have them. Over and over again Ruthless said its relationship with Dre was dead as of December 1991. And the judge said, 'Well, if it was dead in December of 1991, why are you complaining about anything Sony did in 1992?' And they go, 'Holy Cow, we just realized Sony entered into a conspiracy in December 1991'—and they stuck that in the latest complaint. But I don't think that it's going to work, because they've said that by February or March of 1992 Dre said he had no intention of ever working again for Ruthless. They can't have it both ways."

I asked Smith if Sony had any problems dealing with people known to be involved in criminal activity.

"We didn't find any evidence that Knight had any criminal record whatsoever. What do you do with some kid who grew up in the ghetto and got in trouble and has a record and now he's gone to college and is establishing himself in the music business? Are you going to say, 'You're not good enough, you're not lily-white, so we're not going to deal with you'? Should no record company release music or negotiate with Dr. Dre because his chosen manger had some altercations with the law? I don't think that's reasonable. Suge's a big guy. He's quiet, he's soft-spoken. Does he have a dark side? I don't know. But every time I've met him he's a real teddy bear." Smith paused for a moment.

"These are a group of people who make a living producing gangsta music and talking about how tough they are. Did they have a conversation in which everyone talked tough? I'd kind of faint if they didn't. When this lawsuit was filed, they had a press conference with Bourbeau and Wright, and Wright was asked, 'Are you afraid?' And he said, 'I ain't afraid of anyone.' Was he afraid of his old pal Andre Young? Was he afraid of Marion Knight? I don't know. . . . We didn't know the releases were being prepared. We didn't know they were going to get them signed. We weren't there; we didn't witness it. I don't have a clue what happened."

By the summer of 1993, Ruthless Records was less a fully functioning record company than a place under siege—an armed compound where thick complaints, cross-complaints and motions to dismiss came flying in the door. True, some new albums were coming out. A debut by a duo of Jewish rappers called Blood of Abraham was slated to be released, along with a solo album by Eazy-E. A boxed set by N.W.A was on tap and a CD by Above the Law, a hard-core gangsta record, was finally catching fire after Heller had hired someone to convince Giant Records czar Irving Azoff, who was distributing it, to actually work the CD.

But lately, it seemed that in every direction Ruthless turned it was surrounded by enemies. When I show up to spend some time with Heller and Klein in mid-July, the buzz around the office was the failed plot by white supremacists to kill Rodney King, blow up L.A.'s First A.M.E. Church—the congregation instrumental in bringing peace after the riots—and thereby incite a race war.

Eight people, some of whom were skinheads, were picked up and a cache of weapons that included machine guns and pipe bombs was confiscated by undercover federal agents. But neither the FBI nor the U.S. attorney's office had bothered to inform Eazy-E, who was one of a number of African-Americans discussed as possible targets by the Fourth Reich Skinheads and White Aryan Resistance.

"The FBI warned everyone else—why didn't they warn me?" Eazy asked when he was interviewed on KABC radio that afternoon. "I'm reachable. I'm quite sure the FBI could find me. They found me when I did that 'Fuck tha Police' song. There's a lot of people who hate me, so I'm always watching my back."

"Why do you think you're hated?" the KABC host asked.

"First of all, I'm from a group called Niggaz with Attitude. And then I guess because I made a little money, and on the streets a lot of people get jealous when you're makin' money."

Heller thought the FBI agent, who ended up carrying the pipe bombs in his car that might've blown up the church, did a brilliant job, but he was furious that he had received no warning. And he was even more furious after he called a public-affairs officer for the U.S. attorney's office.

The U.S. attorney's office "denied that there was a list or that anyone was warned," Heller said, his voice incredulous. "But it's a matter of public record. Maybe [they were] playing a semantic game with me. But when the federal government chooses not to inform a person who's been marked for death by a serious hate group who obviously can carry out its threat— that's astonishing and horrifying. It makes me think the FBI would love to have these skinheads kill Eazy. They could then kill two birds with one stone: Eazy-E is dead and then they jail the white supremacists for life."

Eazy wasn't the only black not warned. Al Sharpton and Public Enemy received no notification, although the Reverend Cecil Murray, the minister of First A.M.E. Church, and Rodney King were warned.

"But Rodney King is already suing the government," Heller said, a note of cynicism in his voice.

"And the government is afraid to get sued again," said Klein.

"Obviously we weren't surprised that Eazy was a target of white supremacists," said Heller, "because he's been an enemy and foe of theirs all the way back to the beginning of the company. We've had death threats on a very regular basis from the skinheads and the white supremacists."

Usually the threats came in the form of long diatribes left on the Ruthless answering machine, rants filled with vicious bigotry and anti-Semitic slurs. But others were issued by a very articulate Germanic voice. A few dozen came in a year, though Heller wasn't counting.

"They want to know why we deal with niggers and they say they hold us responsible for the deaths of white people. When they do it in person it's usually real short and then they're off the phone. Gary Ballen will play you one now that'll freak you out. Gary, get him that Nazi message we got last month."

A moment later, Ballen, who was Heller's assistant, came in with a cassette of one of the threats. I heard a man with a thick German or Eastern European voice talking: "My name is Helvig," the man said. "You're just a fuckin' Jew, Jerry. Fuckin' shit-ass, shit-ass fuckin' Jew. You should've been killed by Hitler. Yeah, Hitler didn't do his job. You fuckin'-ass Jew. Goddam fuckin' Jew! If I get the chance to kill a Jew I'd kill him with a motherfucking shotgun, sawed-off that is. . . . I ain't got no beef with Jews anyway, but they smell. They smell like shit. . . . You should've been killed at Auschwitz. Yeah, Hitler. I'm Hitler! Fuck Hitler! I'll kill all fuckin' Jews! I can smell you from here. I can smell you all the way from the U.S. of A. . . . You Jews disgust me you, you, you swine-eating, pig-eating . . . bug-ass, shit-ass Jews!"

The RICO lawsuit, the visits by Suge Knight, the threats from Dre on his album and now these Aryan shit-for-brains plotting to blow them up—all this sent Heller's blood pressure through the roof. He took a deep breath, shaking his head.

"The music business is now a small part of my day. The rest of it is dealing with lawsuits and complaints and motions and depositions. And having to go to New York and Birmingham."

Birmingham was another mess, only this time Ruthless was on the other end of the lawsuit. As if Heller didn't have enough things to keep him up late, a woman in Birmingham, Alabama, had filed a lawsuit against N.W.A's MC Ren (real name: Lorenzo Patterson), charging that the rapper had raped and impregnated her back in 1989. The woman, who was sixteen at the time of the alleged rape, now claimed she was raising Ren's three-year-old daughter.[11]

"They haven't offered any blood tests or proof of paternity," said Heller, "so it's been a hodgepodge of legal maneuverings. Ren took a lie-detector test and passed, but he was afraid to go to Alabama, even though it was a civil rape charge. Our attorney settled for three hundred fifty thousand dollars."

The lawyers—a criminal specialist in Boston, a RICO specialist in Washington, a firm in Los Angeles and the attorney in Birmingham—were all clocking hours, costing Ruthless a small fortune, so much money that when Bourbeau, Heller's Boston

---

[11] The paternity complaint, filed against Patterson April 24, 1992, claims that the woman was raped at a party after an N.W.A concert given at the Birmingham-Jefferson Civic Center in July 1989. The rape suit, filed in November 1990, also went after damages based on the misogynistic content of N.W.A's music. Other members of N.W.A, including Dre and Eazy-E, were named in that suit.

attorney, came out to take depositions, Heller put him up at his own house rather than pay out another three thousand dollars a week in hotel bills. At times, the whole world seemed stacked against Heller: one writhing mass of "cocksuckers."

At the top of Heller's list of former associates, now enemies, was the thirtysomething president of Priority Records, Bryan Turner. Turner was the classic example of backdoor, rags-to-riches pop music success. The son of a Canadian Jewish junk peddler and a graduate of the University of British Columbia, he grew up in Winnipeg and then worked for K-tel Records as a vice president of A&R, putting together compilations, as well as records by the California Raisins, before becoming a jetsetter and rap impresario. After learning what he needed to know about distribution, Turner and some partners founded Priority in 1985.

Initially, the company had no rap artists. But when Ruthless, which was just starting up, needed a distributor for its records, Heller and Eazy went to Priority. All of N.W.A's smash albums were distributed by Priority. That alone made Turner a wealthy man, because for every record that Ruthless sold, Heller said, Turner got a far larger profit than Ruthless made. Heller regretted the day he ever laid eyes on Turner. The mere mention of Turner's name, in fact, caused Heller's stomach to cinch up.

"I set him up in business when he worked for K-tel," Heller said one evening, when we were at his house. "Bryan Turner is a little pisher[12] whose only act was the California Raisins when Eazy and I decided to put him in business."

According to Heller, Turner acted when he saw how much of his profit was attributable to Ruthless acts that he didn't control. "He was the one involved in luring Ice Cube away from N.W.A—he helped break up this great group. And he was involved in Dre's unhappiness with his friends. He tried to do the same thing with Eazy and it didn't work. It was because we

[12] *Pisher* means "a nobody" in Yiddish.

controlled so much of his business that he would do anything he could to even out the balance of power.

Turner declined to comment on Heller's allegations other than to refer to an article in *The Bomb* in which Ice Cube blamed Heller for the group's breakup.

In his deposition, Dre said that in 1991, when he was unhappy with the number of points he was getting as a producer—two points on each album—he had discussions with Turner, who gave him more than two hundred thousand dollars. "A hundred thousand of it was for the production on the new album, 'cause I told him I wanted a hundred thousand for producing the album at four points," Dre said. "And a hundred fifty thousand was back payment on the stuff I did before."

Turner claimed in deposition that the money was an advance payment for *The Chronic*. Ruthless ended up authorizing one hundred thousand dollars of the money. But the additional money was what enraged Heller.

"He was obviously trying to induce Dre to leave Ruthless like he did with Ice Cube. There is no legitimate legal explanation for why he offered him this money. And it was our money.

"For Eazy to have done as much as he has for Bryan and Bryan to treat him so badly, with his creative accounting techniques and reserves and free goods, is very shortsighted. The essence of his betrayal was that he saw how much control we had over his company. I've got a whole list of things Bryan Turner has done," Heller said. But Heller wouldn't say if Ruthless was going to sue Turner. And Turner, who was scheduled to be deposed by Bourbeau a few weeks later, wasn't available for interviews.

That day, the only uplifting news Heller received—the only bright spot in his life—was a call about George and Lynwood Stanley, the two rappers who had sued Suge Knight in July 1992, claiming he had threatened to kill them. Knight and his attorney, David Kenner, met with Larry Longo, the DA assigned to the case, at Downtown Superior Court to discuss the charges of battery and assault.

"David Kenner wanted community service. He wanted Suge to plead guilty with no jail time," said Heller. "But Longo said he had one deal only. He said, 'Is your client ready to go to jail today? . . . Because I think he's a menace to society.' " Longo confirmed that he wasn't about to give Knight any lenient plea bargain but was going to go for the maximum sentence. "Just the use of the gun is three to five years," Longo said. According to the Stanley brothers, who attended the meeting, Knight and Kenner were stunned. It suggested that the DA would go after hard jail time, maybe as much as five years in prison.

"I guess it proves that there is a God," Heller said.

But the trial date kept getting delayed and a new defense attorney attached himself to the case. Meanwhile, other people contacted Longo about violent confrontations with Knight, who was still out on bail.

"It's amazing to me Marion Knight is still walking the streets, because he's a one-man crime wave," Longo told me.[13] "It blows me away."

When I first met him, in the spring of 1993, Eazy-E was being mauled in the hip-hop press—being called an Uncle Tom, a sellout, a punk. He'd spent days on end at the second Rodney King trial and was seen a number of times in the company of Theodore Briseno, one of the four LAPD officers accused in the beating of King. Many blacks saw that as a total betrayal, but Eazy couldn't care less.

"I don't really give a shit about what people say," he said, his cunning eyes and sly, mocking smile underscoring his contempt for rival rappers. "You see, most people are followers, but I'm my own man. I don't consider myself a follower. If anything, I be a leader. And if I believe in something, I'll do what-

---

[13] Longo made this comment in the first week of February 1994. At that time, both the civil and criminal cases against Knight were still pending.

ever I believe in. The lawyers sent me the FBI tapes of the videotaped beating, and from what I saw of the videotape, I saw that Briseno was the only one who was trying to stop the beating. He did do that stomp. That wasn't justified. But he was the only one of them all who was trying to stop the beatings. The tape I had had sound on it and you could hear them hollering, 'Stay down.' We don't know what happened before that videotape started. But the police know."

"For some asshole to say that Eazy-E likes the police is fucking ridiculous," Heller said one afternoon. "He had some plan. Eazy doesn't sit around and watch TV. When he gets involved, man, he's involved. He was at the trial every day. Eazy was the first rapper to start his own company. He was the first rapper to press his own records and the first guy to get involved with a white man. Then he was the first guy to make deals with majors.[14] Then he produced the song 'Boyz-N-the-Hood.' We're always on a different level than the other people that do what we do.

"Ice Cube was an athlete. His parents are both educated. Now he lives in Encino. And he went to college. But Eazy is the smartest guy that I've ever met. He's very bright and very Machiavellian. He understands power and the use of power. He's like a study out of *The Prince*. He's very loyal and tough. We're like father and son. He took me under his wing. I was at a bad time in my life. My wife had taken all my money, and I was starting over. I met Eazy and he played me this music that blew my mind.

"A lot of my friends thought I'd lost it. See, I remembered when radio stations wouldn't play the Stones' 'Let's Spend the Night Together.' But when I played 'Coming on the mike is Eazy motherfucking E,' my friends looked at me and said, 'Are

---

[14] Eazy wasn't the first rapper to work with whites. Numerous black rappers had worked with Rick Rubin years earlier. And rappers had worked with major labels before. But Eazy was perhaps the first black rapper to do so as an entrepreneur.

you crazy? You're telling me people are going to listen to this?' And then six months later, all my affluent friends who had car phones would call me and I'd hear *Straight Outta Compton* on their cassette players. All of a sudden rap was chic, the hippest thing in middle-class white America. But of course, the inner-city blacks had been into it long before because they had bought the records at the Compton swap meet. They knew about N.W.A way before suburbia got hip to rap."

That first day I met Heller and Eazy, they and members of the Jewish rap duo Blood of Abraham were hashing out a marketing strategy for the group's Ruthless debut. It was easy to see that a business meeting at Ruthless was nothing like an equivalent session at, say, Warner Bros. Sitting in his long, dark office, dressed in a baseball cap, jersey and baggy jeans, Eazy was finishing off a bucket of Kentucky Fried Chicken wings. He'd signed the group after hearing their tape and now Ruthless was trying to figure out a way to break the band and prevent the media from painting them as a novelty act.

"We should send the record to every kid who has a hip-hop show," Terry Heller, Jerry's nephew, said.

"Are we sending out just vinyl?" Jerry Heller asked.

"We gonna be losing money," said Eazy. "Why don't you sell the muthafuckers for the price it takes to make them?"

"We don't need to be selling the tapes," said Epic, also Jewish, who was producing the CD.

"They're going to get confused," said Terry.

"So this is like throwing away twenty thousand dollars?" Eazy asked. He'd just finished an ear of corn on the cob and he wiped his mouth.

"It's to build more of a buzz on the Blood of Abraham when the album comes out," said Terry. But Eazy wasn't going to give ground. He shook his head in disgust.

"All right. Write a check for twenty thousand dollars since you like to be *givin'* away money."

"It's gonna be going to people like Red Alert in New York who have radio shows," said Terry.

"It's for radios and clubs," said Benyad, Blood of Abraham's Israeli-born rapper, who'd been listening to the whole discussion and getting frustrated.

"Let's do a thousand cassettes, maybe fifteen hundred albums, so radio and promotion people get them," said Eazy. "That's cool. But let the other muthafuckers *buy* that album."

"We need more than that," said Benyad.

"Tell me every place you gonna take 'em," Eazy said, leaning forward in his chair now, eyes mocking.

"Record pools, man," said Benyad.

"You guys know a thousand muthafuckin' *record* pools?" Eazy said, his voice now agitated, for ever since Dre had left and the lawyers had descended, the cash flow at Ruthless had become critical.

"Eazy, let's not talk about the numbers now—let's just agree on the concept," Jerry Heller said diplomatically. "Here's what we'll do: We'll just ask what they need and put twenty-five percent beyond that for ourselves. And that's what we'll press up."

This hardly calmed Eazy. He was making a *point*. He looked away and then looked at Benyad.

"You don't need to be passing out lots of tapes. Let the muthafuckers go out and *buy* that album."

After the meeting ended we went back to Heller's office, where an attractive black woman—one of Eazy's old girlfriends—was waiting with her two kids. When Eazy walked in he talked to her briefly, asked the kids a few questions and then left.

"Your kids look beautiful," Heller said to the woman, smiling at the young girl with pigtails. Then he reached into a locked drawer, pulled out a couple of hundred-dollar bills and handed them to the woman.

"I'm gonna need some more," the woman said. "I got a lot of bills to pay. Car payments, food."

"You got a brand new Acura," Heller said firmly.

"But that don't pay the bills," snapped the woman, who was soon out the door.

A few weeks later, at a recording session for Blood of Abraham, Eazy spent most of his time slicing open cigars, taking out the tobacco and filling them instead with marijuana. One of his girlfriends followed him, hanging on his every move. Maybe Eazy was a great talent scout, but he hardly fulfilled the leadership role you would expect of the man Heller called the smartest guy he'd ever met. There was talk of an N.W.A reunion, and so I asked him if he could ever imagine getting back together with Ice Cube, much less Dre. Eazy-E shot me a cold, stony look.

"They done fucked up the business It makes me feel like one of them postal workers," he said, and flashed one of his dark, inscrutable smiles. "But I can't ever see us getting together again."

Nor, for that matter, could Dre.

"I went to a lot of record companies, tried even to get a little production work to pay for rent and shoes. But nobody wanted to take a chance on me because of all that legal shit, all the cease-and-desist letters," Dre told a reporter for *Rolling Stone* in the summer of 1993, recalling the legal tangles at Ruthless that made 1992 his worst year. "Ruthless did anything and everything they could to fuck me up, and I have hate for everybody there."

But now Dre was having the last laugh. Not only was the triple-platinum *The Chronic* the best-selling gangsta rap record in history, but Dre's protégé, Snoop Doggy Dogg (Calvin Broadus), had also become a major rap star. Months before the November 1993 release of his Dre-produced debut *Doggystyle*, a record laced with tales of guns, gangs, ho's and bitches and full of misogynistic rants, a windstorm of hype had been fanned into existence—helped by the fact that Broadus was wanted in connection with the murder of a man in the Palms district of L.A.

In the world of gangsta rap, where something was always worth the hype, this was a publicist's gold mine. A week after its release, *Doggystyle* was the number one CD on the pop charts. It marked the first time in pop-music history that the artist behind the country's top-selling record was facing murder charges.[15] And it reminded Heller once again of what he'd lost.

"It eats me up because I put those guys in that position . . . I got them to where they would get that kind of attention," Heller said in late November, after the release of Snoop's debut. "But on the other hand, they didn't know how to capitalize on it. All they did was make regular record deals. But it kills me. Because all of this was N.W.A and N.W.A was Ruthless. But these greedy cocksuckers all came in and chipped off their piece of Mount Rushmore."

One afternoon, Heller took me back to his Mountainview Estates house, where I met Gayle Steiner, his twenty-four-year-old girlfriend, and their four dogs: Goo Goo, a bulldog; Roo, a pit bull; a mutt named Skippy; and Missy, a yapping mix of Pekingese and poodle. A platinum blonde with a curvy figure and a Kewpie-doll voice, Steiner was young enough to be Heller's daughter. She was set on marrying him, too. In a few months she would give him an ultimatum for when they were to be engaged *and* married. But Heller, who'd been through one ugly divorce, wasn't too thrilled about the idea of again getting hitched.

"I'm stalling," he said, smiling but not joking. "But she's given me a deadline."

Both of them adored their dogs and let them have the run of the house. The animals were more than pampered. "They sleep with us under the covers," Heller said, playing around with Roo, the Staffordshire pit bull. "We call them coveys."

---

[15] Broadus was arrested for being in the Jeep from which his driver, McKinley Lee, allegedly fired the shots that killed twenty-five-year-old Philip Waldemariam on August 15, 1993. According to police, Lee killed Waldemariam after a car chase. Lee told police he shot Waldemariam in self-defense after Waldemariam allegedly aimed a pistol at their Jeep. Broadus's attorney, David Kenner, said that Waldemariam had previously assaulted Broadus and threatened him with a gun.

"And if you don't let them sleep with you, they cry," said Steiner.

Just then, her mouth full of gooey drool, the bulldog slithered up to Heller.

"Goo Goo. Down. See, she'll get in close like that and rub up against you, and then she'll slime you, and then you got to go change clothes. That's her favorite thing. Then she laughs. She thinks it's so funny. Is that funny, Goo Goo?"

Heller's two-story estate was enormous and ostentatious. There were large abstract expressionist paintings hanging on the walls—Heller fancied himself a serious and budding art collector—including works by one of his favorite painters, who happened to be head of Yale's art department. Outside were a sumptuous garden, a swimming pool, a Jacuzzi and a panoramic view of the Ahmanson ranch and the Hidden Hills. Eazy, who was not around that day, lived a couple of doors down in a similar house. It was hard to believe that Dre, their fearful antagonist, lived so close by—in the same gated community, less than a three-minute walk away.

Though he couldn't prove it, Heller thought he knew who was behind an unsolved robbery of his own house in July 1991. Left behind, scrawled on a bedroom mirror Heller showed me, was a message: "Payback is a bitch, Jerry."

"The burglars took a Corvette convertible, twenty or thirty watches that I'd collected and a safe. If I wouldn't have walked in through the garage I wouldn't have known anything was missing. There wasn't a shirt out of place. They knew where the keys were. Whoever it was had been here before."

Heller and Steiner were in the mood for seafood, so we piled into his white BMW convertible and headed down Las Virgenes Road toward the ocean. It was a beautiful day and a bloodred sun was swelling the horizon, sinking below the hills. When he passed by Dre's house, Heller snorted.

"I came back one day last summer and saw a fire," he said. "It was coming out of one of the houses."

"We saw smoke from a fire and we didn't think it could be somebody we knew," said Steiner.

In fact, the fire was from Dre's house. Flames roared out of the mansion and Dre was outside, Heller said, "laughing with some of his friends."

And now Heller smiled, as if recalling some long-ago enchanted memory—the ghost of a life that might've been.

"Dre was a good kid back when I first met him. He was maybe eighteen years old then. He was in a glam group, the World Class Wreckin' Cru, wearing lace gloves and shirts and G-strings. That was in 1985. I remember one of the guys in the group did a striptease in the show. So it's hard for me to believe that Dre was a gangster."

"He was always so *well* mannered," Steiner added, checking her look in the mirror.

"And he was so thrilled when I bought him his first house in Westlake." Heller's voice sounded happy, as if recalling some treasured time. "I threw his twenty-first birthday."

We'd arrived at the Reel Inn, a roadside fish house on the Pacific Coast Highway, and Heller gave the BMW's keys to the valet. After dinner was ordered, Heller quickly took up his main obsession: the lawsuit and the phalanx of enemies now surrounding him.

"If I lose this case I'll kill myself," he announced dramatically, as his dinner arrived: a plate of steaming fish with Spanish rice and fried potatoes.

"He doesn't mean that," said Steiner, as if explaining the behavior of a misguided five-year-old. Heller looked at her baby-doll face and shook his head. His eyes blackened.

"Yes I *do*. Because that'll mean there's no God and no justice for the little man in this country."

"He's just being dramatic," Steiner said, looping her arms through Heller's elbow and giving him an exaggerated smile. But Heller wasn't in the mood to be cheered up. Every mention of the lawsuit brought up more venom.

"Some guys, if they're told they're gonna die, they want to fuck every woman they meet," Heller said, spearing a forkful of broiled halibut. "But if I were to get cancer, I'd make up a list of people I hated and I'd kill 'em all. Wayne Smith and Suge

Knight would be on it. Smith wouldn't be number one, but he'd be in the top twenty."

"You shouldn't worry so much," Steiner said. "Give me a little kiss." She leaned over and put her lips together the way Marilyn Monroe did for Tony Curtis in *Some Like It Hot*. Heller gave her first one, then two pecks.

"That's it—no more," he said, grimly smiling.

I asked him about the pain and aggravation he'd been living with for two years—was it worth it?

"They nearly ruined us," Heller said. "What they did to our lives should only happen to them. I only hope that Mickey Schulhof, the American president of Sony, goes through the kind of torture and agony and aggravation that we all went through for years of our lives.

"But they will not bury us. We will pursue this if it takes the rest of our lives. Bourbeau is a young, well-known East Coast expert who's defended lots of East Coast figures who were indicted under RICO. The other guy we're using, Ralph Drury Martin, is from Washington, D.C., and he was the senior Justice Department prosecutor who put away this judge in San Francisco. He's a RICO prosecution authority. He helped draft the RICO statute." Heller paused, as if aware that all the high-priced lawyers in the world might not be enough to convince a judge that there was a high-level conspiracy against Ruthless. "Sony's not going to get away with it."

But in fact, the judge dismissed the Ruthless case. On August 9, he threw out the complaint against Sony, effectively exonerating the company from any criminal conspiracy and leaving Ruthless's lawyers no choice but to appeal the ruling or accept it.[16]

---

[16] The entire federal case has been dismissed, though Ruthless is appealing that dismissal. The case contained RICO claims under federal law and claims under state law. The judge dismissed the federal claims. As for the state claims, he dismissed them for lack of jurisdiction, since there were no remaining federal claims. But Ruthless's attorneys could go to state court and pursue their claims alleging contractual interference.

CHAPTER 3

In the Realm of the Shadow Magician

Rick Rubin's Dark Empire

"I look at art and entertainment as one. Is the film of JFK getting shot art? I think there's art to that," Rick Rubin told me one November afternoon as we sat down to lunch at a swank Beverly Hills trattoria. We'd just zoomed up to the restaurant in Rubin's black Rolls-Royce, a tape of gangsta rapper Ice Cube's single "Wicked" blasting out of the window, and naturally people were staring. "There's art to the presentation by the media of anything. It's hard to define, but documenting events is what art is, right?

"Anything could be art. And I don't think there should be any limitations on art. It has nothing to do with morality. There's obviously a demand for violence. If that's what people want to see, they should be able to see it."

As Rubin delivered this blunt, arrogant exegesis on art, violence, entertainment and morality, a tableful of wealthy middle-aged women stared at us. Their faces pinched tight from endless tucks and lifts, they eyed Rubin as butchers might inspect a load of rotten meat. They looked at his mangy beard, his long, black hair, his evil-looking eyes and the bald spot at the back of his head. And when they took in his white denim jacket, torn blue jeans and work shoes, you could almost read their minds: Who allowed this monstrous Charles Manson look-alike to invade our faux-Mediterranean calm?

But Rick Rubin couldn't care less. The thirty-year-old head

of Def American Records[1] loved to mess with people's heads. That's why he drove a black Rolls down Rodeo Drive with gangsta rap blaring out the window. That's why he had a twelve-foot stuffed polar bear in the front hallway of his Mediterranean house up in the Hollywood Hills. And that's why he signed Satanic metal bands like Slayer, horror-rap groups like the Geto Boys, and homophobic, race-baiting comics like Andrew Dice Clay to his label. Other music moguls might try to fit into the respectable world of burghers and businessmen, distancing themselves from the coarseness, violence and misogyny that were part of their working world. But Rick Rubin enjoyed being an outlaw—as long as being an outlaw made him a fortune.

It wasn't that he didn't like mainstream artists. Rubin idolized Neil Young and John Lennon and thought Bob Dylan was a genius. But America, the most violent of Western societies, was a country that celebrated psychopaths and worshiped guns. And what sold in the last years of the twentieth century were entertainment experiences that shocked and appalled. In that realm, Rubin had a genius. Trolling the margins of society, he found misfits who served up such visions, no matter how creepy or downright depraved.

It was Rubin who unleashed the Geto Boys, a Houston-based group led by a vicious four-foot-six-inch rapper named Bushwick Bill, on the Western world. Bushwick, who would eventually have his eye shot out by his own girlfriend after handing her a gun and saying he wanted to die,[2] wrote songs that pushed misogyny and sadism to new depths. In "Mind of a Lunatic," his most infamous song, he spun a rap about murdering a woman and then fucking her corpse—something that

---

[1] The company has since been renamed American Recordings.

[2] Bushwick Bill (real name: Richard Shaw) lost his right eye after his girlfriend, seventeen-year-old Tamika Nicole Randleston, trying to uncock the weapon, accidentally fired a shot on May 10, 1991. According to Bushwick, he threatened Randleston and said he would throw her infant child out the window unless she did his bidding. Bushwick underwent surgery five days later, got a glass eye and said the experience made him believe in God.

Hollywood filmmakers, in their hot pursuit of over-the-top sex and violence, couldn't even begin to contemplate.[3]

But Rubin wasn't bothered by the Geto Boys, though Geffen Records, which was then distributing Def American Records, had another opinion. Eddie Rosenblatt, the label's president, called "Mind of a Lunatic" "the worst thing I ever heard," and David Geffen himself, offended by the song as well as the homophobic rants of Andrew Dice Clay, soon severed his relationship with Rubin.

Before that, Rubin had a similar falling-out over his idea of "brilliant" music. Honchos at CBS, the company with which he had earlier signed a lucrative deal to distribute his first label, Def Jam, were horrified when they got the master tapes of *Reign in Blood*, an album by the band Slayer. Over endlessly dull spasms of thrash, lead singer Tom Araya howled lyrics about everything from virgin sacrifices and Satanism to sadistic mutilation and the atrocities at Auschwitz. Art? Not a chance. What's more, the band wasn't even threatening. Slayer's music was merely stupid and silly, in the tradition of wretched horror flicks. Even so, CBS, then in the middle of fighting two wrongful-death suits involving Ozzy Osbourne and Judas Priest lyrics that had allegedly incited teen suicides, refused to release *Reign in Blood*. With a relationship already poisoned by lawsuits and threats of lawsuits involving the nonpayment of royalties to Def Jam acts like the Beastie Boys, Rubin left searching for another deal and a new record company.

"Maybe I'm the worst case of American youth, but I sign things out of passion," Rubin said, as if announcing a sacred credo. "And I believe in things for entertainment purposes more than anything. If something entertains me, then I'll support it, regardless of what it's saying. But I think that people

---

[3] Subsequent to the shooting incident, the Geto Boys released a truly amazing song called "Mind Playing Tricks on Me," a chilling tale about a gangster who always has to watch his back and lies awake at night wondering just what is true and what is fantasy—what violence he has or hasn't committed.

who are entertained by things but then won't stand by those artists are completely hypocritical," he said when I asked him about his soured deals with CBS (now Sony) and then Geffen. The very mention of David Geffen and his record company brought a pained looked to Rubin's normally inexpressive face.

"They were hypocrites. When Geffen refused to put out the Geto Boys records, the first person I called was [Virgin Records American president] Jeff Ayeroff, because he was behind that whole Censorship Is Un-American program," Rubin said. "I said, 'Jeff, I want you to put out this record. Geffen won't put it out. I'm being censored. What are we gonna do about it?' And he said, 'I don't want to have anything to do with it. It's antiwomen.' And I was shocked.

"Most people in this business don't care about music; they're in the banking business. David Geffen very openly talks about the fact that he doesn't like music and doesn't listen to any of his artists. With him it's solely business.[4]

"Historically, rock and roll is about rebellion," Rubin said, as he dug into a bowlful of penne arrabbiata. "Elvis was called a white nigger. The Beatles in the early days used to play with toilet seats around their necks. And the Doors were completely infamous in their day. So all of the great music of its day was outlaw music. But now the outlaw music is the Geto Boys, Slayer, Danzig."

Just then a luscious-looking blond sylph walked by the table

---

[4] In response to Rubin's accusation that David Geffen was a hypocrite, Geffen Records publicity head Bryn Bridenthal, speaking on behalf of her boss, said the following: "Rick Rubin dropped the Geto Boys even though at Warner Bros. [which agreed to distribute Def American Records after Geffen severed its ties with the label] he was going to be allowed to release whatever he wanted. So when he's talking about hypocrites, perhaps that includes himself as well." Bridenthal said that it was patently false that David Geffen doesn't listen to music on his own label. "He likes some things and doesn't like others. But he does listen to the records on his label. And he's never said he doesn't like music. David said he dropped Def American because of the hypocritical manner in which Rubin dealt with the Geto Boys [incident]."

and gave Rubin a small, folded piece of paper and a seductive smile. Rubin nodded, took the paper and put it in his jacket pocket without looking.

"A socialite," he muttered when she had left the restaurant, as if explaining a nuisance he had to deal with all the time.

In Hollywood, opinions of Rubin varied wildly. Some said he was a genius who'd changed the face of popular music with his early harvesting of New York's rap scene

"Rick Rubin is going to be around for a long time," said Jerry Heller, the cohead of Ruthless Records, the rap label started by N.W.A rapper Eazy-E, "because he's a visionary. He knows music."

"Everyone thought Sir Mix-a-Lot was history—that he was too old," Irving Azoff said, referring to the Seattle rapper who many thought was washed up because of his age. "But Rick signed him and had a huge record."

But not everyone was a Rubin fan. A producer said, "He's good at making money and that's about all, but he has no taste or vision in music. The only reason he's making records in this town is because he's projected an image of being hip."

A onetime friend and rival at another major label said of Rubin, "The whole time his company was distributed through us he was very manipulative and clever. He's smart and good at extracting information out of you. And if he needs you he can be a friend. But once he doesn't need you he drops you like a hot potato."

". . . I think he's one of the most spoiled people I know," said another executive who's known him since his early days at Def Jam. "He expects to have everything the way he wants it. And there's a certain self-fulfilling prophecy in that. If you expect it and you act like you expect it, then you tend to get it. Part of his being a magician is that if he wants something, he thinks he should have it even if it means trying to take an artist from another label.

"He also sees art in everything he does and touches. If it's a commercial failure it's automatically *art*. It was too good for people or it went over their heads. And then if it's very successful he's the brilliant businessman. So he gets one or the other. He doesn't allow himself to lose very often."

For months I'd been trying to spend some time with Rubin, but his assistants said he was always busy. He'd been squirreled away in a studio, producing Mick Jagger's latest record. Before that he had produced the Red Hot Chili Peppers' breakthrough Warner Bros. album. And in between all this, he was running his company, signing bands, buying a European techno-rock label, forming new labels and giving out interviews to all the glitzy magazines and biggest newspapers.

His media campaign was deftly orchestrated and carefully calculated. In each article, Rubin came off as a renegade, a quirky, mysterioso maverick who sometimes arranged deals lying on his bed while the rest of workaday America slogged through days filled with soul-deadening work. Rubin had attached an aura to himself, a calculated image, and the ever-gullible press was gobbling it up.

In a series of profiles in *Vanity Fair*, *The New York Times*, the *Los Angeles Times* Calendar section and *Forbes* magazine, Rubin got what could be described as hagiography: long, glowing profiles of a radical *enfant terrible* who founded Def Jam Records in his NYU dorm room while still an undergrad, making the first L.L. Cool J record for four hundred dollars and selling 120,000 copies of it. The stories told how Rubin took three thousand dollars and parlayed it into an eight-figure joint-venture deal with Warner Bros.,[5] becoming, along the way, a "hot" producer.

Although Rubin came under attack for the performers he signed, he knew how to deflect the criticism. He simply raised the specter of art and censorship, casting himself as one of the oppressed and invoking the constitutional protections of the First Amendment. And most journalists, all too familiar with be-

---

[5] The value of the deal wasn't disclosed. A figure of seventy-five million dollars was reported in many media stories. But record executives I spoke with said that figure grossly exaggerated Rubin's actual deal.

ing muzzled, never bothered to make a distinction between censorship and responsible judgment, much less art and artifice.

But art had specific meaning. It was the conscious production of sounds, colors, forms and movements that affected the sense of *beauty*. As the skillful production of beauty in visible form, art was a revelation that came from contact with Nature. And if art preexisted in Nature, Nature was also reproduced in art. By contrast, artifice, an old word from the same root, was trickery: a subtle, crafty deception.

In twentieth-century Western culture, however, key words no longer held meaning for most people. The crucial distinction between art and artifice could easily be blurred, and Rubin was a master at blurring things. If psychotic murderers like Charles Manson could write songs and rock stars like Axl Rose could record them, leading to reviews and outrage in the national media—wasn't that art? In Rubin's mind it was. Besides, Rubin saw himself as an artist and provocateur, a mixture of Lenny Bruce and Ice Cube, the controversial gangsta rapper from N.W.A: an outlaw fighting the good fight, bedeviled by right-wing forces and persecuted as all true artists and visionaries are persecuted.

Which was strange. Though Rubin was Jewish and Ice Cube whipped up anti-Semitic fervor by exploiting the animosity between blacks and Jews, Rubin saw no irony in his choice of heroes. Maybe that was because he and Ice Cube had manufactured similar personas for the masses. Behind the image that he was the "nigga ya love to hate"—a fierce and courageous urban griot who had come up from South Central L.A.'s gangster culture—Ice Cube was at heart a cunning and wealthy capitalist who'd gone to college and had a good job before he turned into a gunslinging gangster.[6]

---

[6] As Mike Davis observed in his book *City of Quartz:* "Surrounded by benignly smiling white record company execs and PR men, NWA brandish customized assault rifles and talk darkly about recent 'drive-bys' and funerals of friends—a 'polished' image like any other in the business."

Certainly Rubin was no outlaw. The pampered son of a wealthy family living on Long Island's South Shore, Rubin abhorred violence in his own carefully constructed, hermetic world.

"I personally don't like violence in movies," Rubin admitted when the subject came up in relation to his signings. "I like films where two people are sitting in a room and talking for two hours. I like courtroom films. To me, to see a film where people get mowed down with machine guns is senseless violence."

The other impression of Rubin that he helped sustain was that he had rock-solid integrity.

"I believe in honesty and justice. Things like that are really, really important to me. One of my biggest problems with this business is the people who are in it to take from it and not to give to it."

Yet none of what he said jibed with what I'd heard about Rubin. Around Hollywood, he had a reputation for taking *whatever* he wanted—signing predatory deals with performers that paid unconscionably low royalties and deprived the artists of the most lucrative part of being musicians, ownership of their master tapes and the rights to their publishing and merchandising.

The biggest lawsuit filed against Rubin was by Adam Horovitz of the Beastie Boys, a group Rubin was briefly a member of.

"He kept all the money—him and Russell Simmons—so we sued both of them to get our money back," said Horovitz, who filed the multimillion-dollar lawsuit against Rubin and his then-partner at Def Jam Records, Russell Simmons, in 1987, when the band had gotten no royalties though its first album had sold millions of copies.

"There was breach of contract, there was breach of fiduciary duty," said Ken Anderson, who represented the Beastie Boys. "It was large, large amounts of money—in the millions of dollars. We alleged they did a lot of other things in addition to not paying royalties. Rubin [and Simmons] tried to structure everything to benefit themselves rather than the Beastie Boys.

And this was a pattern of abuse. There were other lawsuits already. L.L. Cool J had one.

"Ultimately, the Beastie Boys got everything they wanted and then some," said Anderson. "They got off the label. They got paid a bunch of money that was owed them. They got masters given back to them and their publishing given back to them. Rick may have softened up in his old age—he may not be up to his old shenanigans. At least I hope he's not."

When I asked Rubin about the Beastie Boys' suit, he stiffened.

"Back then, the Beastie Boys said they were going to break up—they said it in the press, that they didn't want to be with us anymore. CBS stopped paying us royalties not only on the Beastie Boys but on everyone on our entire label, because we breached our contract. The Beastie Boys had a contract with us to make records. We had a contract with CBS to deliver records. So if the Beastie Boys didn't deliver us a record, we were breaching our contract with CBS. That's why I couldn't pay them. CBS said, 'You don't get paid on anything because you lost the Beastie Boys record.' This was before we even lost the Beastie Boys."

I asked Rubin if he and Horovitz ever talked to each other. "I miss Adam," Rubin said, as if they were the best of friends who'd fallen out over a silly misunderstanding.

Horovitz and the Beasties weren't the only big-time performers who accused Rubin of cheating them out of millions. In the summer of 1987, L.L. Cool J sued Rubin and Simmons to set aside a recording and management agreement he'd naively signed. At stake was $1.5 million in royalties the rapper should've received from two hit albums.

"They put out the first L.L. record *without* a contract—that's when I came in," said Joseph Giaimo, the attorney who filed the suit and got the contract set aside, forcing Def Jam to come up with seven figures once the royalties were recomputed.

What about L.L. Cool J? Why did he sue you? I asked Rubin. He drew a blank for a moment. Then his memory seemed to clear. "We *were* sued. There was a guy who claimed he was L.L. Cool J. He claimed not only that he wrote all the songs on L.L.'s first album, but he said it was his voice on the record and that we fired him. I remember saying in the press that if this guy wins this case then I am really Bruce Springsteen. It was ridiculous. It cost us three hundred thousand dollars to defend ourselves and they threw it out of court."

Rubin was smiling now, sitting on the green leather sofa in the living room, his face caught in a sliver of late-afternoon sunlight. I glanced at the giant stuffed polar bear and the wall covered with an immense scroll of rare Oriental calligraphy. Instead of answering my question, Rubin had craftily changed the subject—to *another* lawsuit involving the *same* artist.[7]

It wouldn't be the first time Rubin dodged my questions. A master manipulator, he was skilled at verbal sleight of hand. I could imagine him convincing musicians he had what they wanted, but withholding what they actually needed.

He grew up in Lido Beach, Long Island, the only son of an upper-middle-class couple who wanted their son to be a lawyer. His real name was Frederic Jay Rubin and he was fat, lonely and introverted as a youth. His father, who made his money in the shoe and furniture businesses, played jazz and blues records

---

[7] "I don't remember any other lawsuit with L.L. Cool J," Rubin said months later when I again brought the details of the lawsuit to his attention. "I wasn't involved in a lot of those decisions early on. I didn't originally know the [financial and legal] details when we made our deal with Columbia [CBS]. I wasn't all that interested in it, to be honest. What I do remember about our business at that time was that the contracts we did with our artists reflected the contracts we got when we were making our deals [with CBS]. That's what we thought a record deal was." Thus, if the royalty standard Rubin and Simmons gave was low, Rubin claimed, it was because the two of them got the same standard. "That was the nature of the rap business in those days. And that's what we got paid," Rubin said.

around the house. But Rubin had no real desire to become a musician. As a kid, his dream was to become a magician.

"Magic used to be my obsession," Rubin said one afternoon as we sat down to lunch at Hollywood Deli. "I was lonely as a child," Rubin said. "I never really shared the interests of most of the people I knew. Up until the time I was sixteen or seventeen, I'd come home from school and just study my magic books and practice. I loved working with cards. That was my favorite. For close-up magic I had a little table with a mirror built on it so I could just watch my hands from the front. I'd practice for hours in front of the mirror. I always read about sorcery and the spiritual side of magic as well.

"I was shy and did theatrical things to compensate. Anything theatrical was a way of communicating without communicating. If I was a magician I wasn't me, and I could stand up in front of a lot of people and be entertaining and it wasn't me and it was OK.

"I have a theatrical background, whether it was playing the guitar onstage or being in school talent shows. I was *always* performing. I performed in front of people since I was ten years old."

Then, as if offering a clue to his approach to life, Rubin said: "The theatrical side is what magic was about. Physically being able to make the trick happen is not anything. The way it's dressed up, the way you *present* it, is what it's about."

Rubin claimed he could recall little of his youth or childhood, which came back to him as if enshrouded in deep mists. His mother, a housewife, smothered her only child with attention, convincing him that everything he thought and did was brilliant and that nothing was beyond his abilities. And Rubin admitted to being spoiled. Both parents stressed achievement and success—the cornerstones of many an upper-middle-class-Jewish family. But Rubin's formative years may have been highly abnormal. From the time he was a child until the years just before puberty, Rubin reportedly slept with his parents.

"As far as sleeping in my parents' bed, I don't really remember [how long]," Rubin said when I asked him if this was true. "I don't remember how old I was. I remember very little from my childhood. I have poor memory, period. I don't remember much about anything."[8]

There are psychiatrists and psychologists who say family beds can be good for small children, most of whom will want to sleep on their own by age four or five at the latest. But extending such arrangements into early youth, experts say, could cause a child to fail to individuate, affecting everything from sense of worth to sexual identity.

Certainly Rubin showed evidence of that. He seemed to live outside his life and had trouble showing real emotions like joy or sorrow. He dated porn stars and beautiful women and acted as if he had the world in his ass pocket. But underneath the calculatedly arrogant image lurked a needy child trapped in puerile fantasies, yearning for manhood.

In our conversation, Rubin kept returning to the financial security his wealthy parents gave him, but either he'd repressed his formative years or he wasn't willing to explore them.[9] Which was no surprise. To do so would puncture the outlaw-sorcerer mystique he'd spent so much time concocting. When I asked about the dark, perhaps suffocating relationship he hinted that he'd had with his mother, whom he hadn't seen in two years, Rubin first looked troubled and then smirked, carefully weighing his response.

"My mom used to call every day, but now she calls only once a week. She's made me her project" was all Rubin would say.

But months later, when I asked him again about his child-

---

[8] Aside from not being able to remember major lawsuits filed against him, like the one involving L.L. Cool J, Rubin's memory problems extended into all other realms of his past. For instance, he claimed he was thrown out of Hebrew school, but when I asked him for his parents' reaction, he said he couldn't remember. "I can't remember what happened last week. My friend [George Drakoulias] tells me things that happened three or six months ago that regularly shock me. Sometimes he tells these stories and he sounds like he made them up, but eventually they click in my head that they might've happened."

[9] Rubin refused to let me interview his parents, claiming issues of privacy.

hood, he went deeper. "A lot of my mother's happiness hinged on my life and happiness. I've since realized that I have very little self-worth. I've always judged myself on what I'm able to create as opposed to who I am. That's what was stressed in my childhood. Things like taking care of myself were never really important."

If anything, Rubin's father, whom he described as a "workaholic," came off as a remote patriarchal figure.

"He was truthful. He told me I could never do anything wrong as long as I told the truth. And he was musical too. He had a passion for it. He grew up in Brooklyn and the Bronx and he listened to jazz. When he was growing up, he'd go to black jazz clubs and be the only white guy in the place. He liked people like Max Roach, Charlie Parker. But he didn't turn me on to that music. It was there, but I never really focused on it or cared about it until I started hearing rock. The first music I remember loving was the Beatles. Later, I played guitar. I was never really a good player, but I was passionate about playing all the time. I played along with Ramones records. I started in the punk-rock era."

By his late teens, Rubin was listening to the Sex Pistols, AC/DC and Black Flag, a group led by a misfit named Henry Rollins. Such musical interests immediately made Rubin a rebel at his high school.

"I remember being the only kid in my graduating class of four hundred kids who liked punk-rock music. Everyone else liked the Rolling Stones, the Doors, Pink Floyd and Led Zeppelin, none of whom I liked. I liked new, exciting things."

His parents could've never dreamed he would end up in the music business and be making millions of dollars by selling rap music to angry young black kids, many of them gangsters, many of them Jew haters. The Rubins doted on their only child, supporting his every whim. In their eyes he could do no wrong.

"I could do anything I wanted. We were always upper middle class," Rubin remembered. "We were wealthy for the community we lived in. In a sense I was spoiled. But I never took advantage of it. I could have what I wanted, but I didn't often want things that were extravagant. There are people who feel that if they have the ability to take something they take it, but I've never had that feeling. But I've always felt that everything is always there whenever I want it, so whenever I want it I can always get it. The way my parents brought me up—to never worry about anything financial—really allowed me to be concerned with art, without these restrictions of having to make money doing it.

"But I didn't think I could make money creatively or become a musician," he said of his musician years. "It was an unrealistic goal, because I was brought up in a family where success was what mattered. I was going to be a lawyer—that was the plan."

Though Rubin grew up in affluence, Long Beach High School wasn't utopia. Rubin went to a school that was 70 percent white and 30 percent black, where friendships cleaved along racial lines.

"We had race riots at the school," Rubin said. "It was closed several times because of that."

But his life was cushy. When his punk band Pricks played CBGB, his mom would drive him to the gig in the family Lincoln and then wait outside to make sure he got home safely. Meanwhile, the rest of the band's members would take the subway home to their ratty apartments.

It was in high school, when Sugar Hill was putting out its early rap records, that Rubin first heard scratching and mixing. Back then, rap was party music, and Rubin loved the scene.

"I was excited by the newness of rap and the fact that it was accepted in this black community. I mean, as soon as a single came out, that would change the world. A new Treacherous Three record would come out, and that would be *the* group. And a few weeks later, a new Funky Four Plus One record would come out and it was like Treacherous Three never existed. It was an exciting, progressive musical time. Everything happening in rap then was new, whereas the white kids in my high school liked music that came out ten years before."

At NYU, Rubin played in a punk band called Hose, which recorded for a small independent label. But punk was dying out and rap was coming into its own. Blacks spinning dual turntables were creating the first wave of cut-and-paste funk, generating a whole hip-hop subculture that included street poetry, dance (breaking) and art (graffiti). Rubin started hanging out with rappers who were part of the nucleus of the New York rap scene: Kool Moe Dee, Jazzy Jay, Special K, the Treacherous Three.

"The live scratching opened a whole world of possibilities," Rubin would later say in an interview. "That's when I started thinking about producing records rather than being on them. I wanted to put that live sound out on record."

In 1984, while still living in his dorm room at NYU, Rubin produced a record with rapper T. La Rock and DJ Jazzy Jay called "It's Yours." The single, which sold a hundred thousand or so copies, made Rubin reconsider his ambition to become a lawyer. But it hardly made him wealthy.

Even so, Rubin started getting lots of demo tapes, which arrived in his room at NYU's Weinstein dorm. One of the tapes, from a fifteen-year-old kid named James Todd Smith who went by the moniker L.L. Cool J, intrigued Rubin. The two met and signed a deal. Rubin produced L.L.'s first single, "I Need a Beat," which he took to Russell Simmons, then a DJ at Danceteria and the manager of a bunch of rappers that included Run-D.M.C. Soon, Rubin and Simmons were in business and Def Jam was off.

By the time most major labels woke up to the fact that rap was here to stay, the street music of young blacks, Rubin and Simmons had snapped up the cream of New York's rap community. But CBS wasn't stupid. Seeing a potential gold mine in the latest African-American idiom, the company came calling with an offer Rubin couldn't refuse: a distribution deal with a lot of cash. One day Rubin, still living in his dorm, got a large six-figure check. From that day on, he gave up any ideas he may have had of going to law school.

George Drakoulias, who met Rubin at NYU and is now head of A&R for American Recordings, remembers Rubin as being single-minded and obsessed in those days.

"Rick really didn't take into consideration anything but his needs and wants when it came to making records," said Drakoulias. "He expected people to work for him free—that they should just do it because it was the thing to do. He never had any questions of whether the records were successful. At the dorm we used to play Chuck D's tape all the time[10] and Rick would call Chuck every day until he could get him on the phone and convince him to make a record. And eventually Chuck did. Rick graduated from NYU, but he never went to class for the last two years," Drakoulias said, laughing. "He gave one teacher, who was musical, studio time in exchange for extra credit. I really don't know how he did it. I met him when he was a freshman, I think, and he never went to class once. He lived in the dorm until right after graduation and then they kicked him out."

In 1987, Rubin moved to Los Angeles, taking his share of the Def Jam money and letting Simmons run the label. He was glad to leave. The CBS deal had turned sour and Rubin wanted to branch out into other kinds of music. As it turned out, he couldn't have picked a better time. Almost every week, Public Enemy, the rap band he signed, was provoking outrage and being savaged in the media. Professor Griff, the group's minister of information, talked about Jews "perpetrating the majority of wickedness worldwide" when he wasn't raving about the *Protocols of the Elders of Zion,* a notorious anti-Semitic document that dated back to the previous century. Luckily Rubin was in L.A. when a mob from the Jewish Defense Organization pulled up to his pad.

"Two U-Haul trucks with about thirty guys with baseball bats came to my apartment to get me," Rubin said, "but I was angry because they didn't know what they were doing. They

---

[10] Chuck D is the leader of the rap group Public Enemy.

should've talked to me and found out what I felt before coming to attack me, because I was a JDO *supporter*. When I was at NYU I saw [right-wing rabbi] Meir Kahane speak and he *blew* me away—he was amazing. I was not brought up religiously at all, and Israel would probably be the last place I would want to go, but after hearing him speak, I wanted to pack my bags and go home to Israel.

"Kahane said that regardless of what you believe, if you are born into the Jewish faith, when they go to round up Jews they're taking you. It's in your blood and that's all there is to it. I remember him talking about how, five years earlier, in the South, a politician had run for office dressed in full Nazi regalia and lost by only a few percent. 'Well, what's to say he couldn't win by two percent?' Kahane said. Living here, we don't know how racist this country is. But I travel around this country and people look at me like I'm a killer."

Rubin paused. His normally inexpressive face held traces of indignation.

"So here I was, a supporter of Jews. I called the JDO several times, wanting to join, but they never returned my calls. The JDO never did their homework, and it made me lose respect for them. Besides, I had left Def Jam already. And when I signed Public Enemy, Professor Griff didn't exist. When I signed the group they weren't political."

Rap would *become* political: the enraged howl of the black underclass and the expression of a newly revived militant Afrocentric philosophy that scared middle-class whites shitless. But Rubin wasn't interested in politics or deeper meanings. Maybe that was why he couldn't understand, on the most fundamental level, what prompted a truckload of Jews to come for him with baseball bats.

"I've never liked or cared about political music," he said with contempt and disgust. "It's always been completely secondary. I don't believe that political music accomplishes anything other than entertainment. Kids listen to music when they're in a bad mood, and if it helps them deal with their problems, that's good. I don't think that a message even exists.

If you listen to that first Public Enemy album, it wasn't political. In the beginning it was just an act. But Chuck thought, 'Wouldn't it be cool if a rap group talked more about political issues than how big my gold chain is,' and Chuck put that *on* the group. They did it not so much as a revolutionary idea, but more as 'This is a different idea.' But I don't think they did it to change the world. Since then, Chuck has believed the hype and grown into his own character. I hope he knows it. If it were just as trendy to rap about surfing—if a Beach Boys trend of rap came along—then everyone would take off their black medallions and get surfboards.[11]

In Jungian psychology, the Magician archetype carries awareness and insight: deep knowledge into aspects of life that aren't always apparent. It regulates the psyche, embodies thoughtfulness and protects us from other powerful energies. All of us have this positive Magician within—whether we're artists following our muse or doctors looking to cure a disease or parents seeking to invoke our child's sense of wonder.

But there's a Shadow Magician, too, that's cold, cruel and detached. This dark and skillful manipulator uses words and images to deflate others and build himself up. The Shadow Magician thinks he's smarter than everyone else and innocent at the same time. When asked a question that would reveal his true motives, he thinks through all possible answers until he arrives at the one that conceals the most. "Such men are slippery and elusive," psychologists Robert Moore and Douglas Gillette wrote in their classic study, *King, Warrior, Magician, Lover*, their motives "behind an impenetrable wall of feigned naïveté."

When I heard Rubin talk about his obsession with magic

---

[11] I faxed Rubin's comments to Chuck D's management in New York, but he never responded.

and describe his lonely childhood and lack of self-esteem, and when I ran up against the fortress of his distrust and his unexamined life and then looked into his distant, hollow eyes, I knew I was staring at a Shadow Magician.

"I think I'm really an introverted person, and I used to escape that by being theatrical," Rubin told me solemnly one spring afternoon. "Now I sometimes have to talk to a lot of people, and it's really hard for me. I always had lines as a magician or a musician. I don't even like going out to dinner with more than one person. I always feel that if I'm at a dinner with six people and I talk to one person, everyone else is listening to me."

I asked him if he ever examined his life—if he ever thought about things he might've done wrong or right. Rubin's eyes seemed to blacken, and he thought before answering.

"I don't examine anything—I just let it happen. I never think about it. It's weird even being asked a question like that, because I have to think about things that I never think about. I never reflect on how or why anything happens. I just do what I do."

I wasn't surprised by his comment. A lot of the record moguls I'd met did little reflecting. They were, for the most part, narcissists, so self-absorbed and arrogant that the connections between the heart and the soul had yet to fully form. They may have read New Age books and visited spiritualists, palmists, faith healers, yogis and acupuncturists, but their motivation was usually to relieve stress and guilt, not to gain some deep and lasting vision of their own life. Most of their waking time was spent accumulating power and fighting those who might take it away from them. In that game, ruthlessness was a given, the rules being invented as you went along. And it had always been like that.

Hollywood, that all-encompassing place that had emerged in the 1920s as "the most intensely symbolic, emotionally valent landscapes in America . . . an industry, a state of mind, a self-actualizing myth," according to historian Kevin Starr, was not a business run by deep thinkers. Its most successful moguls were the sons of shoemakers, junk peddlers and furriers—riff-raff from the shtetls of Eastern Europe who were searching for some way out of grinding poverty.

Men like Samuel Goldwyn, Louis B. Mayer, Adolph Zukor and Jack Warner, the Jews who invented Hollywood three generations ago, were outsiders, scorned by WASP America. They carved out power in one of the only areas that was available to them: the seedy world of entertainment. They understood people's desires and dreams and systematically exploited them. Most of them had some sort of conscience and a moral code that was mirrored in the films they turned out. Self-made men, they believed that anyone—even the son of a junk peddler—could make it with enough moxie and talent.

In many ways, the pop-music business was run as the film business was in its heyday. It was a club, mostly Jewish, filled with wily impresarios, maverick street fighters and out-and-out operators. Many, like David Geffen, had grown up in Brooklyn, the second generation of poor Eastern European or Russian families who'd worked in sweatshops, peddled fish or sold shoes. When they came of age, the film industry was a largely closed shop. But in the sixties and seventies, a man could make a killing in pop and rock and roll—more money than even a movie-studio president.

Of course, one had to stay away from the Goliaths in the beginning. By the eighties, when Rubin came along, with power concentrated in six major entertainment conglomerates, only those working the margins of pop music could work unhindered. The margins weren't pretty. Rap music was packing a lifetime of rage into tales as ferocious and ugly as the streets of the Bronx or South Central L.A. Some of its biggest stars were former gangsters who used beats and rhymes to glamorize wealth, dope and violence. Deciding whom to sign could be a moral quagmire, as Warner Bros. soon found out with Ice-T's song "Cop Killer." But Rubin wasn't one to be bothered by the trivia of social responsibility.

"Art doesn't even always have to be entertaining. It could be thought-provoking, but it doesn't even have to do that. If the person making it thinks it's art, it's art whether we accept it as such or not. It doesn't matter what it represents. The line is always moving," Rubin said. "Did you ever see the movie *Network?* It's one of my favorite movies. The shows they were talking about in the future—the ones that you were supposed to be shocked by—are what's on now. We're in the time of *Network now.* The media are making deals with people who are murderers to put their stories on the screen and make them stars. That's what *Network* was talking about."

A month after he finished producing Mick Jagger's album, Rubin and I had lunch at a Hollywood joint called Swinger's, a place full of jaded hipsters and musicians. Rubin was wearing blue jeans, camel-colored Ugg boots and a T-shirt with the acupressure meridians of the hand emblazoned on the front.

"I really believe in acupuncture, but I'm afraid of needles," Rubin said. "But I have to get over my fear, because I know it will benefit me."

It was Passover, but Rubin wasn't going to a seder. Looking at the menu, he passed up the matzo brei and the potato latkes for a vegetarian sandwich. For the last few months he'd been eating vegetarian, which helped him battle his lifelong weight problem. Rubin seemed happy to talk about Jagger.

"For the most part he behaved himself in the studio, but there were times when the rock star came out," he said. "Any lead singer, if they're having trouble on a particular day, tends to blame it on someone else in the band—'The mike doesn't sound right'; 'The guitar player's out of tune.' Well, one day Mick wasn't singing that well. We were in this medium-sized recording studio. It wasn't an airplane hangar, but it wasn't a closet. And the whole band was set up and Mick had his whole area with his key and his guitar, his mike and his music stand. But this day he couldn't sing. And he came up to me and said, 'How do you expect me to sing this song when there's no room in there for me to dance?' 'Well,' I said, 'if you'd like I can have the carpenters come in and build you runways just like you have onstage, if that'll make you sing better.' You just can't play into all the craziness. Otherwise, nothing works."

Rubin claimed he didn't know why Jagger picked him, "especially since, as the project went on, our tastes proved to be radically different. But I think a good record came from it."

In fact, the Jagger record sounded derivative, as if a lot of old Stones riffs had been recycled. Oddly, Rubin claimed he had never heard any of the old Stones records, like *Beggars Banquet* or *Exile on Main St*. It was a surprising admission. Was Rubin that stupid? If true, it meant that Rubin had failed to take one of the crucial steps necessary for any producer: familiarizing himself with an artist's history. But someone who knew him smiled when I told the story.

"He's just pretending not to have heard the Stones because he doesn't want anyone to think that he ripped off old Stones records for the new Jagger record—which is what he basically did."

After we finished eating, Rubin invited me to see his new house, a nine-thousand-square-foot mansion up in the Hollywood Hills.

"The guy who owned the Record Plant [recording studio] owned the house," Rubin said as he turned up Roxbury Drive and headed into the hills above Sunset Boulevard. Though summer hadn't yet arrived, it was already smoggy. "He produced Hendrix and made all these other great records. He actually died in the pool—him and his secretary both. There are different stories. Nobody knows how or why."

When we got to the entrance, Rubin pressed a remote and the gate swung open.

"I think an exorcism was done. Supposedly Peter Lorre also died in the house. The Stones and John Lennon stayed here at some point. The last people who owned it had a lot of people stay here: Lauren Hutton, Eric Idle. It's a great old Hollywood house. It's not in Bel Air; it's where people are. I was looking for a house for a few years. There was one other house that I really liked, behind the Beverly Hills Hotel, about eight minutes up.

It doesn't seem like a long ride, but when you get to the top of the hill, after an eight-minute drive, you really don't feel like you want to get down. And I like to go out a lot. I like telling my friends I'll meet them at Damiano's at three A.M. And I can get there in ten minutes. There it is—the pink house. It's a wreck."

Inside, the house was a hive of workers: men putting up drywall, carpenters hammering in struts, plumbers outfitting bathrooms with pipes. There were three stories to the house, as well as an elevator. Huge rooms seemed to spill out into still more immense rooms.

"That's a Bible chest from Burma," Rubin said as we wandered through one room, which held an intricately carved wooden trunk. When we got to the enormous kitchen, he pointed out copper sinks he'd had installed. "I don't like to cook, but I'll probably have somebody cook for me. I like to eat well."

We walked through a cavernous study that had parquet floors, a room with a Javanese daybed and a two-story bathroom that was being outfitted with marble slabs and a Japanese shower. "This"—Rubin pointed up high to the ceiling—"will all be a skylight."

There were still more rooms. One, with carved moldings, Rubin said, would have "an opium-den vibe, with rugs on the wall, like Marrakech."

Rubin stopped in the master bedroom and looked out the window into the haze. We could see the outlines of Century City and all of Hollywood. "You can see the ocean when it's clear," Rubin said.

The master bedroom, with its own spacious balcony, had slanted ceilings with mahogany paneling. On top of a table lay a large picture book opened to a photograph of the bedroom of William Randolph Hearst's San Simeon.

"That's the model for the bedroom," Rubin said blandly, as if this were the most normal thing in the world to do if one had the money. I looked at the photograph: an ornately carved four-poster wooden bed stood in the center of a room filled with art and furniture that only someone who was as rich as a pharaoh could afford.

"I have an 1800s metal four-poster bed, so we'll use that," Rubin said, glancing at the picture of Hearst's bedroom. "In the Hearst Castle, the arches are painted in geometric patterns and mythological biblical scenes."

The moment I'd walked into Rubin's house, I was eerily reminded of San Simeon and of Xanadu, the fabled mansion of Orson Welles's Charles Foster Kane, himself a stand-in for the real-life Hearst. But now, after Rubin had given me the grand tour of his own Xanadu, with peculiarly joyless commentary, the image was complete. Like Kane, Rubin had no traditions; he seemed spiritually desolate, culturally dislocated. And this house, purchased with the millions he'd made from tasteless music, was itself the extension of a lost American psyche searching for meaning in the dead relics of the past.

"I started collecting books on old houses," Rubin said as we left the room. "This house, when it was built, the structure was terrific but the detail wasn't there, so I'm trying to find as many books on old houses as I can to bring it all back."

Back at the old house, the phone had been ringing all morning and Mala, Rubin's assistant, had been taking messages. Rubin made a few phone calls as I walked through the house: In the kitchen hung photos of rock stars like Jim Morrison and John Lennon. Upstairs, in Rubin's bedroom, the four-poster bed was filled with dozens of stuffed bears. Across the hall was an exercise room. I tried to imagine Rubin rattling through his new Xanadu but couldn't.

Downstairs, the bathroom spoke more about Rubin's obsession with rock culture than about the man himself. The entire bathroom was a surreal collage of old magazine photos: pictures of rock stars and naked women, but only those with the most enormous breasts. The breasts exploded out from the walls in all directions, juxtaposed with photographs of Rubin's idols and images from the sixties and seventies: Iggy Pop with a chair over his head, Jim Morrison, the Allman Brothers, AC/DC, Robert Johnson, Neil Young, Jimi Hendrix, John Lennon,

Salvador Dalí, the Sex Pistols. It felt like a teenager's bathroom, a place where horny cravings could be satiated with a quick hand.

Rubin was lighting some incense when I emerged from his bathroom. In his dining room there were five surfboards, surfing being his latest passion. A vase had fresh blue and purple tulips. Rubin seemed anxious to get back to work.

"I was brought up to believe you are what your output is. You get good grades and become a success and that's why you're good, which has made me a crazy workaholic. That's an unhealthy drive. I've gotten a lot of success from it, but at what cost? Lately, since I moved out to L.A., I've learned to take better care of myself. Things like working out. The idea of me spending an hour a day on something that's just for me would have never happened before. Now I'm finding out about me."

Earlier in the day, in fact, we had dropped by a West Side metaphysical bookstore Rubin loved. Though he wasn't at all religious, he said he was interested in yoga and things that were healing. He was especially taken with the Indian doctor Deepak Chopra, the author of the best-selling *Quantum Healing*, a scientific and spiritual exploration of mind-body unity.

"He's amazing. I'll get you his tapes," Rubin had told me.[12]

Now I asked Rubin if he'd ever considered doing anything with all his millions—helping the less fortunate. But Rubin said he hadn't given any money to charity.

"Steven Baker at Warner Bros. recommended we put something together to help clean up the pollution in the water. I think it's a really great idea. But I believe that I don't count. I wonder how much anybody can really do, anyway. I believe a lot of things are the way they're supposed to be, good or bad." Rubin stopped, as if fearful of giving away too much of himself. "That's why I like art so much. It's a controllable world," he said.

---

[12] Rubin purchased them at the time, but I forgot to take them. I later got the two cassettes mailed to me by one of his assistants.

CHAPTER 4

Baby-sitting Satan

Down in the Mosh
Pit with Jonny and
Marsha Zazula

"I'm not gonna play for those Nazi fuckheads!" Jon Zazula screamed into the phone. "M.O.D.'s not going to Hamburg. You hear me? Fuck the Krauts!"

It was only 10:30 A.M. at Crazed Management/Megaforce Records, and already Zazula, or Jonny Z as everyone knew him, had worked himself into a lather. But who could blame him? Young skinheads were marching in Hamburg, beating up immigrants, Jews, Gypsies and any other dark-skinned people in their path. Aryan shit-for-brains, wearing swastikas and armbands, were desecrating Jewish temples and Hebrew cemeteries, painting swastikas on gravestones.

Just a few months earlier, eight hundred Nazis had firebombed a refugee center for guest workers in Rostock, a Baltic seaport in the former East Germany, while police watched. With the locals singing "Deutschland über Alles" and "O Tannenbaum," all that was missing was goose-stepping SS men. And now? The skinheads, some still in high school, were showing up en mass at rock concerts, disrupting shows by bands that Jonny Z managed.

Not that M.O.D., short for Method of Destruction, was some peace-and-love sunshine-vibe band. No, in Canada gays had marched in the streets protesting the group's song "A.I.D.S." (Anally Inflicted Death Sentence), which boasted such memorable lyrics as: "How do you find love in another man's hairy ass? . . . Take the Hershey Highway." And another song by the band's leader, Billy Milano, a snarling blitzkrieg called "Speak English or Die," was ambiguous enough to become a sort of anthem for young fascists everywhere.

"A.I.D.S." was supposed to be a safe-sex song and "Speak English or Die" was intended as nasty satire. But those Nazi assholes didn't get it, and this was just the sort of horseshit Zazula didn't need to be dealing with this morning. So he fired up another cigarette—he'd been chain-smoking all morning— and poured himself a shot of whiskey just to soothe his nerves.

Other rock and roll managers wore natty clothes and put on airs of sophistication. They collected art by Robert Longo or Jasper Johns and hung it on their office walls. But not Jonny Z. Tall and potbellied, with a mat of gray hair that ended in a thin, braided tail, he was built like a brick shithouse. This morning he was wearing black sweatpants emblazoned with the triple-skull logo of Anthrax—one of the bands he managed—and an old sweatshirt. And when he spoke, which was almost always, the words flew out in a torrent, spiced with curses and loud sighs. Born in the Bronx, Jonny Z talked it and walked it.

Art? The overall look at Crazed Management was surreal plastic fantastic anarchy. On one wall was a Ralston cereal box that read: "Wheat Sex—With Piss and Horny Wheat Taste." Near it was a color photograph of Salvador Dalí, Zazula's favorite artist, with a naked woman in the background. Behind Zazula stood a life-size pop-up of Madonna, nude except for a G-string and jewels on her nipples. And underneath his desk was a massive three-foot head of the bald, mustachioed "Not" man[1]—one of many such heads in the room—eyes bugged out grotesquely, looking like some demented, inbred cousin of Mr. Clean.

"I can tell this is gonna be sickness all day long," Zazula

---

[1] Anthrax is widely believed to have started the suburban craze of using the expression "Not," which was popularized by *Wayne's World*. Anthrax fans ritually showed up at gigs with "Not" shirts, "Not" bandannas and different "Not" heads.

announced to no one in particular, though his wife, Marsha, and Milano, the pit-bull-shaped lead singer of M.O.D., were in the room. "I'm feeling it in my neck. This is a war zone! This is a battlefield! I may fuckin' kick someone down a flight of stairs today!"

And with that he took another drag on his cigarette and screamed into the phone.

"We're Jews and two days ago in Hamburg the Nazis blew up an entire sector of homes and killed people," said Marsha, who'd been listening to every word her husband said as she pored over the tour itineraries and chart positions of their bands. A dyed blonde who seemed even tougher than her husband, she was dressed in a long sweatshirt that fell over black stretch pants. She spoke in a thick New Yawk rasp. "It's terrifying. There must've been a thousand of them walkin' down the streets, going, 'Sieg heil, sieg heil,' no different than if it was in 1936."

Milano, who was sitting across from Jonny Z and whose upcoming tour was looking like a nightmare, put it more bluntly.

"I'm on stage and the fuckin' Nazis start getting around me, heads are gonna get racked," Milano said, loud and fast, like a screeching metal solo.

"And now I got to deal with Al Jourgensen," Jonny Z said. He sighed audibly, reaching again for the whiskey bottle, and put on a New Age CD.

The Zazulas had dealt with out-of-control rock and rollers for years. Metallica, Anthrax, M.O.D.—these were Jon and Marsha's babies, and their company wasn't called Crazed Management for nothing. But no artist Jonny Z had ever run across came close to causing him as much aggravation as Jourgensen, the swarthy, dark haired, demonic-looking leader of Ministry and numerous other bands that included Revolting Cocks, 1000 Homo DJs, My Life with the Thrill Kill Kult and Pailhead.

Not that Jonny Z didn't walk into his relationship with Jourgensen with his eyes open. In Chicago, where Ministry was launched, the rocker's exploits were legend. Jourgensen staying up five days in a row at Chicago Trax studio, ripped on acid, heroin, coke or a combination of all three, laying down the diabolical beats and rhythms that were the bands' trademark. Jourgensen inviting journalists to share his well-stocked pharmacopoeia. Jourgensen asking a writer to sit in on a recording session, then getting the poor bastard shitfaced and erasing his interview tape, whispering subliminal messages on it instead.

"Jourgensen's methodology in those days was to go to the studio to get some work done, but he'd soon get bored," said Greg Kot, a music critic for the *Chicago Tribune*, who followed Jourgensen's colorful career. "Al hung out with all these gonzo musicians and they'd end up at the Smart Bar in Cabaret Metro, where the drinks were free, and get roaring drunk. They'd close the place at two or three in the morning. Then someone would say, 'Hey, let's go make some records.' Trax was open twenty-four hours a day, so they could trash the place. Already buzzed from alcohol, they'd start breaking out the heavy drugs. And this would carry on for four or five days at a time."

Jonny Z had heard about the recording sessions: Jourgensen spraying a can of Cheez Whiz down the throat of some musician who wouldn't stop snoring, so that the guy woke up choking, thinking he was dying. Or Jourgensen dumping cans of garbage on an engineer who, unable to stay up for a hundred hours, had finally collapsed from exhaustion.

Two years earlier, when he agreed to manage him, Zazula knew Jourgensen was brilliant, albeit twisted. Metal Maria Ferrero, Zazula's aggressive, plump publicity assistant, had told him as much. But Jonny Z couldn't have fathomed what a madman he'd signed up. Already this year, Jourgensen had punched out a Warner Bros. executive because the guy was acting too self-important and demanding to see him backstage after a show. And when Sire, the Warner Bros. label to which Ministry was signed, allegedly reneged[2] on a promise to give the

---

[2] A source at Sire Records who asked not to be named said this about Jourgensen: "When you're on heroin you can interpret whatever somebody said any way you want."

band sufficient support on the Lollapalooza tour, the summer's hottest concert ticket, Jourgensen snapped out completely. His reaction astonished even Zazula, who could blow a fuse with the best but knew how important it was to have your record company on your side. Confronted with what he saw as double-dealing swine, Jourgensen responded swiftly and with brutal directness: He simply jacked off into a couple of sandwich bags and FedExed one each to Sire president Seymour Stein and general manager Howie Klein, with vicious notes attached.

"We could've gone on our own tour and made millions," Jonny Z said, trying to put a better face on the incident. "I mean, who the *fuck* needed Lollapalooza? Well, this really pissed off Al."

It also enraged Stein. The president of Sire Records, who'd signed everyone from Talking Heads to Madonna, somehow tracked down Zazula in a restaurant. "He'd gotten the package and, whoah, he was *really* pissed," said Zazula. "But that's Al for you. He just whacked off and mailed it to 'em. He doesn't let you get away with shit."

Jourgensen was a challenge, all right, but Zazula loved challenges. When he looked at Jourgensen's pointy face and his beady, evil eyes; when he saw him knocking off fifths of Bushwick whiskey like soda pop and flying into rages when anyone crossed him or didn't do his exact bidding, Zazula saw a little of himself: the wild, angry kid from the Bronx who wouldn't take shit from anyone. Besides, Ministry's latest Sire recording, *Psalm 69: The Way to Succeed and the Way to Suck Eggs*, was nearly gold,[3] the record everyone in college was buzzing about. Jourgensen and Ministry were on the eve of celebrity and Jonny Z was ready to ride that roller coaster to the top. Anyway, when he wasn't giving you an ulcer or kicking you in the nuts, Jourgensen could be hilarious in his own twisted way. Like the time he stopped mixing a Red Hot Chili Peppers song to rid the control room of evil spirits.

---

[3] The CD would eventually sell close to a million copies.

Reid Hyam, owner of Chicago Trax, couldn't forget that day. He'd walked into the control room and found animal skulls and large bones hanging from the ceiling, strobe lights eerily flashing, an exorcism already in progress. Jourgensen had asked for a live chicken—a requirement for the ritual—and now the chicken was walking around the studio, climbing up onto the console, stoned out of its mind and pecking away madly. An engineer fed it some popcorn, but Jourgensen immediately stopped him. "Hey, man, don't give that chicken popcorn," Hyam recalled Jourgensen saying in a completely serious voice. "Everybody knows that chickens don't eat popcorn. Chickens just eat peanuts and drink beer."

"Eventually the chicken took a shit on a rhythm track, and Al took that as a sign," said Hyam. "They threw away the drum track and started over. After that, everything was fine."

So what if Al Jourgensen was whacked out on LSD and heroin? So what if he brought in live chickens for exorcisms? Jonny Z could feel the excitement crackling around Ministry. The same excitement he'd felt with Metallica, a band he and Marsha had guided to the brink of stardom, only to see them snatched away by another manager. But that would never happen again. The truth was, Jourgensen could get away with any kind of insanity because Zazula wasn't about to see him slip out of his hands. Not when Ministry had the potential to sell millions of albums and take everyone on a manic ride. No one had to say it, but everyone at Crazed Management knew it: You couldn't piss off Al, because a performer this charismatic came along only once or twice in a lifetime.

"It's like baby-sitting Satan, isn't it?" Jonny Z said to Michael Jobson, Ministry's Scottish tour manager, who went by the nickname Curly and had dropped by to say hello the day before the big show.

"He's lost his mind," Jobson said, as Zazula offered him a belt of whiskey.

"Al lost his mind long ago," Zazula said, the two managers now sharing a dark laugh.

Zazula needed to laugh. Today, he felt like a Muslim being thrown into a mosh pit with a bunch of crazed Serbian nationalists. For starters, the Ministry show, originally scheduled for Madison Square Garden, was moved at the last minute to the smaller Paramount theater. Not only were thousands of ticket holders, as well as members of the media, now locked out of the show, but the Paramount, located in the Garden complex, was a swank hall unaccustomed to dealing with rock's bottom feeders.

"Not only are the seats plush, but the bathrooms are magnificent. So we got to beef up security or the kids'll destroy the place," Zazula told the promoter over the phone.

Things might've been more promising if there was a mosh pit, the area near the lip of the stage where the hard-core fans violently slammed into each other, working out their boredom and rage to the martial bleat of the music. But tomorrow night there would be no moshing because the promoter didn't want to lose the seats it would've cost him.

"No *mosh* pit?" Zazula asked incredulously when he learned of the decision. "Jesus fucking Christ! They're gonna rip the seats out and I'm gonna lose a hundred thousand dollars. Jesus!! We've got to double security!"

"If you double security, they'll just brutalize the kids," Jobson said in his thick Scottish brogue. He took another belt of whiskey.

Someone mentioned Slayer, a Satanic metal band that caused minimal damage at the Paramount. But Jonny Z sneered.

"Slayer is the New York Philharmonic compared to Ministry," he screamed over the telephone, this time to an ICM agent who was handling the contract and had informed him that each seat cost $150. "I remember at the Clash of the Titans the seats started flying over my head. They destroyed the fucking place! There should be three security guards in each bathroom. I've got to have fifty fucking security men on the floor tomorrow! It's gonna be ugly as hell!"

Hell was a word Zazula used often. It conjured up a place of corrosive intensity where everything went wrong to the sound of beer bottles crashing, seats flying, bones being broken.

"My life is always pretty much hell. But hell is my playground," Zazula said after he hung up the phone. "Without it I'd be bored."

But he was never bored. Even as a child, growing up in the Bronx, Zazula was always restless, angry and pushing the barriers, full of wild, frequently destructive energy that flew out in a thousand different directions. At home he listened to records by the Grateful Dead, the Jefferson Airplane and Quicksilver Messenger Service. But not the way most kids listened to music.

"I had this little stereo as a teenager and I'd come home and try to listen to music, like the Dead, but it sounded like shit," Zazula told me one afternoon during lunch. "So after I did my homework I'd take a tab of acid and turn on this little shitty stereo and it sounded *fantastic!*"

Having just wolfed down a large hero sandwich, Zazula picked up a ball of smoked mozzarella and ate it as if it were a small marshmallow.

"I'd drop acid every night just to *listen* to music. One night me and my cousin did fifteen tabs each of Orange Sunshine— because we were *really* insane. I did about three thousand hits of acid before I quit. But I never freaked until they put STP[4] in the Sunshine. That's when I developed a tic in my neck, because the strychnine and the belladonna were going right to the spinal fluid."

Zazula's memories of music were poignant. He rode the trains to Brooklyn each week to see the bands he loved. He saw Stevie Wonder do "Fingertips" live, and rocked out to Mitch Ryder and the Young Rascals. He saw the Temptations, James Brown and Otis Redding live at Harlem's legendary Apollo Theatre. And when Otis sang "Mr. Pitiful," Zazula remembered, he felt he'd died and gone to heaven.

---

[4] A hallucinogen more powerful than LSD.

If the music was transcendent, his family life brought him only misery. Zazula's mother was a social worker, but his father, a shipping clerk for a giant warehouse, was a mean-tempered man who regularly took it out on his kids, until one day Zazula, the oldest of three brothers, wouldn't take it any longer.

"I just grabbed a knife and put it to his throat and said, 'You're not going to beat up anybody anymore.' Well, it got to be where the house was going to be a war zone, and my mother wanted to leave. So I said, 'Don't worry about it.' And I packed my shit and headed out."

Zazula was fourteen years old then, a runaway, sleeping on the streets and panhandling.

There were crash pads in the Village, and Zazula stayed at many of them, living by his wits. Even so, he went to school every day from the East Village and kept up a B average. On occasion he went back to his parents' house, but the rules were too tight, and he'd soon take off.

"My mother was heartbroken, but I didn't care. I had a job. I did whatever it took to survive."

Surviving wasn't always easy. In the midsixties the male youth of America were all in exile—either feeling betrayed by the lies of politicians and the bad advice of their parents or else fighting and dying in the jungles of Vietnam. In a society without real leaders or elders—a country that had no one to handle the overflowing energies of young men and initiate them into the culture—those who didn't go to war turned to drugs and initiated themselves. To drop LSD, stay stoned four days and become a wanderer seemed like a logical choice. And so Zazula became a nomad.

Angry and confused, looking for meaning, he sought out extreme experiences and outcast cultures. During the late sixties he spent time in San Francisco, dropping acid, listening to Timothy Leary and grooving to the stoned-out jams of the Grateful Dead and the drugstore-cowboy rock of Quicksilver Messenger Service. And in Colorado and New Mexico he hung out with Hell's Angels, hippies, drifters and junkies.

It was at a Colorado ranch that Zazula thinks he encountered Charles Manson, a bearded psychotic who dreamed of murdering actresses and watching girls perform oral sex on dogs.

"He came in one day, wearing these big old Frye boots, with a blade hanging out of the right side of one boot. He looked like he was packing, too. I didn't know it was Charles Manson then. But this guy had an aura that could knock the shit out of you. It got me literally as he walked in the door. People were just scared of him, fear in their eyes. There were two or three girls behind him, but I just looked at his face and said to myself, 'Hey, man, I'm outta here.' Because I would've slept in the canyon with the coyotes before I would've slept in that house."

Like Little Big Man, Zazula acted out and witnessed the crazy energy of the era, running into some of the key people who would shape the pop zeitgeist of that troubled time. He went to Central Park's Sheep Meadow in the Summer of Love, flying kites and joining hands in "love circles." He was at Power Ridge with Wavy Gravy and met Allen Ginsberg. And once he even ran into Ken Kesey and some of the Merry Pranksters.

Kesey also hung out with the Hell's Angels, traveled with the Grateful Dead and entertained his guests by serving Kool-Aid spiked with LSD. But Zazula tried to go Kesey one step further. So when STP surfaced in 1967, Zazula couldn't resist trying this terrifying "caviar of psychedelics." He even considered spending time with the STP Family, a druggy cult that had its own ranch and was led by a witch, but then thought the better of it.

"I didn't want to go with the STP Family because that was another heavy drug/mind control sort of thing," Zazula recalled. "It was almost like they were LSD Moonies. Plus, they were taking this acid that gave you a three-day hallucinogenic trip."

If it was a time of near-apocalyptic wonder and chaos—a time that swallowed some people whole and made others into heroes—it was also a time of violence and hatred. Zazula saw Hell's Angels take over the drug market. In Cheyenne, Wyoming, he got into a brawl with cowboys who used to get a kick out of getting shitfaced Saturday nights and scalping hippies. In New Mexico, near Taos, Zazula saw some poor hippie kid get gunned down in cold blood by some redneck cowboys, just like Peter Fonda and Dennis Hopper in *Easy Rider*.

"There was always danger in New Mexico. That's the way it was back then. They fuckin' hated longhairs."

When he wasn't wandering, Zazula lived in the East Village. There, he saw the rock and roll culture take shape. He went to the Fillmore and the Apollo. He saw the Velvet Underground and James Brown, Tim Hardin and Bob Dylan. There were shows every week by performers who would become legends: Aretha Franklin, Jimi Hendrix and Captain Beefheart. In fact, Beefheart was Zazula's favorite.

"Captain Beefheart, to me, was a god. The Grateful Dead at their *height* played at the level Beefheart *started* from. You'd go hear Beefheart's band and they'd be playing inversions. The bass and the drums would go up the middle and the second drummer would play off the high hat. And then the marimbas would start. Beefheart was a religious experience."

Marsha Rutenberg came from a different background, growing up in a middle-class Jewish family with parents who thought everything should be done for show-and-tell.

"My father was a tough, angry man; my mother swallowed hard and dealt with it because too many divorces had gone down in her family and she didn't want to be the next one in line. I had one sister, older, very meek. And I was the rebellious one."

"Marsha was a friend of a friend. We went to all the Dead shows together—we were big Deadheads," said Jon.

"We met in '76 but just hung out as friends because he was married and I was living with someone," said Marsha.

"But I always really *dug* her—even when I *was* married," said Jon.

When Zazula's marriage ended in 1978, he quickly called up Marsha. And that was it: The two stuck together like glue.

For a while Zazula sold insurance. Then, in the late seventies and early eighties, he sold stocks and commodities on Wall Street. With a gambler's instinct, he quickly made big money at the outset of what would be the decade of greed. Working in what was essentially a clearinghouse for a large firm, Zazula says he earned as much as twenty-five thousand dollars a week. But then, he said, he got sick of it all.

"It was a money-worshiping time. Everything was about greed. And the people were disgusting" was all Jonny Z would say when I asked him where he worked and what he sold. Something told me there was more to the story than that. And there was.

In fact, Zazula had been charged with, and pled guilty to, conspiracy to commit wire fraud in connection with the sale of tantalum, an extremely hard, silver-gray metal principally used in the manufacture of electronic components and aircraft.[5] Zazula was furious when I brought up the six-month sentence he served in a halfway house in New Jersey, a sentence that ended May 24, 1983.[6] He said it was a dark hole in his life that he'd all but erased.

"You're not dealing with a criminal. You're dealing with a person who got caught with people who were, and was guilty by association. . . . That moment in my life was a horrible time," he said. "I don't want to see it in print and I don't want to relive it. It was a trauma."

But eventually, in fits and starts, Jonny Z began to relive it.

"In those days, I was working for a regular investment banking house,[7] and we got involved with a company called, I think, Strategic Minerals—because gold had just finished its run and the big talk on Wall Street was titanium and tantalum. So I went to work for a company that sold tantalum.

"All you read in those days on Wall Street was 'Buy strategic metals.' That's why we were so successful. But we came in

---

[5] By the early eighties it had become a highly speculative commodity.

[6] Zazula says he served only three and a half months of the sentence in a halfway house in New Jersey. His license to sell stocks and commodities was taken away.

[7] Zazula has refused to name the firm, but he did say it was involved in shady transactions that were typical of some major Wall Street firms of the period.

one day and the phones were pulled, and before you knew it we were all arrested. The street was closed off by the time we were inside. And [then] Marsha was watching this on the five o'clock news. . . .

"As far as I was concerned, we were buying and stockpiling tantalum. . . . But once the government calls all your clients on the phone and tells them there's been fraud, your clients panic. They sell everything they have. And when they sell it, they cause a crash—because you've stockpiled. When it crashes, the price goes down to nothing and they've all lost money. And they want your ass because of the money they've lost—so they'll say anything."

Virtually everyone at the company went down, according to Zazula. But he insists that he didn't know he was selling impure tantalum or misrepresenting it to investors. And he contends that he pled guilty only because both the state and the federal authorities were out to make an example of the firm and because paying his legal fees would've left him destitute.

"When you're making too much money for a public defender, you need to hire a lawyer. So over six months, at three thousand dollars a day—you add up the legal bill. And then your lawyer says, 'You better plea bargain because you don't have a rat's chance.' I would've lost my home and my family. That's why I did halfway time and pled—because I didn't want to go inside," Zazula said, referring to the prison sentence that might have been his fate otherwise.

"I was told I'd feel this for thirty years and I didn't believe them. . . . I burnt this chapter in my life. It is something I'm very ashamed of. It's something I'm very unhappy about. And it is so dark that it's buried deep. I developed a nervous twitch that took me five years to get rid of it. It was in my neck from the stress of having to say the words 'I'm guilty,' knowing I wasn't."

Even when he was serving time for conspiracy to commit wire fraud, Zazula was hatching plans for a new life. "I knew that there was only one direction to go—and that was up," he said.

Since his halfway-house sentence allowed him to work, Zazula took what money he had—$180—and decided to open a record store in a flea market in East Brunswick, New Jersey.

"That's how we started Rock N Roll Heaven," Jonny Z said. "Out of that pit of hell came all that we did. That was the *seed*. And the miracle is that while I was serving this sentence everything happened. Metallica exploded. All this from a *pay* phone. I broke Metallica from a pay phone while I was doing halfway time."

Rock N Roll Heaven was just a run-down hole-in-the-wall, a refuge from the soulless world of Wall Street. Metallica didn't happen for a while. The store specialized in heavy metal, a musical subculture that would soon envelop Jon and Marsha's every waking moment.

"People would come from five hundred miles away just to buy records from us," Jon said one evening when he, Marsha and Metal Maria were gathered for dinner at a cozy local restaurant. "We started with a hundred and eighty dollars in our pockets, and within six months we had an eighty-thousand-dollar inventory. And it didn't come from anywhere except self-implosion."

"We were like this mecca," said Marsha. "Metal wasn't even happening in America then."

"And what was happening was stable," said Jon, who was devouring a bowl of fried calamari and zucchini sticks, washing it all down with glasses of white wine. "We started Rock N Roll Heaven out of a love of music. It became a heavy-metal specialty shop. And we became experts in the genre. We loved this music. If you listened to bands like Raven and Motörhead in those days, they were brilliant, adventurous."

The store quickly developed a mythos. Like pilgrims traveling to some sacred shrine, metal fans from all over the world came. All the East Coast metal musicians did their shopping at Jon and Marsha's store. And when Ozzy Osbourne's fabled guitarist Randy Rhoads died, Rock N Roll Heaven was filled to overflowing with mourners. "You'd think it was a church," Jon said, a touch of sadness in his eyes at the memory. "We even had a shirt of all the great rockers who died, like Pigpen and Jimi Hendrix and Janis Joplin. And on the right was a space for Randy."

What the Zazulas had stumbled onto was a burgeoning underground scene that major labels would eventually exploit. In less than five years, heavy metal, though sneered at by critics, would rise again, becoming one of the biggest-selling genres in pop music. And Jonny and Marsha were like the first prospectors panning for gold.

"When albums came in, we'd go out to the airport to pick them up," Jon said, "because everyone wanted them immediately. We were doing major, major business. When *Restless and Wild* came out, by Accept, we sold five hundred copies out of our store. We were the best buyers ever, and I don't mean to brag, but we were. We'd have a hundred twenty-five people lining up before we opened. We were doing better business in a twelve-by-ten-foot flea market than most big record stores. Rock N Roll Heaven was packed to the gills every day. And when we ran out of a record, we would never sell the last one. We'd keep it for in-store play. The people in the stalls near us were always telling us to shut the music down because we were in a marketplace."

Those were the days when labels from all over the world sent their releases to the Zazulas. Rock N Roll Heaven's playlists were printed in England, and fans from Germany and Sweden and Denmark would write Jon and Marsha letters. There were a couple of American labels putting out metal, but most of it was junk.

"Twisted Sister was playing then," Marsha said, a sneer in her voice. "Stupid groups."

One day Jon and Marsha got a tape from a group called Metallica. They listened to the music and neither could believe what they heard: Fast and raw, full of poetry and anarchy, it was the sound of thrash to come.

"Metallica was just a demo tape that came into the store," said Jonny Z, "but the music blew my mind. So we made an

Jory Farr

album, though I don't know how, because we had no money."

A few years later, when Jon and Marsha were broke, Metallica would leave Crazed Management, sign with Elektra Records and become superstars, selling more than twenty-five million records. But in 1983, no one at a major label was interested in the band's ferocious demo, so Zazula said fuck it, and he and Marsha decided to form their own label. They called it Megaforce Records. And to no one's surprise, when Metallica's first album, *Kill 'Em All*, was released, Rock N Roll Heaven couldn't keep it in stock.

Back then, their label was being run out of the Zazula's basement. The house itself was a sanctuary for their bands, who were invariably broke. Metallica slept on their living-room floor for a year and a half.

"We didn't have any money, either," said Jonny Z. "But we were happy because we loved this music. For the first four years, we ate bologna sandwiches."

"Bologna was our filet mignon," said Marsha.

It was an insane time. Some nights the Zazulas would come home and find as many as two dozen long-haired rock musicians in their house—musicians who slept, ate, drank and fucked on their living- or dining-room floor.

"Sometimes we'd find them in our bed," said Marsha. "And they stunk from not taking showers. That's why my kids are six years apart. They were raised between Metallica and Anthrax."

"When I first went down to Megaforce Records, the whole operation was being run out of Jon and Marsha's basement," Rick Downey, who for years was Anthrax's tour manager, said, reflecting on the early days at the company. "He and Marsha didn't sign acts because they wanted to make a lot of money. They just loved the music. They were wild about it."

And the business was run by both of them equally. "Without Marsha I'd be a bum" said Zazula. "We wouldn't exist."

"Without Marsha, Jonny would be the blimp without the tether—no pun intended," said Scott Ian, the leader of Anthrax, a band the Zazulas started managing in the mideighties and guided to thrash stardom and a more-than-ten-million-dollar deal with Elektra Entertainment in 1992. "Marsha brings Jonny back down to Earth. They'll give us Mars and Jonny will ask for Jupiter and Venus, too."

It was no accident that misfits—like S.O.D. (Stormtroopers of Death, Billy Milano's first band), Anthrax and Ministry—gravitated to Crazed/Megaforce; Jon Zazula was as insane as they were. Back in the early days, each time one of his bands finished a recording Zazula would ritually mark the occasion with a brawl—just to get all the repressed rage and tension out. The melee would usually come after everyone got rip-roaring drunk or had chicken fights at a nearby bar, where locals would go to hear country-and-western music.

"We called it the North to Alaska brawl," Zazula said one afternoon, when things were eerily quiet for a moment at Megaforce/Crazed. "Instead of committing murder, because everyone was insane after being cooped up in a studio for months, we'd beat the shit out of each other. I had a three-bedroom apartment up in Ithaca where I kept all the bands when they were recording, and basically we would get fifteen to twenty of us together, then we'd have a massive fist fight and break shit over each other's heads. Frankie Bello, from Anthrax, was the best. Billy Milano, from S.O.D., was a major brawler. I mean, it was no joke. There'd be flesh on the walls, blood flowing. But the next day we'd have dinner."

There was no shortage of fights, but the worst took place when Anthrax played a joint called the Olympic Auditorium, a place where they put on boxing matches. "All the gangs showed up and the security guards were dragging kids out and beating them up," said Jonny Z. "The guys in Suicidal Tendencies came down, and during a jam with Anthrax a riot started.

"There were gang members and fights everywhere you looked," recalled Bello, one of Anthrax's guitarists. "People were stage diving. And Jon was right in the trenches, pushing people off the stage and throwing punches."

"Anthrax had to leave the stage and I ended up fighting with a security guard who was trying to take an amplifier and break it over the head of one of my musicians," said Jonny Z.

"We were duking it out on the fuckin' stage and I just leveled him."

Rick Downey remembered Zazula's brawling abilities. "If someone threw a punch, Jon would throw a punch," said Downey. "He'd jump in and take security matters in his own hands."

Zazula's samurai management style and quick temper, meanwhile, were legend: Zazula hanging some asshole who fucked with him over a spiral staircase five stories high, or suspending some poor schmuck over a deck and listening to him scream.

"I didn't like people double-crossing me or telling me, 'You better do this,'" Zazula said.

The truth was, his moods matched the manic swings of the universe he rotated in. So maybe it wasn't too surprising that in the late eighties, as Megaforce became one of the leading independent labels recording thrash, Jonny Z's ego bloated.

"There was a time when Jon got caught up in the limelight," said Billy Milano, who had known Zazula since the early days, when the Bronx-born manager would ask to split gas money to gigs. "They say musicians are supposed to be rock stars, not their managers, but a few years ago Jon got blown away with himself. He was insane. He used to walk around in a red kimono. It was a fireman's kimono from Japan and he'd show up everywhere, day or night, wearing it. He's pacified now, but he was insane then."

When the Zazulas lost Metallica to Elektra Records and the management company Q Prime, the royalties they got on subsequent albums gave them the money with which to build a franchise. The couple never thought they'd find a band of Metallica's stature. But lately Anthrax was shaping up to be that band.

Back in the early eighties, when the Zazulas were scuffling,

Anthrax were local thrash wanna-bes who pestered them endlessly for a label deal.

"We religiously went to the pancake house for breakfast on Sundays before we opened up Rock N Roll Heaven," Jonny Z said, "and just coincidentally a whole carful of the guys in Anthrax would show up and sit at the next table. I remember their car had an ANTHRAX license plate."

Eventually Megaforce signed the band, and with each record the sound got tighter and the fan base grew. By 1987 Anthrax's albums were turning gold and platinum, and by 1992 Zazula had helped the group negotiate a huge deal at Elektra.

I caught up with Anthrax one January afternoon in 1993, when the band was at Cherokee Recording Studio in Hollywood recording its Elektra debut, *Sound of White Noise*. Ian and Bello seemed happy to take a break and talk about their manager. They immediately told a story about a trick they had played on Zazula.

"We were the cleanest band in the world," Ian said, "and Jonny Z would always joke, 'I can't do anything with you guys! It's like going on tour with Mary Poppins. I can't smoke cigarettes or drink!' So we decided we'd play a joke on him. We'd pretend we were finally hooked on drugs.

"We were playing at all these gigs in Southern California, and we knew Jonny was flying out. So we told him, 'Hey, with all the stress of the road, we couldn't take it anymore. You're probably not going to believe this, but in the past few weeks we started doing blow just to have energy.'

"Jonny didn't believe us. So I said, 'You know us, Jonny. Why we would we lie about it? The hotels suck. We can't sleep. We needed to do lines.' "

"We all had serious faces, too," said Bello.

"And I said, 'As a matter of fact, [guitarist] Danny [Spitz] scored an eight-ball [of coke] today knowing you were going to come out. We'll go nuts. We'll do it together.' "

Now Zazula's disbelief gave way to astonishment, and Ian did a dead-on imitation of his Bronx yowl. " 'If I wudda known,'

Jonny said, 'I wudda bought so much *stuff*. If I only knew!' And he was jumping up and down. 'Where can we get maw?' he asked. And I said, 'Jonny, we got a *lot* already. I don't know how much you do, but we got a *lot*. It's definitely enough for us.' So we went in the back of the bus, and the rest of the guys already had the mirror out and were cutting lines. Jonny's face was all flushed. He was beside himself."

"He was ecstatic," said Bello.

"He said, 'Oh my God, if Marsha could see this!' Well, we were all set to go. So I gave him a rolled-up ten-dollar bill and said, 'Jonny, you be the first one.' And he said, 'No, no. I've got to see this.' And we knew he'd say that. So he handed the bill back to me and says, 'I want to see *you* do it. This is so amazing!'

"So I put the bill up my nostril and bent down like I was going to snort the line—and then I just fake sneezed," Ian said, a mischievous grin spreading across his face. "And all these fat lines of—I guess it was talcum powder—just blew all over the place."

"They went all over the floor," said Bello, who was now howling at the memory.

"And I swear," said Ian, "I got scared for a minute. Because Jonny leaned back, grabbed his heart and his face just drained of color. He looked like he was having a heart attack. But he was OK. We fucking *died!* We did not stop laughing for ten minutes. The look on Jonny's face was unbelievable—I just wished I had a picture of it. It was the Jonny Z windup of all time."

Of course, Zazula could give as good as he got. Art Ring, who toured with various Megaforce bands, could vouch for that.

"I used to have a tendency to treat women with less respect than others would, and Jonny Z has daughters and respects women's rights," Ring said one day. "Well, back in 1988 we were out with Anthrax in Japan and Jonny told me he'd been getting all these calls from the police—that they were after me for treating some girl disrespectfully. Because Anthrax didn't mess around, and all the girls that showed up at the gigs were basically for the pickings of the crew. Well, Jonny basically had me shuttled around, hiding in all these hotel rooms for four days straight, saying the cops were after me. Here I was in a foreign country and I was scared shitless. I thought they were going to come and take me away. So I just hid. The band was in on it, the crew was in on it and the promoter was in on it."

Before Crazed Management came along, plenty of other managers had tried to handle Ministry. None, however, had lasted long. Few could abide Al Jourgensen's strange moods, fueled by whiskey, psychedelics and hard drugs.

Jon and Marsha had first met Jourgensen and his bandmate, keyboardist/programmer Paul Barker, two years earlier when Maria Ferrero, a big Jourgensen fan, learned that the group desperately needed a manager.

"Maria had talked to Al, and what happened was we flew the band in. We were fascinated by the buzz on them," Jonny Z said, recalling the first meeting. "Al and Paul sat down in our office for a while and I didn't even know who they were. We knew of their music, because we'd seen one of their videos that absolutely stunned us, 'In Case You Didn't Feel Like Showing Up.' It was amazing. I thought, 'Why isn't this band the biggest in the world? They should be bigger than Jane's Addiction.'

"Al asked us what do we think about record companies. And we said, 'We hate record companies. Unless you monitor them like the KGB, nothing gets done.' We just hung out and talked, developing a rapport. We knew they were being mishandled. And after two days of mind-melding we had enough to put together a contract that we sent them."

Having done massive quantities of drugs himself, Jonny Z wasn't put off by Jourgensen's reputation. And so what if Jourgensen's loft apartment, chockablock with skulls, bones and Christian statuary, had a huge replica of *The Last Supper* with

Jory Farr

a photo of Charles Manson where Christ's face should be? A lot of artists were eccentric. And for the Zazulas, Jourgensen was just an enchilada away from genius.

No, coming from dysfunctional families, the Zazulas could instantly empathize with Jourgensen's outsider status. Someone who'd initially craved pop celebrity—his first record for Arista cast him as a fey synth-popper with a fake British accent—Jourgensen now looked at every business dealing with a suspicion verging on paranoia. And Jon and Marsha could understand that. Most people in the music business *were* slimeballs.

Once the Zazulas signed on to manage Ministry, they immediately went to work, approaching Sire Records with a plan for breaking the band. The plan included demands for marketing budgets, tour support, awareness campaigns, profiles and trade ads—getting the whole weight of a record company behind them.

"We went to Seymour Stein with a detailed marketing campaign and said we would not manage the band unless Sire did everything we wanted," said Jonny Z. "And Seymour's response was: 'Are you going to be the manager in six months?' Because he couldn't imagine anyone managing Ministry even three *days*. He basically said that if we were going to be the managers for the next year or more, he'd do it."

"I work with Al because I respect his brilliance," Marsha said. "Three quarters of the talent he has people aren't even aware of yet. Ministry's a self-contained entity. In their minds they create the music and make it live, and on the stage they bring it to the audience. As managers, we have nothing to do with that process."

Jonny Z was searching for a word to describe the process of managing Ministry.

"They're *inbred*. It's incestuous," he said a few seconds later. "It's the Ministry *family*. But we were not *in* the Ministry family. We were two sperm trying to get in the egg."

Of course, part of Jourgensen's image was pure hype. If Jourgensen were the cloven-hoofed, blood-sucking, devil-worshiping beast the media made him out to be, he would never have been able to make the carefully crafted music he did. Still, when Zazula woke up the morning of Ministry's New York show, he was worried. The last time he'd talked at any length to Jourgensen, the singer had screamed in his face. Apparently, MTV's *120 Minutes* program had decided to air the wrong edit of Ministry's video of "Just One Fix," a song about drug addiction with a voice-over by William Burroughs. Still up at two in the morning, Jourgensen saw the video on MTV and immediately snapped out.

"Al and I had said, 'Don't play it,' but they did. Monday went by and then Tuesday came. I didn't want to be the one to tell them. I figured, let me just stop it from running on MTV. Why cause everybody a headache? I stopped it on *Headbangers Ball*—a miracle. I stopped it on rotation every night—on a *dime*. But there was no one to talk to on Wednesday for *120 Minutes*.

"Al wanted to know how I could let it run, and he went insane. The phone call was an hour of screaming. It's still burning in him now. What can I say? I dealt with it."

That evening, Zazula felt confident there would be no riots at the Paramount show. A few hours before the concert, dozens of security guards staked out their positions. Some were middle-aged men, and their faces had the bitter expressions of those used to dealing with a higher class of people but now suddenly forced into handling a pack of filthy animals.

At 8:00 P.M., scalpers were doing a brisk business outside the Garden, selling floor seats for $150 a pop. Inside, the Paramount was already mobbed with Ministry's motley fans: sullen youths with bored, empty faces; skinheads, their arms stained with tattoos; college hipsters; and a few fortysomething metalheads. One kid had a skull tattoo emblazoned in his forehead. Almost all of them looked as if they were on some sort of drug, their pupils dilated.

Backstage, Neil Young, who would be playing *Saturday Night Live* a few days later, strolled in, accompanied by his manager, and approached the dressing-room door. But Al wasn't receiving them just then, though ex–Cars leader Ric

Ocasek and his gorgeous wife, the model Paulina, made the A-list.

Outside the dressing rooms of Sepultura and Helmet, who were opening the show, photographers from metal and punk magazines fought for position. And the scenesters were out in force: Sticklike sylphs with rings in their noses, a luscious blonde with an ass that made all the men sigh.

Some forty photographers were jammed into a pit when Sepultura opened the show. But when the lead singer of the Brazilian thrash band made the mistake of jumping into the crowd, security guards pounced on him immediately, forcing him back onstage.

By now, the bouncers had various fans in hammerlocks and were throwing them out of the Paramount. I looked for Zazula but couldn't find him.

After Helmet played, Ministry's roadies set the stage for Jourgensen. I watched as a beefy guy whom everyone called Turner, his arms and neck covered completely with tattoos, brought out the notorious skeletons of the giant Brahma bulls from Texas.[8] Like some aggro-paleontologist, he assembled the bones and fastened them together with steel hooks. Erect, the bulls stood more than ten feet high. And other skulls and vertabrae, wrapped around steel booms and mike stands, gave the stage a menacing, deathlike appearance.

Somewhere around 11:00 P.M. the lights dimmed and Ministry came out to the shattering clang of "N.W.O.," a song that presented George Bush's dream of international prosperity and peace as a fascist-capitalist plot to rule the world. Overhead, two screens pulsed with a stream of hypnotic images: penises with metal rings through them and gruesome stitching; pink vaginas, looking like open gashes; and a box opened with surgical blades, as if in preparation for a savage clitoridectomy.

When the band lurched into "Just One Fix," Jourgensen's take on the addict's convulsive agony and ecstasy, his voice be-

---

[8] Turner supposedly had slaughtered them himself.

came a junkie howl, augmented by a ghostly oration courtesy of the old mugwump himself, William Burroughs. What looked like psychedelic maggots swarmed across the screen. Brahma bulls riding on ball-bearing wheels skidded out across the stage. And I remember wishing that something violent *would* happen. After all, I'd been primed for an eruption, a riot, a melee. But the security force, one hundred strong with more police on alert, was just too intimidating. Each aisle was blocked off, and anyone who wandered out of a section was immediately escorted back.

As for Ministry's performance, it was an act of pure contempt. Jourgensen had absolutely no connection to the thousands of lost souls in the audience, wasted on drugs, looking for someone to absorb their wild rage and alienation. Instead of saying something to stop the thugs who masqueraded as security, the master of aggro-thrash merely scowled.

There was no moshing. And despite all the bones and dread, despite the images of sexual depravity and scarification and sadism on the video monitors, there were no riots at the Paramount. Jonny Z wasn't going to have to shell out a hundred thousand dollars for new seats.

A few days after Christmas, when Ministry was in Los Angeles for one of its last shows, the band and its tour manager went up to Timothy Leary's Beverly Hills house for dinner. Jourgensen had arranged to talk with the grand wizard of LSD himself, who was now seventy-two.

"They came up here and partied," Leary said when I happened to be at his house a few weeks later.[9] Leary wasn't one to waste words. He smiled at me warmly. "Al does a lot of drugs."

One night I got a tour of the Zazulas' sprawling New Jersey house, which is situated in an upper middle-class neighbor-

---

[9] I visited Leary to interview him about his work with virtual reality and computers, not his relationship with Jourgensen.

hood. Like their office, it was a mad pastiche of sixties pop art, surrealism and gobs of rare Disney memorabilia, which Zazula got from a mysterious broker at a discount. There were tiny porcelain Pinocchios and Mickey Mouses, intricately detailed tableaus of Cinderella and Snow White and the Seven Dwarfs, a rare Dumbo teapot and a whole miniature scene out of *Alice in Wonderland:* the Mad Hatter's tea party.

"This stuff is priceless," Jonny Z said. "Look. Here's Mickey in a mirror painting Disney. That's from *The Mickey Mouse Club.*"

The living room had a grand piano, a photo of Dalí and a lithograph by the famous surrealist. But then Zazula flipped on a light and there was another whole display case chock-full of Disney miniatures and Marsha's pride and joy: a rare collection of antique and hand-carved carousel art. Raised on rock and roll, a music all about youth, Jon and Marsha Zazula had made their house a shrine to the fantasy of childhood.

Downstairs, that was even more apparent. The basement, the size of a decent rock and roll club, was jammed with pinball machines from every era, nearly a dozen. We played pinball on one of the oldest, and Jonny Z racked up tens of thousands of points. For a moment he seemed to relax, to be ten years younger, unconcerned with anything except making the balls careen off the bumpers for extra points. But there was another side to the wanderer turned stockbroker turned rock impresario. Upstairs, I noticed a cabinet with a picture of Moses next to Santa Claus and a copy of the Jewish Kabbalah.

"The two books that have influenced me most are the Kabbalah and *The Art of War,*" Zazula said. "Those are heavy, heavy books."

It was hard to imagine Jonny Z following the esoteric path of Jewish mysticism, which called for absolute detachment and subduing the animal self. But then no one can know what someone else is capable of behind closed doors.

At their office the next day, I asked Jon and Marsha what they might be doing if they weren't running a rock and roll label and management company. Marsha smiled and didn't hesitate.

"I'd buy some fabulous house and start an inn somewhere. The food would be incredible and there'd be saunas and massages. That's what I'd really like to do, because our life is so crazy."

"If I wasn't doing this," Jonny Z said, "I'd be running a New Age label and gathering all the acts up, because that's my favorite music. That's what I put on to relax. And Marsha and I have been falling into this whole homeopathic world of medicine. I've been to acupuncturists and chiropractors and I've done tai chi."

I asked Zazula whom he goes to when he needs advice. He leaned his head back and smiled, as if he'd been waiting all night for me to ask him that.

"We're the ones asked all the questions. But where do you go to get answers?" Jonny Z said. And then he paraphrased a line from a Grateful Dead song: Who will answer the answer man? The manager is the person who answers all the questions. But you can't make the walls of Jericho fall.

"There isn't even a psychologist or a psychiatrist that a manager or a power agent can go to, because they can't even clinically figure out what to do. Sure, you can teach somebody to meditate, but how do you tell someone to chill out when they're caught up in a swirl? If I want to cry my heart out or say, 'I've had enough,' no one will have the answer. Who will answer the answer man?"

Just then the phone rang and an assistant came in with a worried look on her face.

"It's for you, Jonny. Something about using the wrong pictures on the new Mindfunk album."

Jonny Z took a deep breath. "Someday I'll start a New Age label and the competition better watch out," he said.

And then he picked up the phone and said, "What the fuck is the problem? I thought we straightened this out."

CHAPTER 5

The Man Who Took the Honk Out of Country

Jimmy Bowen

On a muggy mid-June morning, two New York producers—a short, chunky man named Scott Sanders and Patricia Kellert, his perky assistant—arrived at the sprawling Nashville mansion of Jimmy Bowen.

They waited in Bowen's spacious office and stared at more than four dozen gold and platinum records hanging on the walls. Both seemed edgy, like fish out of water. The day before they'd left the skyscrapers of Manhattan and come to Nashville with a concept that would've been ludicrous a couple of years earlier.

The idea was to bring Garth Brooks, country's reigning superstar, to New York and have him play a concert in Central Park as part of a weeklong country celebration that would include dozens of other events, ranging from dance to art exhibits. The festival, to be called Country Takes Manhattan, conjured up images of gun-toting hillbillies chatting up foul-mouthed cabbies, chicken farmers asking for directions to the Statue of Liberty, yodeling cowboys getting pickpocketed at the Port Authority.

New Yorkers, after all, prided themselves on being sophisticated. They discussed abstract art, listened to jazz and opera and tended to view rural people as one vast swarm of whiskey-drinking, rabbit-hunting hicks. Yet in the summer of 1992, country music had gotten—there was no other word for it—

hip. Wall Street stockbrokers and lawyers were listening to Randy Travis and Clint Black. Dentists and computer programmers were driving home with Travis Tritt and Reba McEntire CDs in their cars. And investment bankers and journalists who'd never smelled cowshit in all their lives were showing up at clubs where down-home country line dancing was the latest rage.

That summer, millions of people would buy an album by a country-styled pinup named Billy Ray Cyrus, whose "Achy Breaky Heart," a song with its own ridiculous dance, would sweep the nation, riding the top of the pop charts and reinforcing the worst hillbilly stereotypes imaginable. But by far the biggest phenomenon was Brooks, a chunky, balding, thirty-year-old Oklahoman who described himself as a "fat boy with a hat." In less than two years, Brooks had sold more than fifteen million records and had negotiated one of the biggest deals in pop music.

You didn't have to be a genius to see that country's image had changed. Sanders and Kellert, who produced concerts for Radio City Music Hall Productions and had a hand in some of the Big Apple's splashiest shows, had major plans. But they needed help and Bowen, the closest thing to a kingpin in Nashville's strange, inbred music scene, was one of the first people they turned to.

That morning, Bowen had already done a segment on NBC's *Today* show, letting the crew set up in his country-French living room. He had on black pants, a black shirt, white tennis shoes and a dark cap—not exactly mogul wear—but his casual style belied a wily, cunning mind. Bowen closed the door behind him, smiled at Sanders and Kellert and walked over to his antique chair.

"Garth's the only person in history who could join the ranks of Diana Ross and Elton John and Simon and Garfunkel," Sanders said after Bowen had sat down, beginning an elaborate pitch that painted a picture of cynical New Yorkers now waking up to the simple pleasures of hillbilly music. Bowen leaned back in his chair and listened to this line of reasoning.

"Taking this stuff to New York City is a waste of time for the most part," he said finally, in a honeyed voice still thick with a West Texas twang. "They look at us as *Hee Haw* up there, bales of *hay* and *bull*shit. If you want to bring this stuff to New York City without the bales of hay, without the cornball shit, well, then you got a prayer. Because this is the music of young America, so you got to dress it like young America and not like what Nashville's image to most people is."

This chilly, no-nonsense assessment wasn't what Sanders had expected. He fidgeted with his fingers before deciding to take another tack to prove that he understood the inherent "image" problems country music had in New York.

"That's not what we have in mind, Jimmy. We're not looking to bring the Grand Ole Opry to Radio City Music Hall," said Sanders, whose black shoes and conservative blazer gave him away as a Yankee carpetbagger.

"I mean, there's a reason country music is exploding. It's not just that all of a sudden we've overturned a rock and found this music. This country is in turmoil. And this music is the music of the working man—the average guy's rap music. Country music is the Ross Perot . . . we're upset . . . what's going on . . . we need to do something . . . we're upset about our quality of life . . . what's happening with this country . . ."

The words flew apart in a puddle of nervous blather, getting more incoherent by the second until Sanders, recognizing that he'd lost his thread, that he was rambling, drowning in non sequiturs, pulled up short.

"Fortunately, people have embraced it. We've always seen that when times have been tough, music has always been a healer, a salvation for people to turn to. And I think that this music is suddenly, thank goodness, becoming accepted. People don't need to be closet country fans in New York City right now. They might not listen to Roy Acuff or like Minnie Pearl. But now you have artists who have an edge to them in their appearance and their style. Now New Yorkers prefer country music and they're gleefully admitting it. . . . This music is not a fad. People like Garth and Travis Tritt and Clint Black are appealing to the sensibility of where America is today. . . . This is like the birth of R&B."

Though Bowen was hardly buying this slick performance, he seemed to soften for a moment. His poker face suddenly turned sympathetic.

"I'm amazed at how much you understand this music— from a New York point of view," he said, the Texas drawl now even thicker to show how fundamentally different their perspectives were. "I mentioned rap music and a guy writing for *The New York Times* called it a racist remark. I said, 'I love rap music because every morning they turn that *shit* on it runs people to country.' "

Now Sanders and Kellert were grinning. Maybe they *could* work with Bowen.

"One of the things we have not penetrated is Madison Avenue," Bowen continued. "We still haven't cracked through like rock and roll has, because the people who are running Madison Avenue grew up with rock and roll. When you go to a Garth Brooks concert you see the kids and the mom and the grandma. . . . "

"You couldn't ask for a better demographic," Sanders said.

"That's why the future is secure . . . and if you were an advertiser, what else could you want?"

"We feel that there's only one guy in country who can play Central Park. If Garth doesn't do Central Park, there will be no Central Park concert," Sanders said finally, trying to sound as simple and plainspoken as Bowen.

"Did you get an audience with Garth?"

"We got an audience with Pam [Lewis] and Joe Harris," Sanders said, referring to one of Brooks's managers and his booking agent.

"The key to Garth is Garth," Bowen said, impatient now to get on with the day, tapping his leg under the table. "It was he who said no to Kentucky Fried Chicken. His instincts are marvelous. Garth said, 'Bowen, I don't want to be remembered for something you can eat.' Revlon made a pitch, but Garth didn't want to be remembered for a fragrance. At some point you're gonna have to sell Garth on it. Talk to me if there's any problem."

"We will. We want to do the concert in Central Park on Saturday," Sanders said, brushing out an imaginary crease in his pants. "We'll own every single newspaper Sunday and Monday. Monday night, we're talking about putting together some kind of dance contest together, with clubs across the country. Maybe we'll take over a restaurant in Central Park and do a dance-oriented thing. . . ."

"You've been to the country dance clubs?" Bowen asked.

"A couple."

"Well, you need to catch up on that phenomenon, because it's quite remarkable. And not just Texas, now. They're in Beverly Hills and San Francisco and New York City. This is another piece of what you're talking about. And this isn't bucking bulls."

"Then we want to do five or six nights at Radio City Music Hall," said Sanders. "We need headliners to pave the way, because we cannot afford failure. But I want enough younger bands on the show so they can be exposed. Then we want to do a country blues night at the Apollo Theatre, maybe something at Carnegie Hall and concerts at clubs. We'll close it out with a jam and get a country version of Paul Shaffer and his band and grab anybody who's still in town.

"We'll have a reception with the mayor at Gracie Mansion and have the mayor proclaim it Country Music Week in New York. We'd have it tied in with retail—Bloomingdale's, Macy's."

"And we'll tie it in with corporate," said Kellert, trying to get a word in edgewise. "We'd have a museum space with country art. . . . "

"There's marvelous country art in this world," Bowen said, "if you get the people to understand it."

Realizing that she hadn't shown Bowen the logo, Kellert pulled out a drawing of a guitar, whose sound hole surrounded the Statue of Liberty's head with its exploding spikes. The logo read: "Country Takes Manhattan."[1]

"We're still working on the typeface," said Kellert.

Bowen looked at the logo and gave an indecipherable expression. Then he grinned.

"Just a little warning so you don't come off elitist: Around here, the Grammys don't mean anything. The Grammys don't give a *shit* about country. They never did and they never will. And just never call the music 'western'—unless you're talking to Roy Rogers. Country's not like rock and roll. The stars don't demand much; they don't ask for one color of M&M in their dressing room. I think you got a handle on it."

With that final advice, Bowen said goodbye and headed out the kitchen door, where his driver, Mike, was waiting to take him to Fanfare, a series of open-air concerts that showcased top artists from each label. Inside the limo, Bowen made a flurry of phone calls to some managers and producers, checked in with his office at Liberty Records and dipped into a bag of Hershey's Kisses.

"I don't know what's to be gained by taking country music to Manhattan," he said after he put down the phone. "If they want it, they'll holler for it, and we'll go. But to force it on them? What's to be gained by it except for publicists and managers who can say, 'Look what we did'?"

The car phone rang and it was Abbey Medic, Bowen's assistant, telling him that Carman would be coming over to the house at 5:00 P.M. Bowen's eyes lit up. He popped another chocolate in his mouth.

"Carman's a preacher who has his own ministry, where he does praises and whatnot. He's Billy Graham—except he sings

---

[1] Held between May 14 and May 23, 1993, and staged at leading venues in New York City, Country Takes Manhattan included concerts by Dolly Parton, Clint Black, Mary-Chapin Carpenter, Willie Nelson, Travis Tritt and the Kentucky Headhunters. Garth Brooks, however, did not participate.

his sermons. He's quite amazing. I'm trying to sign him. You'll get to meet him later this afternoon.

"Christian music's gonna explode just like country did. When I came here, there was about fifty or sixty million dollars' worth of country business a year; now there's four hundred fifty million dollars' worth of business. There's a hundred twenty-five million dollars in the Christian-music business. In five years there'll be five hundred million."

The excited deal maker in Bowen was just getting started when the limo approached the backstage area and was stopped by a guard.

"This car behind me is NBC," Mike told the guard. "They've got press credentials. They're following us in. This here is Mr. Bowen, president of Liberty Records. Major George Currey[2] is meeting us at the backstage parking."

The guard waved us in and a minute later Bowen stepped out, surrounded by a camera crew and a reporter who asked the by now perfunctory question: Why was country so big all of a sudden? Other news crews soon hovered like fruit flies around Bowen, who dutifully gave terse, colorful quotes.

The bleachers held twenty-five thousand people, the hard-core faithful, dressed in polyester and pants suits. Most had come to see Garth Brooks, and thousands had waited hours in the hot sun for an autograph. When Brooks finally came out, the crowd went wild. As he began singing "Shameless," a young woman wormed her way up to the barricade in front of the stage.

"Can I kiss you?" she asked, heart aflutter. And Brooks said, "Yes, you can," giving her a friendly little peck in return, which set off squeals of joy. But not all the fans would get their hearts' desire. When Brooks finished his set, his bodyguards closed around him, escorting him to the trailer, past fans dying for a word, a glimpse, anything. They whisked the star past Julia

---

[2] Currey, a retired police officer, did security work for Liberty Records.

Hayes, who had a gift, a photo album, for Brooks's daughter, Taylor.

"Can't we just talk to him?" she pleaded, her voice anxious, desperate. But the bodyguard shook his head. "Could you at least please see that Garth gets it?" she asked. And then:

"It's a brass photo album with 'TMB'—Taylor Mayne Brooks—engraved on it. We stood in line for eight hours and we couldn't see him. I'm from Athens, Alabama, and I'm too old for this."

"Did you touch him?" a plump woman asked her beak-nosed friend, as Brooks swept by.

"No, I didn't touch him. But I touched him with my eyes," the friend said.

Bowen watched this whole scene with equanimity. This wasn't his favorite place to be, backstage with a swarm of hillbillies clamoring for a moment with their idol; but Brooks had given him his franchise, and this was part of the job. Bowen talked briefly with Major Currey, who scoured the crowd looking for potential crazies. And then the limo came around and we were off again, this time to a Music Row studio to close out a mix.

"Up until 1984, we used to put on all these Fanfare shows free," Bowen said, opening up the bag of Kisses. "Well, that year I called up the Country Music Association a week before and said, 'By the way, I'm pulling MCA out.' Well, they all panicked. The Country Music Association wanted to know why. I told 'em, 'It's costing a fortune to bring in my acts. At least pay for it.' So I *made* them pay. They put up about ten thousand dollars per show. Well, as soon as I got off the phone, I called up all the label heads in Nashville and said, 'Call 'em, you get ten grand from the CMA for your shows.' Well, I guess that irritates people."

Bowen grinned, relishing his role as gadfly and provocateur: the man sticking it to the old-line fat cats.

"Now where did we leave off?" he asked. "Christian music, right? Well, you got seventy-plus million Christians in America and eighty-five percent of them don't go in the bookstores, which is the only place you'll find that music. So the trick is to get the music out where the people are and you'll see a tremendous increase. And unlike country, where the music had to be fixed, Christian music is fine as it is.

"The reason the Christian-music world hasn't exploded yet is that there's no one to bridge those two worlds. The secular people scare them off, and the timidity of that world doesn't fit in pop. The people in Christian music don't make music to sell records. It's their *ministry*, their testimony of what they've found. Most of 'em are singers. Carman's a preacher, but he sings. And his band plays rockin' music—bam-bam-bam-bam.

"He's in his mid-thirties, good-looking, charismatic. Got all the modern moves. I saw him in the Midwest, where sixty percent of the crowd was kids. Carman sells six hundred thousand records, mostly in bookstores. He sells a hundred thousand long-form videos—in the bookstores—and plays in front of a million and a half people a year. He was singing when I saw him, but he did stop for ten minutes to preach, and about eight hundred of his fans came down and got saved—just like Billy Graham. Then they took 'em off to the side and gave 'em counselors from all the local churches. It was amazing."

Ever since I'd arrived in Nashville, I'd felt I was in the heart of white Christian America. There were Baptist hospitals, bookstores and churches almost everywhere I turned. My hotel was overrun with some convention of born-again fundamentalists. And Franklin Road, where Bowen's eight-thousand-square-foot mansion and enormous estate was located, was literally lined with churches for miles. In fact, much of the money and power in Nashville was in the hands of the Christian Right, who had had a notorious reputation for being virulently racist and anti-Semitic.[3] But Bowen wasn't concerned with that. He was interested in bringing Christian music to Targets and Wal-Marts

---

[3] Bowen confirmed that for me. "These people don't *like* the Jews," he said one afternoon just before he was to meet with a powerful group of born-again Christian businessmen and lawyers.

and Kmarts, where it would be like rock and pop—an impulse buy.

And who could doubt that he might pull it off? Ever since Bowen had arrived in Nashville in the midseventies, he'd made successive fortunes at different labels. Between 1978 and 1982, when he headed up Elektra/Asylum's Nashville office, Bowen signed everyone from Crystal Gayle and Conway Twitty to Hank Williams, Jr., and the Bellamy Brothers, transforming the label into a thirty-million-dollar operation. Within a year after taking over as president of MCA Records Nashville in 1984, Bowen had apparently turned the label around. By 1987, when Bowen left, MCA had snagged twenty-three Top Twenty singles, eleven number one hits and six Top Five albums. Record sales tripled and MCA's share of the charts jumped from 12 percent to more than 20 percent.

At both Asylum and MCA, Bowen had fired the existing staff, brought in his own people and created plenty of enemies. He'd aggressively expanded the roster and started releasing lots of records. Some became hits, and Bowen wasn't shy about claiming credit for each success. But not everyone was impressed. Bowen's rivals pointed out that he had a knack for stealing away just before everything unraveled.

"The word on the street was that Bowen would come into a label, take a roster that was maybe twelve artists, expand it to thirty, cut lots of records, ship lots of product and then, when everything would get really big and inflated, leave," one Nashville insider told me.

"The nature of the record business is that the way returns come back, the way royalty money flows, it takes eighteen months to three years for anyone to know whether anything is working. Well, the rumors were that Bowen would escape from these situations just as things would fall apart. And whoever followed him would inherit a huge mess."

Bowen laughed when I told him what some of his critics were saying.

"When I take over a company to fix it I *fix* it. And the owners make *millions* of dollars. When I leave a label, I leave the staff there. Why would you build something and then tear it down?

"When I left MCA, they were making *millions* out of Nashville. And as everything has exploded in the last five years, that good, sound organization has prospered. The MCA roster that's made them all this money in the last five years—I was head of that label when almost every one of them was signed. [George] Strait was there, Reba [McEntire] was there, Wynonna was there, Vince Gill was there. Everyone except Mark Chesnutt and Trisha Yearwood."

Almost everyone I talked to, from managers to producers to rival label executives, conceded that Bowen was one of the shrewdest deal makers in the business, an energetic player who'd made hit records for everyone from Hank Williams, Jr., and Reba McEntire to George Strait and Eddie Rabbitt. Some said he was a "great" producer, but others saw him as a hustler who made slick, vapid records for an audience that had either forgotten or never knew what real country music was all about. Not many people in Nashville liked Bowen. And most weren't willing to talk for the record.

"I think Jimmy Bowen is the single most insensitive person in Nashville," George Massenburg, a top producer who's worked with everyone from Linda Ronstadt to Dolly Parton, told me when I asked him about Bowen's rise to the top.

"Bowen came along at a time when the town was ripe to pillage, and he pillaged what was left. He did increase the recording activity; anyone will warrant that. But he's wrecked the music. He's turned it into a commodity.

"I first met him in L.A. when he was working with Glen Campbell. He was always making stupid records by stupid people. His records have never been artful; there's no cultural imperative to the music and it's not honest. He may be the most powerful guy in Nashville, but that town gave him power."

Depending on whom you talked to, Bowen was either the principal architect of Nashville's current rise to preeminence or a ruthless carpetbagger who had no talent himself, envied true artists and had taken advantage of record-industry economics to become fabulously wealthy. Certainly, his latest and biggest coup had been his role in turning Garth Brooks into a superstar. Having heard some of the music on *No Fences*, Brooks's second album, in May of 1990, Bowen did something only a ballsy executive used to high-stakes gambling would do: he pressed 1.5 million copies of the record and spent millions to buy up premier space in retail all over the country.

By the summer of 1992, Brooks had three records at the top of the charts and had sold more than fifteen million albums. And Bowen, threatening to jump to a rival label, had renegotiated his contract and become even more wealthy, reportedly earning five million dollars a year as an executive and producer. But Bowen's critics quickly pointed out that he hadn't signed Brooks; the singer was already at the label. And according to some wags, if Brooks hadn't taken off, Thorn-EMI, Capitol Nashville's parent company, was set to dump Bowen.

Of course, Brooks's astonishing success made Bowen even more powerful—too powerful for a lot of folks who claimed he was only out to fatten his own pockets. Where other label heads joined the CMA and hobnobbed with Nashville's music elite, Bowen preferred his own counsel. People said he was arrogant, standoffish, bullheaded. Yet Bowen's rivals acknowledged one thing: Bowen had helped transform Nashville from a small-potato satellite industry into the behemoth it was now.

Even before he'd arrived in Tennessee, Bowen had a plan of attack. Instead of moving immediately to Nashville, which tended to distrust outsiders, Bowen headed for Eureka Springs, Arkansas, and spent almost a year traveling the South and Southeast. He talked to the people who listened to country records and watched how they were being made. He hung out at the Glaser brothers' studio in Nashville, which gave birth to the outlaw movement in country music. Above all, Bowen was trying to answer one question: why so few of the tens of millions of country fans actually purchased country albums.

"I was trying to figure out the marketplace. I never was a fan of country music growing up. I was a fan in bits and pieces, but I wasn't a true fan of the music. And I didn't understand the country consumer. So I went to dance halls, listened to radio, talked to people. I wanted to know what they liked, why they liked it, why they didn't buy most of it and why they did buy some of it."

Having worked in L.A., Bowen knew both sides of the business. He knew that successful pop music acts were selling gold and platinum. But what he found out about country wasn't promising.

"I learned that country music didn't sell. The number one album might do sixty thousand. And I knew that wasn't good."

Bowen would find out that the reason country music didn't sell was that the Nashville record business didn't understand how to get its consumer. Worse yet, the industry was turning out bad records.

"The music was made too fast, too cheap and too quick. There were one or two good songs and seven or eight songs that were filler, where you could bet somebody, like the producer, owned the publishing. The music was old, it was ill made, produced in a hurry, with mistakes left in it. Every day it existed it dated itself and set itself backwards as much as it could go forward."

Bowen loved to talk about the dilapidated condition in which he found most Nashville studios. Though most of the studios in New York and L.A. were using digital equipment, Nashville had virtually none. And its engineers and producers seemed to pride themselves on not knowing the new technology.

"That's why if you heard country records then, they sounded little, small, tiny," Bowen said. "You'd punch a country station up after listening to a pop station and the sound would shrink"—Bowen made a sucking sound. "But if you punched up a pop station, the sound would spread out and get depth.

"Everything was behind the times. You'd walk into the studios and all of 'em had so much carpeting that they looked like a carpet warehouse. They must have had a sale on carpeting here one day and all the studios put 'em in as deadening material. Well, there *was* a time when that was the sound. But that time had come and gone.

"The first album I did here was a Mel Tillis album. I was starting to mix it and the engineer in the studio said, 'I noticed you booked two days.' I said, 'Yeah but I'm getting some more time down the road.' And he said, 'Well you don't need that. It only takes forty-five minutes to mix a Mel Tillis song.'" Bowen laughs. "I told him, 'Maybe that's why he hired me.' We didn't get along too well after that. They didn't have any modern equipment. I asked him if he had a keypex, which is a piece of gear that takes out the noise. He said no. I said, 'Never mind, I'll go rent one.' Well, he didn't want to be embarrassed. He said, 'Wait, wait. I got one.' And he did. It was in the back, in a box that had never been opened. They just didn't give a damn." Bowen shook his head and rolled his eyes. "Forty-five minutes to mix a song? I take a day. I sometimes take two days if it calls for it."

"You'll get a lot of opinions about Jimmy Bowen, good and bad," Bill Carter, one of Nashville's most respected and outspoken managers, told me one afternoon. "When Bowen went to MCA, George Strait and Reba McEntire were already there. And when he went to Capitol, Garth Brooks was there. He'll sit and tell you for hours how he broke George and Reba. But all that's really *horseshit*.

"But I know one thing: We were making inferior records in this town, and Bowen came in and said, 'You know what? I'm going to make good records.' Suddenly the budgets skyrocketed, but they were still a third of what pop records cost. If there's one thing I'd remember him for it's that Bowen came in here and forced us to make quality records."

Bowen did help break the grip Nashville's old guard had over the music, a control that dictated not only who got to record, but how the very music sounded. Those were the days when almost all the records out of Nashville sounded as if they were made by the same ten people. And by and large they were.

In the sixties and early seventies an A team of about ten session musicians that included Harold Bradley, Hargus "Pig"

Robbins and Bob Moore were playing on most country records. Their playing started out innovative, but over time, as they cliqued up, it got stale.

Likewise, most of the albums were made by the same producers and publishers, who tended to use the same handful of songwriters. Independent production, a sign of healthy competition, was nonexistent then. At Decca, Owen Bradley produced most of the acts; at Columbia, it was Billy Sherrill; and at RCA it was Chet Atkins.

The truth was, a cadre of about a dozen people controlled the fate of the music through the Country Music Association, a trade organization with far-reaching powers. This old guard— publishing giants like Wesley Rose and Frances Preston and various label heads like MCA's Jim Foglesong and RCA's Jerry Bradley—doled out favors, running the town like a feudal fiefdom.

"Wesley Rose, Bill Hall, Bob Beckham and Jack Stapp— they owned eighty percent of the publishing," said Bill Ivey, an executive with the Country Music Foundation. "They were the power brokers, the ones who could get a single songwriter signed or trade one deal for another. They could say, 'If you take this song, you've got to take four others.' Or, 'If you sign this person, you have to sign her, too.'"

"I remember producers would play you a rhythm track and say, 'Listen to these tracks, man, these are hit tracks. Anybody can sing on 'em.' They thought they could just whip up some tracks that they could then march any kid off the street to sing to," Bill Carter recalled. "Even in the early eighties, the traditional old guard still controlled this town. They got a piece of everything. And they simply wouldn't let outsiders in."

A perfect example of the inbred nature of the business was MCA Records, where Bowen served a brief stint in 1978 as vice-president and general manager.

"Half of the people MCA had shouldn't have been on record in the first place," said Bowen, who went in and cleaned house. "I think Conway [Twitty] and Loretta [Lynn] between their two families had ten acts. People'd come in and say they want to be on the label and the executives were afraid to tell 'em no, so they put 'em on the label, not realizing that they were cluttering things up and diminishing any efforts they could make.

"I went to the A&R department and started looking. I'd take out a file and see"—Bowen lapsed into a thick good-ole-boy drawl—"'The producer gets a royalty, OK. And—whoops—he owns the studio. And—whoops—he owns the song. And, well, looky here, he was AF of M[4] leader.' Well, damn, they were choking down the creativity. No wonder the artists would show up drunk at half the sessions and didn't enjoy the process. They had nothing to do with it except the words."

Since songwriting and music publishing have always been where the money is, it wasn't surprising that everyone wanted a piece of that action. And it wasn't just publishers, but record companies wanting to be publishers. It was record producers, too, who wanted a piece of the publishing if they were going to cut your song, and record labels wanting you to place your songs with their in-house publishing divisions.

"The only way the system works is if everyone is separate and everyone is making their money out of what they do as a specialty. As soon as you start to combine it," said Ivey, "even when you have a singer/songwriter, you start to compromise the system a bit because you're going to get an album with songs by that artist only."

And that's what had happened in Nashville. As the functions got intertwined, corruption set in. The music got worse, but a bunch of people got rich in the short run. Why didn't Nashville sell lots of albums? Bowen's analysis was simple.

"The powers that be were too concerned about who published the songs as opposed to what's thirty-five to forty minutes' worth of magic. They were into a three-minutes-of-magic mentality. Get a hit and then add eight or nine other songs.

---

[4] Bowen is referring to the American Federation of Musicians union.

Singles were going away and they were still making singles. They weren't making albums that were worth seven ninety-eight, which is what they were going for then. The CMA controlled the music real well, but when country music had to grow and had to change, they couldn't help it and in many cases wouldn't let it."

If he was going to compete with pop and rock, and he knew he'd have to, Bowen had to upgrade the quality of the music. And he wasn't shy about taking credit for this. He insisted on digital recording and taking more time to make albums. And he ensured that there was plenty of preproduction, time spent planning long before the artist and producers set foot in the studio. That was to underscore that the making of a record "was a big event in the artist's life, something that everyone anticipated." All this took money and time, something Nashville wasn't used to spending.

"They thought I was nuts, of course," said Bowen. "They thought I spent so much time in the studio I must be doing drugs. But according to my peers in New York I was doing things in a *hurry*. And I wasn't spending a lot of money. I came to a town that spent fifteen thousand to twenty thousand dollars on an album, and here I was spending fifty thousand and a hundred thousand." Bowen shook his head and smiled. "One of the newspapers said, 'He came here and taught us how to make a thirty-thousand-dollar album for a hundred thirty thousand dollars.' "

But no one denied that Bowen's albums were getting played on country radio, a powerful, conservative format that now exerted a stranglehold on creativity and innovation.

"Nashville makes the rest of radio seem like Amsterdam on a Saturday night," Dave Alvin, a founder of the Blasters, had told me once after he'd spent a year as a songwriter in Nashville. "They're incredibly closed to new music. They want songs about Mom, God and apple pie."

From Bowen's vantage point, country radio was a mess when he arrived in Nashville. Pop-music radio stations were segmented by genre and age, reaching maximum demographics, and playing predominantly new music; but country stations were playing 60–70 percent oldies and 30–40 percent new material. Worse yet, from Bowen's viewpoint, the artists were all wadded together, diluting the ability to stimulate advertising.

The format reflected the aging stock of performers. These days, Merle Haggard and George Jones can scarcely be heard on country radio, whose airwaves are clogged with dozens of performers in their late twenties. But less than twenty years ago, country music had almost no young audience.

"Back then, a performer at age thirty-five was considered young. There were no twenty-two-year-old singers like there are today," said Bowen. "They wouldn't have a prayer. And I knew that had to change."

It became obvious to Bowen that the music had to be *fixed*—that younger artists had to be developed to change the balance of power.

"It had nothing to do with radio," Bowen told me one afternoon at a studio, after he'd just finished hearing a few cuts from a forthcoming Charlie Daniels album. "That wasn't why country was selling so poorly. They didn't have enough killer new records to play. I said all along that as soon as you give radio enough good music, you'd see the proportions of oldies to new songs flip."

Which is exactly what started happening, though not everyone was willing to concede that Bowen's "new" music was good, much less killer. In fact, most of it sounded like deracinated junk: country music stripped of its true roots and power.

Historically, country music had been the soul music of rural America, a chronicle of its joys and sorrows. When Jimmie Rodgers sang "Moonlight and Skies," his popular convict ballad and one of his best-selling records, he was singing about the hardscrabble lives of a whole generation of rural Americans. And when Merle Haggard sang "They're Tearin' the Labor Camps Down," he was speaking of the transplanted Okies who'd migrated to the arid plains of Bakersfield, California, in search of work and a better life.

But Bowen had no knowledge or love of country's deep roots, symbolic meanings and radical genius. Amid the music he was writing off as worthless honky-tonk were some of the masterpieces of country and bluegrass music—records like Haggard's *Songs I'll Always Sing*, George Jones's *The Battle*, Waylon Jennings's seminal outlaw sessions, Bill Monroe's astonishing *Bean Blossom*, and Loretta Lynn's *When the Tingle Becomes a Chill*.[5]

All of these artists and others, from Steve Earle and Lucinda Williams to Dwight Yoakam and ex-"outlaw" and singer/songwriter Billy Joe Shaver, gave a new voice to music and stories that were timeless: echoes of deep ancestral wounds that were already widening cracks in the American psyche. When Hank Williams sang "I'm So Lonesome I Could Cry" or "Cold, Cold Heart," the hairs on the back of your neck stood up. And when Lester Flatt and Bill Monroe entwined their voices in aching harmony on "It's Mighty Dark to Travel," with Monroe's fingers flying over the mandolin's fretboard—the instrument itself a direct descendant of the medieval lute—you heard the ecstasy, pain and resilience in this great music: a mystery as deep as life itself.

Listening to Monroe, Hank Williams, Lefty Frizzell or Haggard, you realized they couldn't have lived any other life, for their songs and voices were an expression of their culture—something that had to come out lest keeping it in corrode their very souls. And listening to the wild, beautiful honky-tonk of Texas's Jimmie Dale Gilmore and Lucinda Williams, you came away with a vision of country music as a rich, still-evolving portrait of America.

But Bowen had no time for mystery or tradition. And he loathed bluegrass and down-and-dirty honky-tonk, which, with

---

[5] This is not to deny the fact that there was much bad music coming out of Nashville throughout the early seventies, when producers put treacly sing-along choruses on songs, leading to the inanities of the "urban cowboy" era.

its deep backwoods moan, couldn't make pop inroads and was too strong a reminder for countrypolitan people of their hillbilly roots.

The few who complained in the nineties that country was sounding hollow and phony—that it had cornball keyboard parts, tasteless rock solos, jingoistic blather and vapid singing that had nothing to do with the radical roots of the music— were drowned out in the celebration of success.

"Nashville thrives on monotony," said Shaver, who'd re- sisted offers to write songs by committee—the typical approach of big publishers—and whose acclaimed 1993 honky-tonk al- bum, *Tramp on Your Street*, wasn't even released by a country label.[6] "What they're doing now is not going to make a mark on the music. We're dealing with art and they're dealing with quick bucks."

But people like Shaver were all disposable has-beens for moguls like Bowen, representing what needed to be changed and eradicated. For ever since he'd arrived, Bowen had been tireless in his quest to "fix" country music, to bring in the huge audience—even if that meant robbing it of its authentic rural voice.

"I call it the honk factor," Bowen said one afternoon, back at his mansion. He paused dramatically, sounding like an inven- tor who'd stumbled onto the secret for making a noiseless vac- uum cleaner. "It's about three thousand cycles and it comes from singing through the head voice and singing hard through the nose. But to the average buyer, it hurts your ears. That's why bluegrass has a very limited reach. It's very nasal. So one of the things we did, those of us who came from L.A., was to dehonk this stuff—actually go in with EQ and soften it, so it'll appeal to everyone in the room and not just those hard of hearing."

Hearing Bowen proudly crow about dehonking country mu-

---

[6] No label in Nashville would even give Shaver, in his fifties now, a record deal. Zoo Entertainment, a pop-rock division of BMG, ended up releas- ing the CD.

sic left me stunned, for the nasal tonality he was describing was the very soul of country and bluegrass—what made a Hank Williams or Bill Monroe vocal give you the shivers. In fact, the honk was *the* most soulful aspect of the human voice singing in every culture.

From the high-pitched moan of the great Cajun and zydeco singers to the haunting Siberian throat-singing in Tuva to the mystical Qawwali singing of the Sufis, the honk was the deep, ancient voice that came up from the gut and took you into the realm of spirit. But for Jimmy Bowen it was just an annoyance, something that got in the way of marketing country music to the masses. And so he cut it out like a cancer.

Bill Carter, an attorney who represented the Rolling Stones for years and was one of Nashville's most outspoken critics, laughed when I told him of Bowen's boast. "Bowen's famous for taking the realism out of the music," said Carter, who manages Rodney Crowell. "You can hear it in his records. He's the guy who created Pirates of the Mississippi."

Carter was referring to one of the lamest acts to ever hit country music: a manufactured group that rivaled New Kids on the Block for soullessness. But Bowen showed no embarrassment over Pirates of the Mississippi or even Billy Ray Cyrus, whose "Achy Breaky Heart" dance routine on the Grammys had made Nashville the laughing stock of the music awards show.

"Billy Ray Cyrus is *great* for country. I wished *I'd* signed him. It's just what this music needs." Bowen grinned, as if explaining something obvious. "Taking out the honk—why, that's the best thing that could've happened to the music. We're no longer a country of farmers as we once were. Things don't come from the dirt anymore; they're made out of plastic. And they come by boat to get here from the Orient or Europe. This is the world we live in *today*. And if the music is gonna exist in the global entertainment market today, it's got to have *mass* appeal, or else its profits shrink and you can't have new acts. When that happens, the music just withers away to become a cult thing.

"I'm not one to look back and say, 'I sure miss this.' I'd much rather fly to L.A. than drive. You should take the good part of yesterday and apply it to today, but make sure it's a small portion, because the only thing that matters about today and tomorrow is today and tomorrow. The hell with the old."

Three months passed before I saw Bowen again. It was late October in Nashville, and the leaves were starting to turn colors. Bowen had pressed five million copies of *The Chase*, Garth Brooks's latest album, and to no one's surprise it had stormed up the charts, past Billy Ray Cyrus and the rest of the pop competition. That night Brooks was playing in Wichita, Kansas, where scalper tickets were going for as much as $750 a pop.

Since the summer, Bowen had been busy. After vacationing at one of his two homes in Maui, he'd traveled to Europe and New York for meetings with Capitol-EMI's top brass. For the past two years, Liberty Records had been EMI's biggest profit-making arm and Bowen was basking in the power that came with that. With country music slaughtering the competition, lawyers, managers, producers and agents were descending on the town from New York and L.A., and many of them wanted an audience with Bowen.

Yet with all the success he'd had with country, it was the nascent world of Christian music that raised his pulse now. In the fall, Bowen had signed Carman, the evangelical pop singer he was determined to make into a star, stealing him away from Warner Bros.

It was a classic Bowen move. Most of the labels in Nashville were satellite divisions that had to go through New York or L.A. to make big decisions, but Bowen, knowing how cutthroat the competition was and how important decisions had to be made quickly, had convinced EMI to make Capitol Nashville an autonomous label (reflected later in its new name, Liberty).

"If we have to commit a hundred thousand dollars to get

something done I can say yes or no. Everywhere else, that decision is made in New York by the VP of sales and marketing and it's not a priority for them," Bowen said. "They all should have their own business-affairs and finance people here, but none of them do. So while they're all dillydallying back and forth to the West Coast, I'm going in and snatching acts away from them. That's what I did with Carman. Warners delayed too long."

What's more, Bowen had purchased Sparrow Records, a renowned gospel record and publishing company.

"I'm kind of the heathen coming into their world," Bowen joked. "Tomorrow morning I'm goin' golfing with some of those folks—*Christian* golfing. Means I can't swear. Got to say 'Darn' if I foul up a shot."

Bowen could kid about hanging out with the straitlaced set—people who were cleaner, as the saying goes, than a preacher's peter—but you could tell he was dead serious about breaking Christian music, even if he had to put on appearances. That afternoon, at one of the studios on Music Row where he'd stopped off to check out a mix, the president of Liberty Records kept talking about this new, virgin market.

"I believe that if you put this product out there, people are gonna buy it," Bowen said, munching on some catfish and black-eyed peas that had been brought in by a catering service. "We have a young man named Steven Curtis Chapman on Sparrow Records. He's gonna be a superstar. He played to eighty-five hundred people at the Starwood Amphitheatre here and he blew 'em away. It was just like a rock show—except the lyrics were different. You've got the smoke and the lights and the guitars and the drums.

"I had some Kmart people with me and some executives from Handleman, which is a big one-stop that sells to Kmarts and Wal-Marts. They'd never been to a Christian concert before—I'd only been to a few—and they couldn't believe what they saw. A third of the audience were high school, a third of them were college. They went away from that con-

Jory Farr

cert and said, 'I think you're right. We're gonna go along with you.' "[7]

A short time later, Bowen's general manager, Wayne Halper, came in and introduced two New York lawyers to his boss. The lawyers had come to schmooze Bowen, but Nashville's kingpin had heard it all before.

"If you want to do business down here," he told them flatly, "learn the *market*. Learn how things are done. This isn't New *York*. We don't play these six-month negotiating games. If you're gonna *deal* with us, know up front you're gonna make a deal or not. A good deal's only good if it's good for both sides."

One of the lawyers wore jeans with a blazer, an attempt at fitting into the casual world of Nashville entertainment.

"We're not trying to take a carpetbagger approach," he said, suddenly defensive. "We just want to do business here."

"Richie Furay, of Buffalo Springfield, is a Christian-music artist who we represent," the other lawyer chimed in. "When he dropped out of the music business he became a born-again Christian. We just want to know if we can pitch some songs with you."

Sure, Bowen said, now that he had intimidated them a bit. And soon he was telling them about Christian music, how it was going to break big and be in Kmarts and Wal-Marts, selling in the millions. When the New York lawyers left, Bowen made some calls and came back to talk.

"All the lawyers in New York and L.A. in the music industry see the big money, the big sales, and they want to come here and represent acts," Bowen said. "But where were they ten years ago? You have to understand the market. Any genre of

---

[7] For the record, Carman's first album for Bowen, *The Absolute Best*, sold more than 150,000 copies in secular stores, according to Bowen. Just before Christmas 1993, Bowen released Carman's album *The Standard*. As of February 1994, the CD had sold 125,000 copies in the secular marketplace. "But you're talking about four or five times as many sales as previously in the secular world. The bookstore sales are still solid. I'm pleased about the acceptance. It's in Wal-Marts, ·Kmarts, Camelots."

music will be hurt if the people who make the deals don't understand the music."

In Nashville, all the label executives came from music backgrounds. Warner Bros. president Jim Ed Norman had been a producer, and Tony Brown, head of A&R at MCA, was both a top-flight keyboardist and producer. On the other hand, as Bowen loved to point out, the people in charge of the pop music business these days frequently didn't know a C major from a C minor chord. Run by promotion and marketing men, most of the pop labels tried to buy the marketplace: to influence consumers through gimmicks, attitude and promotion.

"The country-music business is like the pop-music business of the sixties and early seventies," Bowen said one afternoon. "It's nothing like the pop-music business of today, where radio is controlled by the independent promoters and the tip-sheet people. There, you got old people tryin' to figure out what kids want. Every label has too many artists. It's just 'Throw 'em against the wall and hope something sticks.'

"We know our bottom line. We know what we're gonna spend before we go to the marketplace. The key difference is, we don't try to drive the marketplace with money. We wait until the music catches on and then we try to maximize the popularity. We market it to the masses. Therefore, when we're wrong three times a year, we're only wrong in the production costs. We're not wrong in the marketing spend, which can be three or four times as high as the production costs of a piece of music."

Bowen certainly wasn't wrong with Garth Brooks, who he saw perform a few weeks after he took over as president of Capitol Nashville.

"The first week I was there, Brooks's producer, Allen Reynolds, came up to me and said, 'Bowen, this is the exceptional one. Go look at him.' So I did. I saw him open for the Statler Brothers in a small town in Tennessee. Well, after I saw Garth work, I turned to my wife and said, 'He's gonna be the biggest ever.'

"I came back and called all my department heads and said,

'We got the franchise. I don't care what you do for the next few years, but I want seventy-five to eighty percent of your energy to go into this kid because he's a monster.' They all looked at me funny. And I said, 'By the way, you got thirty days to see him perform live if you want to still work here.' Of course, I only kept three people out of the whole company. I had a lot of my own people, from Universal.''

Brooks's first video was "The Dance." At that point, his first album had sold five hundred thousand copies and Bowen had heard five sides from *No Fences.*

"I said, 'Go buy every available slot for the months of October, November and December.' Well, my man asked: 'You're not gonna put out another album? This one's starting to sell.' I said, 'No, no. "The Dance" is the last single from this album. But we need the next album and it needs to be better.' So Joe went to buy every spot there is. Garth got price and position as a rock star.''

Bowen also met with Brooks and told him that it was very important that he deliver a record a year. He'd seen the way it was done in rock and roll, with pampered artists taking three years and spending five hundred thousand dollars to make a record.

"Every two and a half or three years they put out an album and so they're starting over every time with an audience," Bowen said. "So I told Garth, 'You can't get a roll that way. Elvis didn't do it that way. He put out two or three a year. And the Beatles had seven in the first six months.' I said, 'You want to be a household name, a superstar? Steady flow of product.' He heard me.''

Now, with six albums out that have sold more than thirty-eight million copies, Brooks is a power unto himself. In the fall of 1992 he negotiated what would be one of the biggest deals in pop music.

"But he had to go over my head for that. I wouldn't have given him that much money," Bowen said, likening the Brooks deal to Michael Jackson's. "But Garth is so smart. He's negotiating the contract himself.''

Bowen could appreciate the moxie of a country boy like Brooks. He himself had grown up in Dumas, in the panhandle of Texas, a town of about six thousand people.

"I liked music, but as a kid not all that much, because the music we had was for old people," he said.

When his parents split up, Bowen was raised by his dad, who bought him a ukulele. Soon the young boy was playing electric guitar, jamming with friends. But when he saw Elvis Presley perform in Amarillo, Texas, in the fifties, his ideas about music were forever changed.

"I had a balcony seat and all I remember was that the girls went berserk even before Elvis came on. Colonel Parker's theory was that he wanted a juggler out front, so that the anticipation would build and build and then explode. That night he had a classical violinist open for Elvis, and people threw stuff at the poor guy. When Elvis came on you couldn't hear a word for the next hour.

"I couldn't believe it. This was when rock and roll was first starting, and for the first time in our lives we had music we could relate to, instead of old people's music. You didn't have to dress like our parents or Eisenhower, you could have long hair, you could wiggle your butt. Within three years, Elvis changed everything."

Bowen learned another lesson when he saw Roy Orbison perform later. "Roy Orbison wasn't the best-looking guy, but he was the best singer of his era," Bowen said. "And I went to school on that. Hearing him, I realized that talent was the most important thing, not looks."

For a while, Bowen pursued dreams of being a pop star. At West Texas State College, where he went on a basketball scholarship, Bowen met Buddy Knox, a singer/guitarist, and the two started working on music together. Almost on a lark Bowen, Knox and a third friend traveled to Clovis, New Mexico, where Norman Petty had worked with Buddy Holly, and cut two songs, "Party Doll" and "I'm Stickin' with You," using Petty's drummer.

They sent the record out to various companies but got no

action until Morris Levy, then head of Rama Records, heard it and wired them one thousand dollars to come to New York.

"It took all day for us to cash the check, it was so big," Bowen says. "It was a Friday in August when we met with Morris to make the deal. And he said, 'Well, boys, I gotta run. We'll finish this up on Monday.' Well, that weekend we spent nearly all of the money, drinking and eating and tipping. Come Monday, we had to make a deal."

Bowen and Knox had a hit with "Party Doll." They even played on one of Alan Freed's legendary rock shows at New York's Paramount Theater. He knew his talent was unexceptional, but already he was learning some important lessons: how records got made and artists got screwed. For Levy, a fast-talking music publisher turned operator—he owned New York's famed Birdland—had screwed the Texas pop-rockers.

"We sold Morris everything—publishing, management, all of it," said Bowen, smiling at the memory of being so naive. "I walked into his office one day later and said, 'You can't do what you did—it's not legal.' And Morris opened the drawer, ripped up a contract and threw it in the trash, and said, 'What else can I do for you?' I said, "Nothing, that'll do today.' And to this day, I don't know whether that was our contract or not."

For a while Bowen worked in radio, as a DJ in Colorado Springs, and in publishing, learning those crucial parts of the business. By 1960, he was living in L.A. and working as a staff writer at America Music Publishing Company. He wrote songs with Glen Campbell, another staff writer, turning in five dem-oed tunes a week.

A year later, Bowen was working for Chancellor Records, whose artist roster had teen heartthrobs Frankie Avalon and Fabian. But it wasn't until 1963, when he started working for Reprise, Frank Sinatra's label, that his career took off.

As an A&R man/producer now, Bowen got to work with Ol' Blue Eyes. One of the first songs he did was "Softly, as I Leave You." When Sinatra asked Bowen what he thought of the tune, Bowen shot back: "I think you got about a number thirty record, but it'll get you back on the charts."

Sinatra wasn't too thrilled with that assessment. But as it happened, the song went to twenty-seven and Bowen gained Sinatra's confidence. It was Bowen who produced Sinatra's big hits "Strangers in the Night" and "That's Life."

Bowen remembers the day Sinatra was set to record "That's Life." The singer showed up earlier than usual and things started immediately going wrong.

"We'd just put the music on the stands, and when I went to the control room, the engineer's face went white. I asked what was wrong. Well, none of the microphones were working. I asked if anything was working, and he said, 'Just the rhythm-section mikes.'"

Sensing a catastrophe, Bowen went out and took one of the only working mikes and plugged it in for Sinatra's voice.

"The musicians could hear themselves but we couldn't. Well, Sinatra recorded the song and it was real breezy and hip. We played it back and I told 'em, 'You're not gonna hear what you heard in the phones.' Mo Ostin [the head of Warner Bros. Records, Reprise's distributor] said, 'Well, that's a hit.' And Sinatra turned to me and said, 'We got it, huh?' And I said, 'Not if you want a hit. If you want a hit, you gotta do it again.'

"Well, nobody had ever said that to him, and he was pissed. So on the next take he growled 'That's Life.' He put all his anger into it. I got a call the next day and he said, 'James, that sounds absolutely great. Thanks.'"

The fame was nice, but Bowen was learning that A&R men and producers didn't make anything unless they had a share in the profits. In 1963, Ostin offered Bowen $150 a week to do A&R at Reprise.

"I told him I'd take a hundred dollars a week and one percent of anything I produced," Bowen said. "I think I was the first person to get that—it wasn't done back then. And every time I had a number one record, I had to quit to get more points."

When Dean Martin's career took a nosedive, Bowen revived it with "Everybody Loves Somebody," a huge hit. Together he and Martin had twenty-six hit singles, fifteen gold albums and five platinum records.

Bowen left Reprise in 1968 and formed his own company, Amos Productions. He recorded Kenny Rogers, Mason Williams and soon-to-be-Eagles Glenn Frey and Don Henley. But by 1970 Bowen was back producing Campbell and Martin. Rock and roll was the dominant music then, but Bowen knew he wasn't cut out for that world.

"I didn't have the patience to sit inside a studio for a week while five or six long-haired kids tried to figure out an eight-bar intro. So I said, 'Where can I go to produce music and get my family out of the smog and the traffic?' I looked at the Northwest; I looked at Albuquerque, Santa Fe. But really all along I knew it had to be Nashville—adult artist, adult consumer, adult music. And that's what I was. If anybody was gonna hire me it was gonna be for that kind of act."

In 1976, after a brief stint as president of MGM Records, Bowen left California for good and headed to Arkansas.

When I first took over MCA I had to fire everybody, I had to cut about eighty percent of the roster. In a little town like this, you fire nine people, you've touched twenty-seven. Drop twenty acts, you've touched sixty people.

"At Elektra, I had to clean shop and get rid of most of its roster. And at Warners, I got rid of most everyone because I had my own people. Did the same thing at MCA, because most of them weren't any good. Shit, I've fired some of these people two or three times! And that doesn't make you best friends with everyone."

It was a crisp, beautiful fall day in Nashville and we were sitting in Bowen's immense living room, a testament to his power. The walls were full of musical memorabilia: a shot of Bowen looking cool and sharp, with a full head of hair, next to Frank Sinatra; a picture of Bowen and a young, albeit still dissipated, Dean Martin; shots with Kenny Rogers and George Strait.

At one end of the living room a vintage Wurlitzer jukebox

was filled with many of the country and pop tunes Bowen's been associated with down the years: songs like George Strait's "All My Ex's Live in Texas," Mel Tillis's "Coca-Cola Cowboy," Frank Sinatra's "That's Life," Reba McEntire's "Have I Got a Deal for You."

Bowen was wearing an expensive print shirt, black pants and designer gym shoes. He seemed to have put on a few pounds since we had last talked.

"I got the first digital two-track and the first Mitsubishi thirty-two-track and I had the studios buy big new boards. That made me a radical. When I came here, the CMA said, 'You're full of shit. You don't do anything for country music. You do stuff for yourself.' They had four board meetings a year—one in town, when we're too busy to mess with it, and the other three were in exotic places like London and Denver. All that did was keep the youth out of it, because they couldn't afford it. I told them that but they didn't like it.

"In 1982 I started the Nashville Music Organization, which is now called Nashville Entertainment Association. Well, that irritated the shit out of the CMA. How could I have the audacity to form another organization? Well, I had to," Bowen says, leaning forward now to emphasize his point. "If you weren't in the CMA power clique—and most weren't—you had no voice. Secondly, if you had any kind of music that wasn't accepted outside of Nashville, the CMA said, 'Oh well, it was from Nashville.' And they accepted that. But it was bullshit, because the truth was the music just wasn't good enough. They just had a scapegoat."

Bowen liked to talk about how he changed the balance of power: how he put trust in, and control of the music back with, the artist.

"That's the most lasting thing that I've done. The producer should work for the artist and not the other way around. They should cut the ten best songs to create the best thirty-five minutes of music they can. Forget who wrote it or published it. That's what I set out to do and it was just self-preservation, because I couldn't join the system. They didn't want me. And

I couldn't have lived with the system, because it's not the right way to do music. As a twenty-six-year-old I worked with Frank Sinatra, who right away let me know that it was his music, not mine. And I never forgot that."

Yet Bowen wasn't perceived as some benevolent advocate for the artists, as BMI president Frances Preston was. Her influence was so great at one point that it was said she ran the town, arranging contracts, helping writers get loans against royalties, mending rifts at record companies. By contrast, Bowen is seen as someone whose every relationship is designed to aggrandize himself and maximize the money that flows to him.

"I've done as Bowen said, not as he *did*," said Tony Brown, who worked under Bowen for years at MCA before they had a falling-out that allegedly led to Bowen's ouster. "He used to tell me that record labels and producers shouldn't own the publishing. But Bowen owns the publishing on most everything he does."

"When Bowen first came to town, the word was that he insisted on a piece of the publishing for everything that got cut," a veteran of the music business told me. "His deals were so structured that he got a piece of what would go for studio costs. In general, everything was structured so that the cash went to him. Bowen's an extraordinarily charming person, if you're the person he needs. And he's got all the resources to bring you around, whether that's cajoling you, threatening you or bullying you. It works in this town. And it works with the people in New York and L.A. who see Nashville as this exotic town that doesn't make any sense. Bowen's the perfect guy to manipulate their lack of understanding."[8]

Certainly Bowen's rise to power in Nashville was helped by a profound shift in popular taste. Even as far back as the sev-

---

[8] Bowen said he does have a joint-venture publishing deal with EMI, but denied he abuses the power that comes from that. "It's how you handle it when it cross-pollinates that says whether you will fail or not fail. If I handle it wrong, it'll destroy me. If I handle it right, everybody wins. You'd be a fool to take a great song and cut it with the wrong artist."

enties, the rock audience had been fracturing. And in the eighties, rock sounded as if it were creatively played out.

"[Rock] no longer seems to speak in unknown tongues that turn into new and common languages, to say anything that is not instantly translated back into the dominant discourse of our day," the critic Greil Marcus wrote in "Notes on the Life and Death and Incandescent Banality of Rock 'n' Roll." "The discourse of corporatism, selfishness, crime, racism, sexism, homophobia, government propaganda, scapegoating and happy endings."

During the late eighties, the only popular music that consistently spoke directly to youth about subjects that mattered—from racism to sexism—was rap, in which story and meaning, even if they repulsed you, were dominant. Rap at least addressed the rage of millions of disempowered African-Americans, and there were plenty of whites who bought the music as well. By contrast, during the late eighties, when country music started taking off, much of pop and rock had sacrificed story and melody for attitude and rhythm.

Not surprisingly, Americans started tuning out, and not just the baby boomers, who were seeing in country a return to the melodic and lyrical music they grew up on with the Beatles and Bob Dylan. Kids, too, were turned off. As Bowen liked to point out, Garth Brooks's "Friends in Low Places," a defiant song about recovering from a broken heart, was a huge hit among junior high school students.

Maybe this new country music wasn't all that thrilling; it didn't generally have the excitement of great rock and roll, and some of it was downright idiotic. But it had melody and a story line, something pop music had nearly forgotten about. You could understand the lyrics, even if they were a little corny at times. And most country music wasn't threatening, like rap or hard rock, to people in their thirties or forties. Why were aging hippies and stockbrokers buying country? Bowen answered with a question:

"How does a thirty-year-old white person with two cars and a house relate to Michael Jackson or Guns N' Roses?"

"Country music is real—it has a history that goes way back," said Tony Brown. "Pop music just doesn't have that."

"I think we're at a turning point in popular music," Bill Ivey said when I asked him about country's ever-widening appeal. "The music shifts every few decades and I would say that we're at the end of the rock and roll era as we know it. It's as painful a transition for the industry as it was when the Mitch Miller era ended and rock came along. At that time you had this whole big-band outlook.

"I think the rock world is just as baffled by this country phenomenon as the big-band guys were when rock came along. Of America's ethnic musics, country is the least explored. We've worked the black tradition a lot of different ways in this country in terms of jazz, R&B, blues, rock and rap, and I think that maybe we're going to work with the Anglo side of our Southern music heritage a little more. We may be working towards a folk revival or a revitalizing of great pop songs."

Would Nashville be able to sustain this? Bowen thought so. But in Nashville, people had their doubts. They'd seen the city poised before to become a truly dominant center for American music, only to fumble the chance.

If Nashville had been comfortable in the late fifties and early sixties with black music, it might well have become what Memphis became: a melting pot for black and white traditions and the site of a musical renaissance. But the people who controlled Nashville back then caved in to the racist sensibilities that had always ruled the town and prevented blacks from gaining access to the music.

"They weren't comfortable working anything other than the Anglo side of Southern music. That's why Motown happened and Memphis happened," Ivey said. "Had people been enlightened, Nashville really could've become Music City, USA."

"Are we going to sustain this?" Bill Carter posed the question one afternoon in his office, which was appointed with modern art. "We're caught up in our own success, but is that accurate? I've managed Rodney Crowell, and when his record started crossing over to pop music I started talking to the radio people there, asking them what happened to pop music. And they said they ran off the number one demographic in the country—twenty-five-to-forty-year-old females. 'We lost them to country music,' they said. We didn't *steal* them. They *lost* them. People are over here out of curiosity right now, but they won't stay unless we give them something with substance."

Bowen put it another way.

"There was a time when you could walk up and down Music Row and pop in and say hello to people and have a cup of coffee. But that was another era. That was when it was a fifty-million-dollar-a-year industry. Now it's a five-hundred- to six-hundred-million-dollar industry. And in ten years it'll probably double again.

"Pop-music people are so absorbed with their own little tunnel that they don't see other things coming. They're trying to blame the rise of country on SoundScan.[9] But this has been building for a long time. And it's not going to go away. But for us to be right, there's got to be more than one Garth Brooks."

[9] By tallying the number of records sold in stores across the country, SoundScan accurately reported sales of country music, which had long been underreported. As a result, country albums that were best-sellers zoomed up the charts.

CHAPTER 6

A Hillbilly Becomes a Mogul

Tony Brown

Hank Williams, Johnny Cash, George Jones, Merle Haggard and Waylon Jennings—the towering male figures in country music were all outlaws and demon seeds. They played in honky-tonks, once known as blood buckets, and sang about hobos and whores, love and death, sex and salvation. They weren't *nice* people. If you wanted decent folks, you could go to the church social. But they were burningly, ferociously alive. Down at the local bar was where you'd find them, getting shitfaced on whiskey and grabbing as much pussy as they could. And when Sunday morning rolled around, they tried to shake down the devil and repent for their sins.

Nowadays almost nobody in Nashville wants anything to do with hell-raisers. The country record moguls, who've seen profits soar through the roof the last few years, prefer their stars to be morally upright, God-fearing and sexy in a wholesome way—so wholesome that when rumors first started surfacing in Nashville that a leading country star was gay, he quickly married his manager to end speculation. Whether he was or wasn't gay was beside the point. The fact was, one of Nashville's superstars, whose audience was predominantly female—most country fans, in fact, are women—couldn't take a chance that his millions of followers would put a new interpretation on his romantic hits.

For all the talk about a revolution in country music, much

Jory Farr

of what I was hearing on country radio in the 1990s sounded bland and calculated: leeched of all its deviltry, marked by a kind of dull competence and safe enough for born-again Christians, who happened to form a huge portion of the country audience. The best country music was being made outside of Nashville, in places like Austin, Texas. Yet at least one powerful Nashville music man was trying at times to go against the grain.

"When I signed Steve Earle, I didn't think he was going to be the next Springsteen or the next John Cougar Mellencamp," Tony Brown, then the head of A&R[1] for MCA Nashville, told me one afternoon. "I thought he was the next Waylon [Jennings]. I kept thinking that's what I'd found. But then the press got a hold of him and they kind of screwed everything up, because then Nashville started getting scared that he might be a rock artist. Well, they kind of ran him off and he started believing his own press. And then everything went haywire."

Sitting on the steps of Woodland Recording Studio, where Brown was producing Kelly Willis's third album, the forty-seven-year-old executive didn't look as if he belonged in Nashville. With black jeans, spiky black hair, a loose-fitting green shirt and natty sunglasses, Brown cut an exotic figure. Small and slight, he might've passed for a New York film director or a Hollywood actor. But once you heard his high-pitched musical drawl, there was no doubting that Brown grew up in rural North Carolina, the breeding ground for many great country musicians.

As for Steve Earle, the memory still vexed Brown. Though *Guitar Town*, which Brown coproduced, was easily the best country album of the eighties, earning raves across the board, it sold pitifully. Brown and Earle made other records, but the singer/songwriter thereafter plunged into self-destructive behavior. He married an A&R woman, lived out in L.A. and took to not showing up at gigs or showing up late.

"The last time I saw Steve he looked really bad. But I hear

---

[1] Brown would be named president of MCA Nashville in 1993.

he's now straight and writing again. Willie and Waylon got involved with drugs for a while, too," Brown said as we headed back into the studio. "And Hank [Williams,] Sr. It seems like addiction is always involved with these great artists who do things on the edge. I'm attracted to these people. And usually if their music's on the edge, their life's on the edge. But here's the scary part of it: When these people get straight, they lose something. When Waylon got straight, I missed the *old* Waylon."

Most Nashville executives wouldn't be caught dead talking like this. But then, Tony Brown was an anomaly. The son of a Baptist evangelist, he knew firsthand that part of country music—its hymnal harmonies, family themes and spiritual lyrics—came directly from gospel music. But Brown also knew that the other part of the music—the rocking rhythms that made girls shudder—came from black blues and back-alley honky-tonks and had more to do with sin, sex and damnation than anything else. Brown had been in both worlds. Part of a touring gospel family, he'd sung for congregations of Pentecostal snakehandlers, whipped up sanctified fever with the Oak Ridge Boys, played piano with Elvis Presley and been part of Emmylou Harris's Hot Band, a rebel collective that fifteen years earlier had forged the sound that many young country artists were imitating.

But now, at forty-seven, Tony Brown had become a major player. In less than five years he'd made MCA the best country label in America, with a roster that far outshone those of rival labels. And for two years running, in 1990 and 1991, *Billboard* magazine had named him the number one country singles producer. It was Brown who produced records for Earle, Lyle Lovett and Nanci Griffith, three singer/songwriters he'd signed because he thought their talents were great. All three, along with singers like k. d. lang, had opened up doors for more adventurous country artists—even though many of those doors soon closed again.

Not everything he touched turned to gold. Brown signed a pure-voiced hayseed named Marty Brown, grizzled Texas honky-tonker Joe Ely and hell-raising country rockers the Mavericks. All got acclaim from the press but went nowhere on the country charts—though Brown knew you needed patience in a town like Nashville, where musical conservatism and suspicion were the ruling principles.

It wasn't as if the man was some wide-eyed radical. For every band he signed that carried a big risk, he had other artists who were commercial slam dunks. Brown knew Trisha Yearwood would be a star the moment he signed her. And when her second album, *Hearts in Armor*, went platinum, Brown wasn't surprised. Soon Yearwood became the darling of rock and rollers as well.

"I'm not stupid enough to ignore the mainstream," Brown said, as John Hiatt walked into the studio and started talking to some of the musicians. "I mean, I work with Reba McEntire. And I just helped George Strait do his movie soundtrack. That's as mainstream as it gets. But I still have this burning desire to turn people on to Kelly Willis, Marty Brown, the Mavericks and Joe Ely. I keep saying to myself, 'This isn't that different. Country fans should like this.' And I've tried to figure out why these performers had trouble connecting with a big audience.

"What I realized is that it had to do with image, not music. You see, that real youthful, rebellious image continues to scare the country-music industry. And it always has. When Waylon Jennings and Willie Nelson shook things up and made it as outlaws they were *old* men being rebellious. Country music has not learned how to deal with rebellious youth. And there happens to be a lot of that around right now."

Willis was the perfect example. At twenty-three, she was poised for stardom. Her voice reminded you of Patsy Cline, Emmylou Harris and ex–Lone Justice singer Maria McKee. But it also had hints of rock and roll's rebelliousness to it, a fact underscored by Willis's refusal to give in to some image consultant's idea of what a female country singer should look like.

"I told Kelly, 'If I don't make you a star, somebody else will.' And I truly·believe she will be," Brown said. "They're gonna give Kelly a lot of problems about the way she dresses and her attitude. It's a Chrissie Hynde kind of attitude. And she looks young, like a girl. But see, in Nashville, men want to perceive singers as women—as young ladies. And Kelly doesn't have that stereotyped look. We did a poster of her for her last album and she absolutely hated it. But she's not gonna change. And I firmly believe that's why she's gonna make it—on her own terms. 'Cause if an artist makes it on his or her own terms—if they're patient—it's a little sweeter."

Brown had fallen in love with Willis's voice the first time he'd heard her. He immediately signed the twenty-year-old singer. But neither of the two MCA albums he had produced for her had done very well.

"The first album, I basically recorded ten or so songs Kelly did live with her band. But on the second album, she and I were manipulated into doing something the label and radio liked," Brown said. "So for the third record we decided we were going to let it rip. I said, 'Kelly, you tell me what you want to do. You pick the musicians and you come in with five songs in October and I'll be there to help you do it.' "

The session, which had begun the day before, was a good glimpse into how Brown worked. Instead of using hired-gun studio players who came with a stock bag of slick licks, Brown had let Willis pick her own band. Even more daring—by Nashville standards—he'd invited the well-known L.A. rock producer Don Was to coproduce Willis's record.

"I was in L.A. a couple of months ago and saw Don at a meeting and basically as a joke asked what he was doing October twelfth and thirteenth," Brown said, offhandedly. "And Don said, 'Why?' So I said, 'Why don't you come to Nashville and coproduce Kelly Willis?' And he said, 'You know, if I wasn't busy I'd do it.' Well, I didn't think anything about it. And then about a week ago he called and said, 'If you're serious, I'll be there.' And I said, 'I'm not sure I can afford you.' But he came."

With a mop of long, kinky hair, bare feet, ratty blue jeans and a dirty gray sweatshirt, Was looked like the antithesis of Nashville. He didn't wear rattlesnake boots and sport big silver buckles. He looked like a hippie ragamuffin as he positioned himself between the monitors and listened carefully to the band's first take of "That'll Be Me," a duet between Willis and Kevin Welch, her MCA labelmate and boyfriend.

As Michael Henderson's slide meshed with Kieran Kane's mandolin, Willis, dressed in blue jeans, sang the opening verse with a sad, yearning ache. It was easy to see why Brown believed she'd be a star. Not only was Willis drop-dead gorgeous, she also had a voice most singers would kill for. By the time she hit the chorus, Willis's voice was melting into Welch's low harmony.

"I remember the first take as being slicker," Was said after he heard two full run-throughs, "but the second take sounds way better."

Brown, who was standing behind the console and letting Was do his thing, smiled. Looking at Welch, he said, "Yeah, there's a big difference."

"I wished I could *hear* the difference," said Welch, who was wearing jeans and a flannel shirt and had his arm around Willis. He spoke with the warm Midwestern twang common to Oklahoma, where he'd grown up. "I hate being an idiot."

"That other verse doesn't have any power to it," Brown said. "This one sounds more anchored."

"And I didn't feel you were really locked in on that other chorus," said Was.

"This was an attempt to put together a band that would give a live sound," Brown said when everyone went to take a lunch break. "It's basically Kevin Welch's band, so they have played together. But they've never played together for anyone except Kevin, so to play for Kelly was important. That little fine line between what session players bring to an artist and what road players who play on records bring to an artist is important. Some artists don't like this kind of a band. It's a fly-by-the-seat-of-your-pants band. But this is a very crucial record for her.

"Most of these guys are just playing what comes to them, whereas most session players learn a part and play it over and over again and perfect it. But here, every solo is different. And everyone's on edge to make sure that they don't mess up because if the performance is happening you can be the one person who destroys it all. So the edge is there."

What Was's presence had done was to raise the stakes for everyone concerned. One of the hottest producers in pop music, he'd worked with everyone from Bonnie Raitt to Bob Dylan, but now he was producing records for Tammy Wynette and Willie Nelson. In Nashville, Was commanded respect. But though Brown was a fan, the two producers had radically different styles of getting the best performance: Brown rarely interfered with a band's take, but as the session progressed Was would constantly stop the musicians midtake, to work out intros, turnarounds and push beats, until the musicians had the arrangement down solid.

"He sits down on the floor and won't let the musicians play a song from top to bottom," Brown said. He told me, 'Don't ever let the band play a song completely until they know the arrangement really well, because that's how you get those first and second takes that are so strong—you work out the trouble spots.'

"Don works out the arrangements with the band more than I would, because I'm a fan of spontaneity. But of all the producers from L.A., Don makes the most sense. He works with roots artists. Don looks at these players in a different way. It's very easy for me to take players for granted—to make things move a little faster than they should. But him walking into the room ... I watch him and it's like he's in this candy store, because all these guys have raised their level of playing just by him being in the room. And his admiration of them and their admiration of him—those are the ingredients that create magic."

Pleased with that insight, Brown stopped for a moment to think. Then, as if acknowledging the riskiness of it all anyway, he grinned: "But this is a gamble for Don and me. I never even worked with him before. It was impulsive."

"Tony Brown signed Lyle Lovett when no one else was interested in him—and he made it work. He signed Steve Earle, who made *Guitar Town*, one of the most brilliant country records of the past decade. It didn't work. But Tony had the guts to try," Bill Carter, a widely respected entertainment lawyer who managed Rodney Crowell and had known Brown for years, told me one afternoon. Sitting in his Music Row office, Carter, who had run one of Jimmy Carter's campaigns in Arkansas and been an attorney for the Rolling Stones at one point in his life, spoke in a thick, honeyed Arkansas drawl. From time to time he would suddenly erupt into a big, wide-mouthed grin and laugh at the strange, arcane methods of Nashville. In town he was known as someone who went against the grain, unafraid to take on the big boys even if it cost him.

"Historically, Nashville has been a conservative town. When one thing works, everybody goes out and does it. And while it's hot, they stay on it and won't do anything but what's working. But Tony tried things that didn't work. If he'd have been here any sooner he'd have failed, because the town was too closed. He'd have done the same thing, but Nashville wasn't ready for that. So the thing that distinguishes him is his courage. A lot of us have convictions, but most keep quiet and don't make waves."

"I always thought his musical instincts for songs, writers and singers were dead-on," David Conrad, a powerful executive with Almo-Irving Publishing who's known Brown for years, said when I asked him to assess Brown's talents. "He's a lot like Chet Atkins was when he was running RCA. They both had an eye for what was genuine and what artist had a vision.

"Tony turned MCA around in four years and he's clearly given it the best roster in country music. There aren't many true, experienced musicians running record companies, but he's one of them. And he can move in any circle. He can hang with Reba and Lyle, with George Strait and with hillbillies. He's a hipster."

Tony Brown's biggest rival is Jimmy Bowen, whom he worked under between 1984 and 1987, when Bowen was the president of MCA Nashville. For a while, Brown was the dutiful student and Bowen the prodding teacher. But the relationship soon got strained when Brown saw the direction in which Bowen was taking the label.

"I actually did learn the basics of producing from Bowen, and some of the things he taught me that I've applied to the craft work," Brown said one Saturday afternoon as we sat in an enormous downstairs room in his brand-new house. "Bowen's one of those 'Do as I say, not as I do' guys. The reason we sort of parted ways creatively is because he had ceased to like music anymore. He liked deals. At that time, none of the artists I was producing was making any money. What got me high was a story in the press. So when [a record by] someone like Steve Earle had sold only twelve thousand copies but *Rolling Stone* loved it, it was like I had just made twelve thousand dollars.

"When I was working for Bowen I wanted to sign Steve Earle, but Bowen didn't like him. He said, 'If you can make me and Bruce Hinton [then the vice-president and general manager of MCA Nashville, now its chairman] like one of his songs, then you can sign him.' So me and Emory Gordy, Jr., who produced the album with me, cut 'Guitar Town.' That's the one song we concentrated on; we made Steve pronounce every word correctly. Then we took the song to Bowen and he said, 'Well, that sounds OK.'" Imitating Bowen, Brown's voice carried a tone of disgust.

Bowen left MCA around 1987 to run an MCA subsidiary, Universal Records, leaving Bruce Hinton and Brown to run the company. But then he asked to come back, deciding he wanted to merge Universal back into MCA. In his gut, Brown knew that would spell trouble.

"I knew if he came back in, both for me and Bruce, our futures would look pretty bleak," Brown said. "I knew Bowen would probably fire us soon, because creatively he and I didn't see eye to eye. The toughest thing I ever had to do was stand up to Bowen. But I stood my ground. I knew I had to. I told Al Teller [then the president of MCA Records] that if Bowen came back I'd leave. MCA said I was taking this way too seriously. But I told them, 'I know exactly the way it is.' And they stood by me."

"Bowen and Tony got at odds at MCA" was the way Bill Carter put it one afternoon. "Tony was signing the Lyle Lovetts and Nanci Griffiths. Bowen wanted mainstream acts. Well, the situation got so tense that Brown called a meeting with Al Teller, the chairman [sic] of MCA. Tony went up to New York and told Al what was happening. And Teller made a decision. He went with Tony Brown.

"The town saw it as a Jimmy Bowen–Tony Brown conflict that Tony won. Now, as time has passed, Bowen would have you believe he walked from a bad situation and went over to Capitol and Garth Brooks and made much more money. And the facts would support him on that. Bowen came out smelling like a rose. But the truth is, he was forced out."

As it turned out, Capitol[2] benefited from Bowen going over there and MCA benefited from Brown standing his ground. When I brought up Brown's astonishing success to Bowen, he praised his former colleague's savvy producing abilities. But when their feud at MCA was mentioned, Bowen's eyes went momentarily cold.

"Tony's doing a magnificent job at MCA," Bowen said, all diplomacy. "But anyone who walks into a label with George and Reba there has got the situation of a lifetime."

Brown rolled his eyes when I told him what Bowen had said.

"When Bowen came to MCA, George Strait was basically gold, so he didn't actually break George Strait. Reba McEntire he actually did take to another level, but after he left, what Reba and I did was the next plateau. I spent a lot of time with Reba before we cut that first album, because I knew that if we failed it could finish me—not only at the label, but everyone in town would know that I didn't have the goods. So I drove out to her house a lot. And that became the focal point at that time. And the album we made has sold almost two million copies—which is bigger than anything Bowen ever cut."

In appreciation of that feat, in fact, McEntire had recently

---

[2] Bowen would later change Capitol Nashville to Liberty Records.

given Brown a gift: a brand-new Harley-Davidson motorcycle.

"When Bowen left MCA, he basically got to take the acts that we didn't want. We got left with a very small roster with only two strong acts—George and Reba," Brown said. "We let him take Eddie Rabbitt, Glen Campbell, the Nitty Gritty Dirt Band and a whole lot of other artists.

"People thought we were crazy. It emptied our roster out for two quarters. But we created a new label. It took around a year for us to turn around. But now we have the best label in country music. If Bowen's lost something, he's lost the desire to understand what a Steve Earle or a Marty Brown is about. He really prefers to be around the country-club set. I like the country-club set for a few hours, but I was raised around people like Marty Brown, and so I understand what he's all about."

And now Brown's eyes flickered mischievously.

"Now I just live to kick Bowen's ass," he said, busting out in a quick, whinnying laugh.

Tony Brown was born in Greensboro, North Carolina, and was raised in nearby Walkertown, the son of dirt-poor, hard-shell Baptists.

"My father had a handkerchief in one hand, which he used to wipe off the sweat, and he'd be frothing at the mouth and scaring you. He was an evangelist—a hellfire-and-brimstone kind of guy—and we sang. We were called the Brown Family and we traveled around the South. I started playing piano when I was thirteen. One day I played this gospel song called 'All the Way' in the church we went to. Well, the people started going crazy. That's when I got my first indication of what it was like to be a celebrity. So then at every revival meeting there was a special request for me to play that song. I said to myself, 'I should learn two songs.' "

It was a stern, strict upbringing. Brown's father kept his brood on a relentless schedule. And no one questioned whether he was right. The children just obeyed, lest they end up in the hellfire their father so eloquently conjured up behind the pulpit.

"I went to church three times on Sunday. Tuesday night I'd visit the rest home. Wednesday night it was prayer meetings. Thursday night it was visitation at people's homes. Usually Saturday night we were singing at a revival. And then on Sunday it was church. We'd go to our aunt's house and watch *The Lone Ranger*, but we never had a TV. At school, people would talk about Elvis Presley. I'd ask my dad about him and he'd say, 'That's awful stuff.' I missed Elvis and even missed the first wave of the Beatles. I couldn't listen to secular music. Couldn't listen to the ball games either."

We were sitting in Brown's living room, where a shaft of late-fall sunlight was warming the room. Other men might've relayed such childhood tales with bitterness, but Brown wasn't one to dwell on regrets or misfortune.

"There were four kids—three boys and a girl. My father worked for a dairy company—it was called Farmer's Dairy. It was like Sealtest, but it was a local company. Anyway, he developed lung cancer, so they laid him off. We lived at the poverty level. We didn't have in-house plumbing. We had a four-room house. Three boys slept in one room, and my sister slept in a room with Mom and Dad. All we had was one spigot with cold water.

"My mother worked at a dress shop. So, needless to say, there wasn't much money. Our Christmas presents would come from Goodwill. The truck would pull up and we'd get bicycles with no fenders. That's the way I was raised until I left home when I was fifteen. But I didn't know the difference. I was happy. As I look back on this, I realize that until I got out in the world I didn't really know we were poor. Now that there's satellite dishes and everyone can see what rich is, you can know you're poor. But we didn't."

Living around Winston-Salem, nearly all of Brown's relatives grew tobacco for R. J. Reynolds. As a youngster, he worked weekends in the summertime to help them. Frequently, he'd work from five in the morning until nine at night, hanging, priming and curing tobacco.

"I remember at day's end my uncles would say, 'How much do we owe your boys for working all day?' And before I could say a word, my father would say, 'You don't owe my boys a dime.' And that's the way my dad was. He believed you helped your family. Besides, they did give us food. Whatever my dad said, went. We all believed him."

Even though the Brown clan were strict Baptists and so couldn't dance, drink or carouse, Tony's father took the family out on the road, to churches all around the Virginias and the Carolinas and to Pentecostal revivals. "We'd go to sing where these people lived and they spoke in tongues and threw babies in the air," Brown recalls. "I went to revivals where a woman fainted and threw her baby in the air, and somebody caught it.

"And even though it was a small world, there were star preachers and people who would stand out. That's when I started noticing that people had different talents. This preacher, I realized, could really get people motivated, whereas that one couldn't do anything. My father would say, 'We're going to play at the Pentecostal church in Greensboro, North Carolina, this afternoon,' and I'd go, 'Yeah, that's where that wild preacher is.' All that was like being on the edge."

Growing up around gospel, Brown could see that country music, R&B and rock and roll were all extensions of church music. At that point, the Brown Family was singing modern gospel songs, stylistically the beginning of what would become contemporary Christian music.

"And I liked that," Brown said. "We'd go to see the Blackwood Brothers and the Statesmen Quartet. And back in those days all those acts were on RCA Records. That was what I wanted to do: to be in white gospel music, thinking that was the pinnacle of the entertainment business, because my parents did not allow me to listen to any popular music."

In fact, it wasn't until Brown played gospel music with the Oak Ridge Boys and J. D. Sumner, Elvis's bass singer, that he realized how gospel could interact with popular music.

"I was with the Oak Ridge Boys when they were starting to go country, and I realized *I* could leave gospel," Brown said, as if that leap of logic, so clear to most people, was a dangerous heresy to contemplate. But Brown had a pinch of the wild-eyed rebel in him even then.

With the Oak Ridge Boys, who were anything but pure gospel, the plucky pianist bucked the stylistic traditions of the genre. Whereas most gospel bands used acoustic piano, Brown used an electric—a little Wurlitzer with a chorus and an amp on it. And where most white gospel groups had only a piano player, the Oak Ridge Boys added a whole band to their arsenal.

"They had long hair, too, so they were sort of like the Nirvana of white Southern gospel music," Brown said, laughing at his own analogy. "And I liked that. There was some radical thing in me. I had my beard and my long hair. So we shook things up a bit. When I was with the Oak Ridge Boys we swept the Dove awards, which are the gospel equivalent of the Grammys. And people hated us. They thought we were trying to be rock stars."

Sometime around 1974, Brown hooked up with a group of gospel musicians called Voice, whom Elvis Presley had started singing with. Elvis was way past his prime—his 1968 comeback, his last great moment, was years behind him—but Brown still was awed in the presence of rock's supremely mythic figure.

"We'd sing around the house," Brown said, soft-pedaling the whole experience. "Then Elvis put us on the tour to open for the Sweet Inspirations. If you ever saw an Elvis show then, there were a lot of people in the band. There was an orchestra; a conductor; J. D. Sumner and the Stamps, which had six people: three Sweet Inspirations and three guys in Voice. Those were all background singers. Well, on the tour we'd do secular songs, and the Sweet Inspirations didn't have a piano player. An orchestra player would sit at the piano for a few songs. Eventually, I started playing with the Sweet Inspirations, just because it was fun."

When Brown wasn't touring with Elvis, he was playing low-rent nightclubs, doing Top Forty. "I thought to myself, 'This is amazing. I've gone to the depths.' But I lived for the nights we played with Elvis and I could play three songs with the Sweet Inspirations."

Those were the days when Elvis had let himself go, busting out of his pants, pitching tantrums onstage, wearing white jumpsuits, looking grotesque and singing strange, horrible songs amid the classics. He was, in a sense, a parody of himself already: the drugged zombie who would show up, after death, at trailer parks, part of the slipstream of pop culture. But onstage, Elvis could seem rejuvenated singing gospel hymns like "Precious Lord, Take My Hand."

Brown played with Voice for a short while, but then Elvis's manager convinced him that the group was a stupid idea and they disbanded it. A month later, Glen D. Hardin, Presley's bandleader and keyboardist, would leave and arrange for Brown to take over. But for a month Brown had no job, no wife, nothing.

"I thought this was God telling me to get back in gospel music. That was the lowest point in my life because my first marriage was falling apart from me being on the road too much. Getting out of gospel music and getting into secular music gave me loads of guilt. But I didn't go back."

For the last year and half of Elvis's life, Brown played every show, an eyewitness to the decline of a legend. The music was a joke, but the band still boasted some of the greatest country musicians. And nothing was ever boring.

"My first night, I remember, [there] was no rehearsal It was an arena in Kansas City and Felton Jarvis said, 'Don't worry. Just get "Teddy Bear" and "I Can't Help Falling in Love with You," and James Burton has the rest of it. And when Elvis points at you, just hit dun-dun-dun-dun dun-dun-dun-dun-dun. But if you miss it, you're in trouble.' The first song was 'Mystery Train' and then the next song was 'Teddy Bear.' Needless to say, my heart was pounding. Well, Elvis pointed at me and I got it and, whew, I felt like the weight of the world was off my shoulders."

Those were wild days. Elvis was usually zonked on pills and

might call songs the band had never rehearsed. The musicians had to wing it. One night in Las Vegas, Presley pointed to Tony and said, " 'Blueberry Hill.' "

"And I said, 'What key?' because we'd never done it. In fact, I didn't remember the intro to 'Blueberry Hill' at all. So I was sitting on stage in this big arena, trying to figure out what to do. I played something finally, but Elvis turned toward me and went, 'Thaaat's wrong.' And he walked over to the piano, sat down, made me move over and showed me the intro. Everyone was trying to help me out and I was just sweating. Elvis ended up singing maybe one verse of the song and then he was off to something else."

Six months before our interview, some Elvis Fan Club member came to town and told Brown about a tape he had of some old Elvis show from 1977. "He called me and said, 'I've got some video of Elvis introducing you and you playing a solo. Would you like a copy of it?' And I said, 'Absolutely.' Because the cameraman on my side of the stage had the camera focused on me. And this guy also had a cassette of Elvis singing 'Happy Birthday' on my thirty-third birthday. He said, 'We trade Elvis paraphernalia between here and Europe just like drugs. There's so much stuff we have it'd blow your mind.' "

Brown got up, rummaged through a video cart, pulled out a tape and fast-forwarded it. Suddenly we were watching a bloated Elvis decked out in his fabled white jumpsuit, which had been made even more famous by a thousand and one Elvis impersonators. There behind him was Tony Brown, his hair all long and shaggy, also dressed in a white jumpsuit. Brown laughed out loud as I pointed him out.

"From Nashville, it's Tony Brown," said the King in that slurred, druggy drawl he had in his last year of life. And he was huddled over the piano, right next to Brown, with Charlie Hodges and Jerry Scheff nearby. Soon Elvis was singing "I Really Don't Want to Know."

"Now watch him," Brown instructed me, pointing to the top of the screen. "He stands and faces *me*—as opposed to the *crowd*. This is one of those impromptu things he always did.

Anyway, at the end of the song, instead of thanking the crowd, if you listen real closely you can hear what he says."

I leaned in close, and under the wave of applause I heard Elvis half mumble, "Thank ya, Tony," as if he were performing in his living room. "And he thanked the crowd. Which really goes to show that he was *into* that moment.

"Elvis used to come in just before we'd go onstage," Brown said, shutting off the VCR, suddenly remembering another mythical Elvis encounter. "We'd be leaving the dressing room to prepare and he'd come in with that huge entourage. There were maybe ten horn players and fifteen backup singers all these people everywhere. And inevitably Elvis'd look across that group of people and single out one person. One night, on that last tour, I was ready to go on the stage. And"—Brown turned on Elvis's stoned, slurred drawl—" 'Hey, Tony. . . . ' I'm thinking, 'Whoah, the King has called.' So I turned around and walked back towards him. And he looked at me and said, 'Er, damn. I forgot what I was going to say.' "

Working for Elvis opened more doors for Brown than anything else in his life, for it introduced the pianist and aspiring producer to both Hardin and Emory Gordy, Jr., part of the core of Emmylou Harris's group of people.

"That shaped my whole taste in music," Brown told me a few months after we'd first talked. "And whatever benchmark was set for me was set by Emmylou Harris and Brian Ahern and Rodney Crowell. Through Rodney I met Guy Clark. And through Guy I met Lyle Lovett. And through Lyle I met Nanci Griffith. So to play with Elvis was nothing more than a calling card that let me meet a different level of people."

After Elvis died, in 1977, Brown joined Emmylou's band, and for the first time he realized what it was like to be with musicians who were playing a groundbreaking kind of music.

"It was just like 'Fasten your seat belt and hang on,' " he said of those years. "To be a sideman in a great band, there was nothing else left after all that was over."

If Dwight Yoakam pays his allegiance to Buck Owens, and Randy Travis and Alan Jackson were disciples of George Jones, then Nashville right now must owe its respect to Emmylou Harris. In the beginning, Harris's feathery soprano floated angelically over country-pop music full of quavering pedal-steel guitar. But in 1980, with *Roses in the Snow*, Harris and her husband, producer Brian Ahern, moved toward traditional bluegrass arrangements, incorporating the innovations of pioneers like Bill Monroe with a flair for fast and furious playing.

"I think Emmylou is like the earth mother of this whole new resurgence in traditional music," Brown said. "That track Kelly does, 'That'll Be Me,' reminds me of a song from *Elite Hotel*, which Emmy did in 1976. All those little what I call dig-diga-diga-diga songs, full of fast playing—well, Emmylou and the Hot Band invented that. They owned it. It's like turbocharged bluegrass. And another thing Emmylou Harris brought to the table was Rodney Crowell. Rodney is another one of those people who inspired a whole generation of songwriters, like Ricky Skaggs and Kevin Welch. So Emmylou became a breeding ground for a lot of great musicians.

"Her group really opened up the doors, even though the Judds and Randy Travis made the biggest impact as far as sales. Ricky Skaggs sprung of Emmylou's Hot Band and brought the traditional thing back on the scene even stronger. Ricky took credit for it. He was aggressive and he was living here in Nashville and all of a sudden it became his thing according to all the press. But Emmylou started it.

"Her influence is huge and underrated. Rodney is one of the best songwriters and producers in town. I'm an A&R man and producer. Vince Gill is now a star. Hank DeVito has become one of the best songwriters in town. So the tentacles of Emmylou's band have stretched a long ways and influenced a lot of people in Nashville. Someday I hope all of us can get together and pay her allegiance, like we have done for Johnny Cash and George Jones."

In 1978, Brown headed up Free Flight Records, an RCA pop venture out in Los Angeles, where he and members of the Emmylou circle were then living. When the label shut down two years later, Brown came back to Nashville and worked for

RCA, where he signed Alabama, among other groups. But when he tried to break into producing and session work, he found the town to be a closed shop.

"It was really hard. The person who gave me my first shot was Jerry Bradley, the guy who started the whole outlaw thing. But even he was leery of letting me do too much. They thought I was a pop guy, that I didn't know anything about what was going on in Nashville. And I could never play any session here either."

Out of frustration, Brown quit RCA in 1980 and went back out on the road with Crowell, a gifted songwriter whose tunes Emmylou Harris covered, and his wife, Rosanne Cash, daughter of country legend Johnny Cash. It was a time Brown remembers warmly.

"With Rodney and Rosanne I could actually *play* on their records. They let me spend all the time I needed to get the parts right. And I thought, 'There's something to this.' Nashville's mentality of 'Do it good, do it right now, or I'll never call you again' is stifling.

"I wanted to be part of the Nashville thing. I wanted to work in the industry. But it was hard. All the people I knew who were creative were the L.A. bunch, which were Emmylou, Rodney, Rosanne, Mary Martin.[3] To me they were the hippest.

"There's strength in numbers," Brown said, grinning. "All of a sudden we became a factor for Music Row to deal with."

Vince Gill was part of that clique, but for years, until very recently, fame and fortune eluded him.

"I was always infatuated with Vince's voice," Brown said, so I talked him into moving here. I left RCA and thought he'd be OK, but I watched him flounder there for years. He and [label president] Joe Galante got sideways a bit over his writing. But when I found he was leaving RCA, I made a phone call. I said, 'Vince, give me another chance.' So he did. And I found out

---

[3] Martin, who's been an A&R executive and a manager, was the person who introduced Bob Dylan to the Band.

what the problem was. Joe didn't want him to write his own songs, but Vince was such a proud guy. So I said, 'I'll listen to every song you got, and if we're missing a certain song, we can cut an outside song. Otherwise, I'll let you do whatever you want to do.' "

Sure enough, Gill turned up one day and played Brown some forty songs he'd written in one marathon session. Brown just listened and made notes, amazed at Gill's energy.

"I sort of gave Vince two hours of my time. And you know what? Vince *did* have a lot of good songs. Joe Galante just didn't have the time to give him. So we picked some songs out for an album. I felt like I was patronizing him at first, but I thought that was what he needed. And my gut instinct was right. Vince had the goods."

Gill's 1990 album, *When I Call Your Name*, contained a lot of the songs Brown had heard in his office that day. When the record took off, flying out of stores, selling more than a million copies, it made Gill, who had all-American good looks, a superstar. The follow-up, *Pocket Full of Gold*, also went platinum, and Gill's third MCA album, *I Still Believe in You*, has sold close to three million copies and was the CMA album of the year.

"RCA had Vince Gill for years and didn't succeed," Bill Carter said. "But Tony hung in there. He didn't give up. And his faith paid off."

Brown would've liked to do the same trick for Kelly Willis and Marty Brown, but he knew the odds were always against success. After Willis's third album sold poorly, Brown dropped her.

"She wasn't able to get out and play live. And we weren't able to get the word out that she was not only a good recording artist but a good live artist," Brown said. "We'll just have to let somebody else take a shot at it.

"Someone told me to get Marty to cover mainstream songs," Brown had said after the first record sold dismally and the singer was reduced to playing in Wal-Marts. "But I wouldn't do it, because he wouldn't be Marty Brown anymore. He either makes it on his own terms or he ain't gonna make it. But I will not give up until the label says, 'Tony, it's over.'

"People think that if [Jimmy] Bowen or I sign you, you're in. But it's not a given that it's going to happen. Some of my favorite bands *never* happen. The Mavericks are great, but they're getting nowhere. Marty Brown hasn't gone anywhere. And with Kelly we're on the third album. Nobody's tried as hard as I have. I've lobbied within the label, and I've lobbied any way I could, so if I had power, she'd be a star now. But maybe because Kelly is actually credible, because she's gotten all this press, because she's great and has some kind of celebrity, she'll maybe break soon.

"But as far as star-making power, in Nashville it doesn't work that way. Here, the band managed by the most Mickey Mouse person and produced by a nobody can have a double-platinum record."

Not all that long ago, New York and Los Angeles, historically the country's music and entertainment capitals, scoffed at Nashville. The place was considered a hillbilly backwater that every so often erupted and produced revenue, but certainly not an epicenter for music. Yet by the spring of 1993, Nashville was the hottest music city in the world and a veritable cash cow for money-starved major parent companies. No less than three of the country's biggest record companies—Capitol-EMI, MCA and RCA—were seeing a large percentage of their profits, if not all of them, coming from country.

Between 1990 and 1992, Brown had been red hot, the only man in Nashville with a sure Midas touch. In that time he'd produced four gold albums, five platinum albums and three double-platinum albums. Reba McEntire's second album with Brown, *For My Broken Heart*, had gone double platinum, and Trisha Yearwood, a Brown signing, was on her way to becoming a superstar, admired by country and rock fans alike. By November 1992, Brown-produced CDs had sold some thirteen million copies for MCA. Those were the kinds of numbers that made record moguls drool and pull out huge bonuses. Not surprisingly, in December, persistent rumors that Brown was preparing to defect to a rival label were spreading like wildfire through Nashville.

Some thought he would go to Sony Records and take over its ailing Nashville division. And there was talk that he might jump to RCA, where he'd done A&R more than ten years earlier. Others bet that he would go to Mercury, where he might build a real roster on the millions country hunk Billy Ray Cyrus had brought the label.

"I got to thinking that because the MCA [Nashville] president spot wasn't open, I'd try for it at another label," Brown said when I asked him about all the rumors. "So I had my attorney look into the possibilities of getting out of my contract. Well, John Mason is such a high-profile lawyer in Nashville—he renegotiated Bowen's contract—that as soon as I hired him it raised flags.

"The rumor mill just blew my mind. In any other year it wouldn't be quite as sensational, but with country music so big, the rumors flew. Thing is, I was really not unhappy at MCA. I loved the artists. But once I started looking, I had to follow through and think about what I was going to do for the rest of my life."

MCA wasn't about to let Brown go. In the end, the company bumped Bruce Hinton, who was then MCA Nashville's president, to chairman and gave Brown the presidency with a whopping raise and a bigger incentive package. "I signed a firm five-year contract, so I've definitely become a company man. Now I report directly to [MCA chairman] Al Teller instead of Bruce. It gives me a lot more autonomy. If I get a harebrained idea I can talk to Al and Bruce."

Though Brown constantly got offers to cross over into pop and rock, he had no interest. He laughed at the wags who were predicting that country music was merely the latest fad or that its inability to create huge sales abroad meant it was bad for the global music economy so widely touted of late. And Brown dismissed critics who said the new country wasn't as powerful or significant as the old country music.

"Hey, this is the *best* period of country music, because you've got everything from Marty Brown to Garth Brooks to Mary-Chapin Carpenter. The music is more diversified than ever. People say that there are more things we can do in country. Well, that's bullshit, because the bottom line is that the music has expanded as far as it can. There comes a point when it's not country anymore.

"It's like saying that some of this hip-hop is real R&B. Well, it's not really. It's just basic pop music. Because real R&B is like country music. There comes a point where you've crossed the line and the music is no longer true to the tradition. And pretty soon the intentions of the person playing it get muddled."

Certainly, some of the most acclaimed new country artists felt confined by the genre and the conservative power structure of Nashville. k. d. lang, one of the best singers of her generation, switched over to the pop division and won enormous success. And Lyle Lovett, whom Brown worked with, did the same. When Lovett's name came up, Brown smiled tolerantly.

"As far as Lyle goes, he never *claimed* he was country. He just happened to stumble into our A&R department. And we didn't *lose* Lyle. He did what he did and moved on. As for k. d. lang, she was never a country artist to start with. She's a cabaret singer who can be everything from Sarah Vaughan to Patsy Cline. So she was basically a carpetbagger. And she made such a big splash that she caused a controversy that served her career well, because now she's become a pop star and critical favorite.

"See, country music is actually a legitimate genre of music—an original art, like blues and R&B," Brown said, as if to explain why he would never be seduced by the glitter of New York or L.A. "But nobody knows what pop music is anymore. Is it Creedence Clearwater or Poison? Pop music used to be a melting pot of all forms of music. Rock and roll *was* a culture; it was really a fusion of rock and country. But I don't know what it is anymore. Now they've sort of made it a fashion club. That's why Garth Brooks hasn't crossed over. He's not as fashionable as Kris Kross, even though he's sold more music. Whereas in country we're not about fashion.

"It seems like in pop music the idea is to push the envelope on purpose and see how far you can push it, and the one who pushes it the furthest and succeeds is the one in fashion. But in country, the people who have always pushed the envelope, like Waylon Jennings or Hank Williams, they weren't trying to start something on purpose—to be something *new*. They were just doing things different, and fighting against country's conservatism.

"To me a lot of current contemporary pop music is not about feeling. It's about rhythms and attitude. Whereas in country music, what's happening now is people are pulled in by the feeling in the music. Human beings expressing themselves. I think pop music has gone back to being dance music, disco. So where do you turn to for great singers and great songs? Well, the only people doing that are country singers. The reason we've done so well now is that the last time we had a big country music boom, in the late seventies, there weren't that many songs to choose from. The big hits were 'Lookin' for Love' by Johnny Lee and 'Stand by Me' by Mickey Gilley. There was nothing else to choose from. Now, though, you have Garth Brooks, Alan Jackson, Vince Gill, Clint Black, Pam Tillis, Trisha Yearwood. All of a sudden there's a bigger selection."

I asked Brown what gospel music taught him. He looked down for a moment before answering.

"I grew up around bluegrass-gospel and Southern gospel music. If you listen to Vince Gill's 'When I Call Your Name,' you hear Southern gospel mixed in with bluegrass gospel music, too. A lot of people in the business today came from gospel backgrounds. You know, white gospel music is not that far off from country music. It's basically simple music, simple chord structures, simple lyrics for the most part. Even though country is a secular form of music, for the most part it's also very conservative. They're kissing cousins. So I think what it taught

227

Moguls and Madmen

me is about harmonies, how to appreciate harmonies, because country music borrowed from bluegrass harmonies.

"There are certain secular country tunes that have nothing to do lyrically or spiritually with anything, but at the same time there's something spiritual in these songs, because that's where it's coming from. When you hear a great gospel song, it can make you cry. And in country music, there are some songs that carry that same emotion, like 'I Will Always Love You' by Dolly Parton or 'He Stopped Loving Her Today' by George Jones. A lot of Emmylou Harris's music does that for me. Like 'Boulder to Birmingham'—that's one of the best spiritual songs I've heard. It has that power."

Down in Winston-Salem, where Brown grew up, tobacco raising is a summerlong event. If you grew up in the fifties, the son of a poor family, you spent long hours in the burning sun working the crop, fighting off mosquitoes. You kept the worms off the leaves, hung the tobacco, cured it, dried it. Back then, when you drove into town, one of the first things you saw was a big billboard for Winston and Salem cigarettes.

Tony Brown had no reason to think he'd ever escape that culture. And he never dreamed that he'd be a millionaire, hanging out with country stars, getting motorcycles from Reba McEntire. But success comes with its own burden: guilt.

"There's a bit of guilt there about how successful I've become," Brown told me one night, a few weeks before he was scheduled to come out for Academy of Country Music awards, which were being held in Los Angeles. "My two brothers and sisters are like the way we were raised. One of my brothers is a preacher and lives in Savannah, Georgia. And my other brother has been a preacher off and on. He works with mentally handicapped people and lives in South Carolina. My sister, who works for the post office, lives in Winston-Salem with my mother.

"It's funny. There's this satisfaction on the one hand, but there is this guilt thinking about my brothers and sisters. I could go over there and play Elvis and buy them cars and things, but I'd never go and try to flaunt my money in front of my family. I bought my mother a car for her birthday, but I could tell it felt a bit strange. *They* couldn't do that, so it didn't give me as much satisfaction as I thought it would. But if anyone in my family got in dire straits they could call me.

"There's this guilt. But I've worked really hard and nobody ever gave me anything. I've been through two marriages, and both of my jobs took their toll, as a musician with the first one and as an executive with the second one. I'm not proud of that. I have two children, a son, twenty, and a daughter, twenty-one, by my first wife. She moved to Colorado and left this hick town. My second wife, Gina, we were married thirteen years. Her father was Harold Morrison, who played with Kitty Wells and George Jones and Tammy Wynette and came out of that Grand Ole Opry tradition. But things just didn't work out between us.

"This business is hard on marriages. It's easy to be consumed by what you do. That happened to me in my first marriage, when I was on the road as a musician. And then getting back in town, getting caught up in my career and producing, you're talking working day and night and a lot of weekends, and there isn't much free time. Now that I'm divorced, I must tell you I'm taking a whole new look at my priorities. It's a little late, but I'm thinking there's a whole lot more to life than work. I don't ever want to lose that person in me that loves music. I don't ever want to turn into a deal maker. I don't mind running a label, but I wouldn't ever want to be a *mogul* mogul. I don't want to be so busy for the rest of my life that I lose the musician in me, just like I don't want to ever forget where I came from, which is from a very poor family. I was raised so poor that I could be poor again, though I don't want to be. The thought distresses me. But having some money for the first time in my life, being able to buy what I want without thinking about it—I take it all with a grain of salt because I know that, basically, that's not what life is all about. It's like that cliché, 'Money can't buy you happiness.' Well, I'm actually experiencing that. I sit here thinking, 'I've got all this money that I've worked so hard to get and I don't have a companion to share it with.' And that's what I really want."

I asked Brown if having power was worth the price. Brown thought about that for a moment.

"The one thing about power is that it causes people to become jealous of you and not like you. With people who used to like me I now have to be very careful, because things are exaggerated. Every move I make is exaggerated and that's something I've never experienced before, because I've never been high-profile enough in my mind to think that anybody would not like me. But now I can sense their envy. And I hate that, because I want people to like me. . . . Sometimes I have to make decisions that make me appear as a hard-ass. But the power's worth having, because the good things you can do with it far outweigh the bad things that come with it."

CHAPTER 7

The Scholar and the Warrior

Cliff Burnstein
and
Peter Mensch

Ever since Colonel Tom Parker managed Elvis Presley—
helping to transform him from primordial rock and roll rebel
into tabloid totem, drugged-out icon and trailer-park vampire—
the pop-music business has been filled with hustlers.

Heir to the Great Parker Pony Circus, the colonel was a
figure straight out of a medicine show: clever carny barker,
ingenious self-promoter and ruthless Svengali. Nor was he unusual. Back in the sixties and seventies, before rock became a
multibillion-dollar business, the numerous roles managers
played made the potential for trickery great. Frequently, the
agent—the person who booked a show—the accountant, the
merchandiser and the manager were one and the same person.
As a result, there were no checks and balances and chicanery
was rife. By the 1980s, a typical successful band had a manager,
a road manager, a business manager, an agent, a lawyer and a
merchandiser. But the field was still full of operators.

The truth was, many managers were less-than-savory
characters—larger-than-life figures who smelled the easy money
and glamorous thrills that rock and roll promised and occasionally delivered. Masters of cunning chatter, they could prey on
innocent rockers, rookie rappers and grizzled veterans alike.
And each one had his own come-on. Some signed their victims
to unscrupulous management deals and charged up dubious

commissions, while others kept a double set of books or sold away a band's publishing.

Since most artists had no head for business, it was easy to outwit them, and both small-time operators and major moguls could play the game. Every town had a band whose destiny was controlled by the proverbial sharpie: a guy thick around the middle, sporting rock clothes, a slicked-back ponytail and a diamond pinkie ring. And some of the biggest players were notorious for following the practice of Motown Records founder Berry Gordy, who often signed his artists to deals that made Motown the artists' manager.[1]

Every day incompetent managers could ruin bands in a dozen ways, giving them the wrong image, the wrong haircuts, the wrong tour, the wrong songs or the wrong vision. Or maybe no vision at all. The field demanded intelligence, but it didn't necessarily attract the best, the brightest and the most honest. Doc McGhee, who managed Bon Jovi, Mötley Crüe and the Scorpions at the height of their success, was a money launderer who got busted in 1988 for helping one of the country's largest drug-smuggling rings import forty-five thousand pounds of marijuana from Colombia to North Carolina.[2] And Billy Joel found out that having a family member as his manager didn't mean anything: In 1989, Joel filed a ninety-million-dollar lawsuit against former brother-in-law Frank Weber, claiming he ran off with millions and lost millions more in risky investments like horse breeding.

"You want a picture of the typical megalomaniac manager?" Cliff Burnstein said the first afternoon I met him and his

---

[1] The classic case is Teena Marie, who was signed to Motown in 1976 by Gordy. Marie had no attorney and Motown had her managed by the common-law wife of Berry Gordy's brother, according to Fredric Dannen's Hit Men.

[2] McGhee took $10 for every pound brought in, or $450,000. He pled guilty in 1988, but in an unusual probation agreement was allowed to set up an antidrug charity instead of going to prison. The drug ring he worked with was the Kalish-Vogel-Ritch organization, which had connections to Manuel Noriega, among others.

partner, Peter Mensch, who managed Metallica, Def Leppard, Bruce Hornsby and seven other bands. "OK. First, he sells himself to the band as God's gift. He says, 'I'm gonna make it happen for you.' Then he's helping the band in the studio. And before you know it, he's coproducing or executive-producing the albums. This is the kind of manager who tells the band how to write songs, how to record them.

"When the band is out at the bar and going after chicks, this guy is going after chicks at the *same* rate. And whatever the musicians are doing, he's got to have it *better*. He's convinced himself he's part of the band. And at the same time, he's always telling them, 'You'd be nowhere without me.' He tries to become indispensable to them—by being there all the time, making all the decisions and not letting anyone else know what's going on."

"Meanwhile, you *should* have all the answers," said Mensch. "Because you've got to let the band members know what's going on at the end of the day."

"The other style," said Burnstein, "is the manager who asks somebody *else* what's going on. This guy sees himself as just a conduit. When the band asks him something, he says, 'I'll get back to you.' He doesn't have his own opinion. He's asking somebody else. Which is why you see more lawyers and agents managing bands. There are a couple of really big rock bands where the manager is just one quarter of the decision-making team."

Burnstein, who was talking in rapid gusts, paused for a moment. Rail thin, dressed in a cyberpunk T-shirt and ratty jeans, with an overgrown beard and frizzy gray hair that exploded in all directions, he might've passed for a sixties dope dealer, an ex-Hasid or a wild mountain man. Mensch, by contrast, with his square jaw, short, thinning hair, mischievous eyes and ready sarcasm, came off as a privileged, fortysomething yuppie.

But appearances were deceiving. Though he looked like some *ur*-hippie, Burnstein had the mind and ambition of a Wall Street financier. And with three years of graduate school at the University of Pennsylvania in demography he was a match for anyone in the entertainment business. As for Mensch, underneath the bluster, the tough talk, the impatience and the quick temper was a river of pain and self-doubt.

"I struggle with insecurity. I will never believe that I'm really good at what I'm doing," Mensch said when I asked him what his demons were. "The issue that gets me every day is looking in the mirror and going, 'When are they going to discover that it's all a fraud?' "

In their twelve years at Q Prime, both had run across scads of managers, and classifying them now seemed amusing. If nothing else, Mensch and Burnstein themselves were nothing like the image most people had of rock and roll managers. Neither champed on a cigar or had walked into a record company president's office and climbed on a desk, screaming out demands.

Most managers thought of themselves as stars and lived in Los Angeles, the world's rock and roll power epicenter. They traveled by limo with a retinue of flunkies and assistants in tow. But Burnstein and Mensch lived in Manhattan and rode the subway[3] almost everywhere, taking in the parade of crackheads, panhandlers, hipsters, janitors, immigrants, teachers, students and other commuters. Both Mensch and Burnstein were multimillionaires, but Burnstein drove a Toyota and lived modestly in a five-bedroom house in Queens that was certainly no palace. And if Mensch's Greenwich Village townhouse cost more, it wasn't a mogul's pad. Q Prime itself, located near seedy Times Square, looked more like the headquarters for a Kmart than the office complex of rock's most powerful managers.

Most managers looked for the band that filled the niche of what was currently popular. But Burnstein and Mensch didn't follow trends. They weren't hustling to sign tomorrow's grunge

---

[3] Taking the subway was a point of pride with Burnstein and Mensch, who got their employees discounts on rides through a token-purchase program run by the New York City Transit Authority.

band today just because grunge bands like Nirvana and Pearl Jam happened to be selling millions of records. When Q Prime signed Metallica and Def Leppard, who turned into two of the biggest groups in the history of rock, the charts were dominated by new wave and dance-pop. And now that metal and grunge were everywhere, Q Prime was signing bands like the Screaming Trees and Hash, groups that drew on everything from psyche-delic pop to punk.

Multiple-act managers—and there were very few who were successful—were lucky if they had two big bands. But Q Prime, which was managing ten acts in 1993, had four huge bands— Metallica, Def Leppard, Queensrÿche and Tesla—that regularly sold millions of records. And if pop star Bruce Hornsby, a new client, wasn't doing as well as in the past it was probably be-cause his jazzy record *Harbor Lights* was a hard sell in the current pop marketplace.

In fact, Q Prime was more than a management company. Burnstein and Mensch could see a time when the great bands might not come to them, and if and when that happened they wanted to be ready. They already owned three radio stations in California—one in Bakersfield, one in San Luis Obispo and one in Fresno. However, their most daring—you could even call it visionary—move was into an arena that made them Davids in the land of the Goliaths: In the spring and summer of 1993, Burnstein and Mensch had suddenly found themselves talking to scientists and engineers in the wake of filing an application to participate in satellite radio broadcasting. Three other applicants—a consortium of the American Mobile Satellite Corporation, Hughes Aircraft and McCaw Cellular Communi-cations; a company called CD Radio; and a group called the Digital Satellite Broadcasting Corporation—had met the FCC filing deadline that was the first hurdle in becoming eligible to broadcast radio nationally via satellite.

"We don't know who's going to be granted a license," Burn-stein said. "We could all get it or only one or two of us could get it. And whoever is picked has to put up a satellite, which means we'll have to raise six hundred million dollars. But this is the future of radio. It'll be a national radio—something that you could get in your car or your home." For Burnstein, just talking about the proposed satellite network, called Primosphere, was exhilarating.

"I was telling Peter we can't even have an intelligent discussion with people in the music business—the people that we deal with—but here, in a period of a month, we've had three or four really intelligent people call us. If we were playing in that arena, we would have to be much better." Burnstein paused for a moment, trying to put things in perspective.

"We've had some luck as managers, but mostly you just need to be smart. Every Wednesday we get the sales figures and airplay figures on everything. You're constantly being tested. It's public knowledge how well your acts are doing all the time. The grosses are printed up. I could give you statistics all day long on how we do. The music business is something where you don't have to ask someone else how you're doing. You can rate yourself, because everything is right there."

"There are some people who may bullshit themselves into power, but I'm not capable of doing that. You do great work and then the power *comes* to you. And as long as you continue doing great work, then you'll maintain that power. Behind Primosphere is the idea that we'll have something unique and important. If it really is important and we do a great job at it, then we will be powerful. But we didn't pursue the power; we're just pursuing the idea because it's a challenge. If we wanted the most power we would've moved to Los Angeles. New York is real second-rate in this business; we feel pretty lonely here. But we enjoy living here."

By any measure, Q Prime was powerful. In 1992, during a recession that had devastated the industry, scuttling tours and sending record sales plummeting, Q Prime–managed bands like Metallica and Def Leppard had sold more than twenty million records. When the *Los Angeles Times* came out with its 1992 ranking of the forty most powerful people in pop music, only one other manager besides Burnstein and Mensch made the "Rock's New World Order" list—this despite the fact that most of their clients were bands that played the sort of molar-twisting music that most adults held in contempt. Even Rick Rubin, not one to freely pass out compliments, had called Burnstein "the smartest guy in the record business."

What's more, Burnstein and Mensch made it all seem easy. Neither led the kind of workaholic life endemic to the profession. Burnstein rarely came to the office earlier than 10:00 A.M. and almost never left later than 5:30 P.M.—in plenty of time to get home to his wife and two kids in the Kew Gardens neighborhood of Queens. And if Mensch stayed later—he was married with no children—he rarely let work interfere with pleasure.

"We don't baby-sit bands," Mensch said when I asked if anything got them bent out of shape. "If we get a call from one of our bands playing in Saskatchewan and they say, 'I'm freezing. All I got is my leather jacket,' I'll say 'Go buy another jacket.' And they know that Cliff is not going to go down to the store, buy a coat and FedEx it to them. They'll freeze to death before he does that."

Yet things could get tense at Q Prime. As if to prove that point, the phone rang a few minutes later with Guns N' Roses' manager, Doug Goldstein, on the line. Mensch took the call, and when he came back his habitually mischievous grin was gone.

"That was Goldstein. Guns N' Roses is really pissed at us over something Metallica said about Axl in the video," Mensch announced, referring to Metallica's recently released two-hour home video culled from the stadium tour the two supergroups coheadlined. "I think Metallica had a copy of the Guns N' Roses contract rider and James Hetfield [Metallica's lead singer/guitarist] read it on camera. . . . We should let them sue us, Cliff."

"Yeah, it's great publicity," Burnstein said.

"What's the worst they could do? Make us change it?"

It was no secret that Metallica despised Axl Rose, whose egomania was rivaled only by his obnoxious onstage tantrums. But the thought of being sued by Guns N' Roses was not a pleasant one.

"Here's what can happen," Burnstein said after a few seconds. "They can get an injunction and we'll have to take all the videos off the market. This is what happened in the Biz Markie case last year with the samples.[4] They actually had to go to retailers and get them returned. It's incredibly costly. And then the video would have to be reedited. That'll cost a fucking fortune! We're churning these videos out like crazy—it's the middle of the Christmas season. If you were going to go in and reedit the thing, you probably couldn't get the time for a few days. So we'd probably lose a couple of weeks."

"Right now there's not much we can do about it," Mensch said.

"But no matter what James did, Guns N' Roses are public figures—the court will know that," said Burnstein, who was now nervously drumming his fingers, clearly vexed. "This is social commentary. Let's see what he says. Does he actually say anything about Axl, like 'You're a fucking asshole,' or does he just read the rider and look up quizzically? If they say they want Slash out of there, we have to deal with that," the forty-five-year-old manager said, referring to a possible appearance—without a signed release—by Guns N' Roses' guitarist. "But I don't know how fast they can get an injunction. Conceivably they could get one by tomorrow. What you want to do at a time like this is get it removed."

"We should talk to Gary Casson now," said Mensch, referring to the head of business affairs at Elektra. The two managers looked at each other for a moment.

"I don't think James will apologize," Mensch said, "though Goldstein said that would be OK."

A short while later, after taking a flurry of calls from the Guns N' Roses camp, Mensch seemed even edgier.

"Now Slash is saying he hasn't signed the release."

---

[4] Biz Markie was a rapper who was successfully sued for unauthorized use of Gilbert O'Sullivan's song "Alone Again (Naturally)" on his album *I Need a Haircut.*

"Let's look at the video," Burnstein said, as George Kne- meyer, a Q Prime employee, fast-forwarded through the foot- age until he came to the offending passage. James Hetfield was staring mischievously into the camera, surrounded by some bandmates, reading from the Guns N' Roses contract rider.

" 'Axl Rose, dressing room requirements. . . . There will be no substitutions. . . . One cup of cubed ham'—and it's got to be cubed fucking *right* so it'll get down his little neck . . . 'a steak dinner'—I didn't even know the guy ate meat; he looks like a fucking vegemetarian . . . 'one gourmet cheese tray, pepperoni pizza . . . cans of assorted Pringles chips'—you know, greasy shit, to slick his hair back . . . 'Sue Bee honey'—that makes him SING LIKE THIS!!" And here Hetfield screamed the last three words in clear imitation of Axl's artery-popping banshee howl.

The effect was hilarious: Hetfield had exposed the rock star for the spoiled baby he was in public. Even Burnstein and Mensch couldn't help laughing, though a moment later, with more calls and threats of a lawsuit, all smiles vanished. Mensch disappeared into his office and Burnstein looked annoyed.

"I have to go deal with this. We'll have to set something up later," Burnstein told me tensely, and joined Mensch, closing the door behind him.

It wasn't until four months later that I was in New York again. By then Axl Rose had whipped himself into a full-scale rage over Metallica's "treachery." At a mid-April show at Sac- ramento's Arco Arena, Rose stormed off the stage ninety min- utes into Guns N' Roses' set—but not before he went into a long, poisonous, frequently incomprehensible tirade against Metallica.

"Let me tell you a couple of things about Metallica. First off, they do a lot of bitching for a band who got paid about twenty-thirty percent more than fuckin' what they deserved at a show—because they didn't bring that much," snarled Rose, who was wearing a T-shirt with a picture of Charles Manson on it. Then, as many of the sixteen thousand fans started booing, Rose descended into the waters of paranoia and rage that swirled in his psyche. He accused Hetfield of being a racist ("I watched him be really shitty with black people") and the band of cruelty to their roadies, who supposedly slaved all year long with no bonuses ("There was nobody in their crew that had ever gotten a bonus or [was] paid anything extra for working their fuckin' ass off and slaving for that band"). When I asked Burnstein about what had happened since we last talked, he grinned.

"Axl was pissed at James reading the rider. But he didn't even see it. Someone had called him and said, 'They're fucking you, man,' and so then Axl went crazy and he drove his manager, Doug Goldstein, crazy. The first question was, could they slap an injunction on us? Slash appeared in part of the video. Now, if we didn't have a clearance—a signed release—they could fuck with us. But we had a clearance on Slash. After we found our clearance, a signed release, we said to Geffen, 'Do as you want to do, but my guy reading Axl's rider is not something that our lawyer thinks you will find the basis for an injunction on.' Because James didn't libel him.

"Goldstein wanted Geffen to make us pull the videos and reedit them. But we told Geffen, 'You've got no case. And we're not going to pull anything voluntarily to change this video. We're happy with it. You're going to have to come after us legally.' And they didn't. Axl tries to intimidate everybody, but I don't want to be intimidated by him. Normally he gets what he wants by intimidation. But we don't intimidate. And Metallica doesn't intimidate."

And the charges of racism?

"Listen, James doesn't like rap music. It's just a personal taste. If a black person doesn't like country music, does that make him a racist? Axl's full of shit. They wanted to have Ice-T's group, Body Count, open a bunch of dates, but James didn't think that was appropriate. Metallica wanted Motörhead, which was one of their idols. So we split the opening slots—half went to Body Count and half to Motörhead. And if we're not treating our crew properly, why are they sticking around? We have guys who've worked for us for many, many years. But showing up three hours late for a show or walking off in the middle of a show—how's that showing respect for a crew? The way Axl makes up for all the shit he puts people through is by throwing a party afterwards. He gives everybody food and drink. Meanwhile, he blanks out the fact that he put them through hell and physical danger because he walked off stage. We don't put on a party every night because it's a *business*. We put on a show and it goes on. And it's nothing to celebrate. People have work to do and they go on to the next city. With Axl it's like, 'Wow, we got through a show! Let's celebrate!' Or 'We didn't get through one, so let's make everybody feel better about it.' "

What about the millions of dollars paid to Metallica that the band didn't deserve, according to Rose?

"He's crazy. Axl claimed that Metallica got more than they deserved as coheadliners on this tour. But I'm like, 'Whoah, wait a minute.' I told their manager, 'I don't think you'd want the financial numbers to come out on this tour. I mean, I'd be happy to publish them if you want to make it public, but I think if we made it public you'd be very embarrassed about who got what on this tour.' Because everybody was supposed to see it as being fifty-fifty split; it was a coheadlining tour, both bands playing their full set. Axl said he thought we got paid twenty to thirty percent *more* than we deserved, and I'm telling you we got *less* than half. We take less than half and subtract twenty to thirty percent from that. So Axl thinks Metallica should've earned what—ten or fifteen percent? Is that what he thinks we should've gotten for these shows? The new Metallica album has sold eleven million copies—almost six million when we went out on this fucking tour." Burnstein mockingly knocked on Axl Rose's imaginary forehead. "Hello? Is anybody home?"

Most big rock management partners had separate offices and divvied up the bands they handled, but Burnstein and Mensch worked from two couches in the same cluttered office, their rapid-fire phone conversations bleeding into one another's.

Both shared a passion for music, baseball and films—especially violent films, by directors like John Woo, that their wives were sure to hate. And both consumed mass quantities of chocolate all day long. Yet their differences were also dramatic.

"Peter's impulsive and I'm cautious. Peter's a pessimist and I'm an optimist. I have a real good bullshit detector and he doesn't," Burnstein said when I asked him about their differences. "Peter wants control and I want chaos. And he's very sociable in a nonbusiness setting, whereas I'm not particularly. These are extremes, but with a kernel of truth."

Mensch loved the theater—he and his wife went to dozens of plays a year—and loved to travel. He went scuba diving, he had traveled to Africa and he had just been river rafting in New Mexico. But Burnstein, who thought almost nothing, least of all a play, ever lived up to the hype it received, couldn't care less about theater. He rarely took vacations, much less went on adventures. At forty-five, his passions were his family, music and the stock market.

"Mensch is the creative guy when it comes to packaging and staging. Burnstein deals more with the record companies, the contracts, the songs, and radio. I go to them for different things," Lars Ulrich, Metallica's blond-haired drummer, said when I asked him about the differences between the two managers. "I would never call up Cliff and ask him what he thinks of a lighting diagram. And I would never call up Peter and ask what he thinks about some radio track. I've probably had more ups and downs with Peter. He tends to get more emotional. He and I have had some less-than-great times. I've had to go to Cliff and say, 'I'm having a tough time dealing with Peter over such and such.' But now me and Peter have a really good relationship. And it goes outside the business. We go diving together. We hang out. Before he got married and started having kids, Cliff and I had that. I'd spend a week in New York and me and Cliff would hang out every day and go to movies. But now he spends time with his family."

"Cliff's more of the visionary and I'm more of the guy who schleps out to the road. He's Mr. Inside and I'm Mr. Outside,"

Mensch said dismissively when I asked him to describe their differences. "Cliff's more uncomfortable being in Italy with Metallica, whereas I can go and know all the crew guys in the band and know the inside jokes. I schmooze better, maybe. A lot of people think Cliff is carrying me."

"See, Peter's being too modest," Burnstein said when I mentioned Mensch's description of himself as the "schlep." "He does more with touring and staging—he sees the bands more. And I do more with promotion, getting the albums made. I'm doing more with the satellite network and Peter does more with the international side of the business. But there's a give-and-take on each thing. He's brilliant at what he does."

"If you're managed by Q Prime, it's sort of like having an Hasidic scholar whose partner is Attila the Hun," said Peter Lubin, who does merchandising for Giant Records and has known Burnstein and Mensch since the 1980s, when they worked for the management company Leber-Krebs. "Peter's the guy who calls and gives you shit all day long. But if Cliff calls to give you shit, your life's over. They're brilliant managers. They both believe there is a way to do things, and if you're managed by them they have expectations of you and they're not shy about telling you."

"A lot of people are in this business for the glamour, but Cliff doesn't care about all the flash that goes with rock and roll. This is a guy who's taken dates on the subway," said Bob Pfiefer, an A&R man for Hollywood Records and a friend to both managers. "He may be a genius—a real genius. And a lot of people think Mensch is a tough guy—even an asshole. But last year I came down with a severe case of Bell's palsy. The doctors said I was screwed for life. And Peter Mensch called me every day—to the point of driving me fucking *crazy!* Both Peter and he are totally honest. That sounds like a trivial statement, but in this business it's not."

"I know he'll never try to fuck me, and he knows I'll never try to fuck him," Burnstein said, summing up whatever alchemy he and Mensch had. "And most partnerships break up because of just that—because someone thinks that they're getting fucked. We're complementary and we don't compete with each other. We have a company together and we try to do it for our acts."

Burnstein had grown up in the affluent Chicago suburb of Highland Park, the son of a tax lawyer and the grandson of Eastern European Jewish immigrants.

"All my grandparents were from Russia, the Ukraine, Latvia—depending on what borders they had that day. My mother's parents were garment workers. But my father's father was extremely bright. He came over from Russia when he was thirteen or fourteen. He was already a black-market player in Russia. He came over here not knowing any English and learned typesetting for Yiddish newspapers. He made some money and started retail stores where they sold ladies' undergarments. And my grandmother worked there, too. They sold off the stores one by one. Like a lot of first-generation immigrants, my parents eventually settled in Chicago and wanted to make sure that their children did better than they did."

Highland Park was the kind of place where people trained for years to become something—doctors, dentists, lawyers, accountants. Frequently, families would spend their money ostentatiously—on fancy cars and clothes. But Burnstein's parents eschewed conspicuous consumption and never channeled their son in any one direction. They told him there were lots of options.

"My father would say, 'Just because you get a law degree doesn't mean you have to be a lawyer.' He never pushed me in his footsteps but encouraged me to think that I had lots of options every step along the way—that I could do some indirect thinking in order to get to another place."

In high school, Burnstein was in all the advanced classes, and his College Boards put him nearly at the top of his class. But as a student he was an underachiever. And his radical ideas put him at odds with both his family and most of his classmates.

"I was difficult. I'd grow everything right out to the edge—my hair, my sideburns, my beard. And this was 1966, before you could do what you wanted. At home, we'd get into screaming fights because my parents were fairly mainstream. But I would take a radical position that probably forced them further to the right."

Burnstein might never have ended up in the music business if he hadn't fallen sick for two weeks with chicken pox and listened to radio. But his early passion for music took an odd form. While other fifteen-year-olds were busy playing their favorite records, Burnstein turned his love for pop music into a statistical ritual. Each week, he sent away to twenty or more stations for their local surveys.

"Then I'd compile them into my own national survey—a crudely weighted Top One Hundred. I was obsessed. And it was a tremendous amount of work. But I did this all through high school."

Mensch's roots were also in Eastern Europe, and his grandparents had also made the archetypal migration to America in the early part of the century. His parents quickly made the leap to prosperity that was the goal of all first-generation Jewish immigrants.

"We went from Levittown, Long Island, which is one sociological phenomenon, to Scarsdale, a second sociological phenomenon, to Park Avenue. We were the classic *arriviste* Jewish family. My grandparents couldn't speak English and came from Poland, Austria, Lithuania. My mother, who was a teacher, went to Hunter College. And my father went to Yale Law School and became a corporate attorney."

At Scarsdale's elite high school, from which virtually every kid went to college, Mensch was pushed to succeed. But though he was part of the high-school intelligentsia—the top tier of kids who got into first-rate colleges—he wasn't popular.

"My group was kind of nerdy. We all got involved in student government. I was a campaign manager for the guy who became class president. But then I got pushed out, because I wasn't as smart."

Mensch worked high-school summers as a cashier at a local clothing store. At the end of each workweek, he'd take the money, stop off at a record store and spend it all. "I ended up going to college with four hundred records—which was more than my whole college dorm combined," Mensch said. "I was listening to Jefferson Airplane, the Byrds, the Procol Harum, Jethro Tull. Whatever WNEW was pounding, I'd listen to it incessantly. And I also had done a radio show while I was going to high school in Westchester County."

Burnstein first met Mensch in 1973 after Mensch had transferred from the University of Chicago, where he'd been the program director of WHBK, to Brandeis University, where he'd become the music director of WBRS, the school's radio station.

"They were the only ones who would take me with my shitty grade-point average," Mensch recalled with a laugh. "And I got to be music director of WBRS because I claimed I had all this knowledge and knew all these people in promotion, which wasn't really true."

College radio was in its infancy then and WBRS was just a tiny ten-watt radio station, but it reported to *Walrus*, an early tip sheet, which ran playlists from radio stations along with commentary.

"Well, Burnstein was a promotion man then, and what he would do—more thoroughly than anyone else, I might add—was call every reporter," said Mensch. "He'd find, for instance, that seventy percent of all reported stations were playing Thin Lizzy. And he'd promote his records. Now, when you're working for a dinky radio station like WBRS, where the signal hits a wall and it dies, and you get a call from a national promotion guy, you'll run *anything*, because you know no one's listening to your radio station anyway. So I'd put down whatever people wanted me to put—heavy, medium or light rotation.

"Anyway, Cliff would call me up and hype me on his English rock records. I invited him to come by if he was ever around. This was 1974. So midnight one Friday night, forgetting I'd even asked him to come, in comes the station's program director with this hippie. And it's Cliff Burnstein." Mensch stopped, leaned forward on his elbows, ran his fingers quickly through his hair and smiled. "I had short hair back then too and I was the ultimate yuppie. After I got over my initial shock, Burnstein asked me what I wanted to play, and I pointed him to the record library and said, 'Play whatever you want.' Well, he picked out a lot of the same records I would've picked."

By any measure, Burnstein was ridiculously overqualified when he entered the music business. Before he'd talked his way into an entry-level job at Mercury Records, he'd done three years of graduate school. It wasn't long before the Mercury bigwigs realized they had a prodigy on their hands. When a position in rock promotion opened up, Burnstein was tapped for it.

"I'd never done promotion before, so I thought, 'Well, fine, this is great,' but I didn't know anybody and I had no idea how to do the job. So I just worked my ass off. I would come in every weekend and arrange the mailing lists and go through all the stations. I mean, I certainly worked every day for two years doing this. I never thought I could deal with the public too well—I'm very introverted—but I was forced to make all these phone calls to people I didn't know, some of whom were legends, like Kid Leo, the Cleveland DJ. Every time I had to talk to somebody I was nervous and I had laryngitis for six months. But I just kept doing it."

"Mercury had given Burnstein his own extension at home," Mensch remembered, "which was a WATS line. And it got to the point where Burnstein would give me his home phone number. So I would call him at home collect and he'd deny the charges, then he'd call me back on the WATS line. We talked until all hours of the night. I was in Boston and he was in Chicago."

From that point on their lives were enmeshed, though in ways neither could envision. Burnstein made the leap from promotion to A&R in 1976, two years after he signed Rush. By then, Mensch, realizing there were no jobs for him when he finished Brandeis, had returned to the Windy City, where he at least knew Burnstein, to go to graduate school at the University of Chicago.

"I'd designed this master's program in communications—but it was one of the softest programs ever," Mensch said. "Really, I was just marking time until I could get into the music business."

At Chicago, Mensch literally had to stage a campaign of terror to get back his old job as program director of WHBK, a position then held by a woman named Jane Ginsburg, the daughter of the future Supreme Court justice Ruth Bader Ginsburg.

"So I duked it out with her daughter Jane through faculty tribunals to take over the radio station," Mensch said, laughing. "It was some bullshit strategy some of us concocted to wrest control of the station. It got really bitter. But I *had* to be music director—that was my whole connection to the music business. I didn't give a damn about grad school."

Around the time Mensch finished his master's program, Burnstein had convinced Mercury to give him his own punk label. When he needed an assistant to help run things in New York for the label, Blank Records, Burnstein immediately called Mensch.

"Cliff was into Pere Ubu and the Suicide Commandos. Punk was OK—but I just wanted a job. I was more of a metal fan. But I took the job, which paid fifteen thousand dollars a year, and I moved back to New York, which is where I had to be as label manager. That whole scene was happening around CB-GB's, Irving Plaza. I saw Talking Heads, met my first girlfriend there. When we broke up she'd be playing Elvis Costello songs and I'd be playing Aerosmith songs."

Pere Ubu didn't turn out to be the Sex Pistols. The bean counters at Mercury pulled the plug on Blank Records, and for a while Burnstein managed Ubu. But soon afterward he was back at his old A&R job at Mercury. By then, Mensch had moved on to Leber-Krebs, then one of the biggest management companies in rock, whose clients included Aerosmith and Ted Nugent.

A major booking agent and executive with the William Morris Agency, Steve Leber had been involved with putting together the mother of all clone plays, *Beatlemania*. And David Krebs, the firm's idea man, would later be one of the people behind the now-defunct magazine *The National Times*.

"You'd go to David Krebs's office and you'd sit there and tell him who you were," Mensch recalled. "The phone would ring constantly and he'd be talking for four hours, during which time you got maybe thirty minutes with him. You'd get up to go and Krebs would say, 'No, no, sit down. I'll be right with you.' I was very impressed. There were lights everywhere, everyone was running around. Krebs was a smart guy, but too smart for his own good."

"Krebs was really imaginative—he had a hundred ideas a day that were often original. Five of them might be brilliant," said Burnstein, who worked there for two years also. "What he needed was a guy to tell him the other ninety-five would not work out well. If Krebs was a dreamer, Leber was the ball-buster."

"People had offices in the hallways," said Mensch. "It was an insane place."

In the spring of 1978, Krebs offered Mensch a position as tour accountant for Aerosmith. "Well, that was one of my favorite bands of all time," said Mensch. "So I called up Burnstein at Mercury and asked what a tour accountant was." A week later, Mensch was on the road with one of hard rock's most notorious acts.

"I settled the shows—got the money from the promoters and mailed it back to Krebs. I'd handle the receipts and give people drug money and personal money. I had an Aerosmith credit card. I got laid a lot," Mensch said, grinning. "This wasn't the height of the band's popularity. This was five drug-crazed people whose wives hated each other's guts. There was more cocaine than you'd see in an entire lifetime. And by this time they were throwing things at each other. Two of the band members got divorced on my tour. I saw the band break up for the first time. I saw all these vicious fights."

While touring with Aerosmith, Mensch met AC/DC, the Australian hard-rock band that was opening some of the shows.

Fronted by leather-lunged singer Bon Scott and powered by Angus and Malcolm Young, two Scots-born brothers who played blazing fast guitar, the group wasn't famous yet. But Mensch was in awe. "I'd never seen anything like it before. If you think Angus Young is fast now, he was twice as quick as he is now."

Mensch was doing marketing for Krebs and trying to figure out his future when Burnstein called telling him he'd just signed the Scorpions, a German metal band.

"Cliff said he'd be their A&R man and that I should quit and be their manager," said Mensch. "The Scorpions wanted someone really heavy as their manager. But even then, these guys were in their early thirties. Some of them had no hair. And they spoke German."

While Mensch tried to convince the Scorpions' lawyer that he was management material, he got a call from Malcolm Young of AC/DC. The band Mensch loved was having problems with its manager, which was making it difficult to finish its album, *Highway to Hell*.

"Malcolm said, 'Peter, we don't know where the money's gone. Do you want to come on the road with us and be our tour accountant?' But I said I already had a job. Then he called me up again, after they'd finished *Highway to Hell*, and said, 'Come to New York.' "

By June of 1979, about two months after he'd gotten the call from Young, Mensch was managing AC/DC. But Krebs was pissed off. "He'd wanted to manage AC/DC himself—he'd put them on the Aerosmith tour," said Mensch. "But now this upstart, me, got the deal. Anyway, Krebs made a deal with me. He gave me a piece of his piece. Then I told him I wanted to manage the Scorpions, too. By this time, Krebs was so happy, he would've let me manage the Turds."

Having gone from promotion to A&R to managing, Burnstein had learned a few lessons. If he hadn't been the most effective A&R man, it was because he'd fallen into the trap of trying to sign bands he thought people would like. "But now I had a new resolve in 1979, which was: sign what I like, forget about the rest."

Burnstein had signed the Scorpions, but even more interesting was the new generation of British metal. A voracious reader, Burnstein regularly scoured all the British and American music magazines. He'd visited England, where heavy-metal discos were all the rage. And then he heard an EP by a group called Def Leppard. The record was so good that in September 1979, Burnstein flew over to England, where he met Mensch and the two checked out Def Leppard's show in Wolverhampton.

"Burnstein's theory," said Mensch, "was that whoever their manager was, we should get rid of him. And by the fifth show, Richard Allen, all of fifteen, came up to me and said, would I mind going to the Def Leppard dressing room and hanging out there?" Three months later, the band asked Mensch to manage them.

Knowing he had to be based in Europe, Mensch moved to London and rented a flat. He was all of twenty-six then and managing four bands, including the Michael Schenker Group, which was led by the former lead guitarist of UFO. In less than a year, he'd gone from making fifteen thousand dollars a year to pulling down more than three hundred thousand dollars a year.

"I was envious of Peter," Burnstein admitted. "One day he's working for me, the next day he's a tour accountant for Aerosmith and the next day he's managing four bands. I mean, I was five years older, but here he was, on the fast track. He was kicking ass."

"Michael Schenker was my roommate," Mensch recalled of his early years in London, where he had his own town house. "Def Leppard would come by the house, and so would AC/DC, so for about a year and a half I was in heaven. *Highway to Hell* was double platinum. But I was nervous, all by myself in a flat in London. I used to hang out with [record producer] Mutt Lange and I'd talk to Cliff all the time. I met a woman who ended up being my first wife."

When *Back in Black*, the next AC/DC album, came out, it

was even bigger than *Highway to Hell*. And each Scorpions album did big business. Def Leppard was beginning to break. By 1980, Mensch had no trouble convincing Burnstein to join him at Leber-Krebs, working the bands in America. But what seemed like a good move soon turned sour. When Mensch had a falling-out with AC/DC, who fired him in 1981, Krebs decided he no longer needed to pay Burnstein and Mensch their AC/DC commission anymore.

"As a team we were managing four acts and getting a percentage—a third of the commission from four bands," said Burnstein. "And AC/DC was huge, so they owed us a lot of money. They felt they shouldn't have to pay us on AC/DC because of the falling-out. Our position was that Peter had picked the band—that was the most important thing. It always is. For that alone he should've gotten his third. And on our watch AC/DC had sold five million albums with *Back in Black* in the United States."

The upshot was that Mensch and Burnstein were fired and took Leber and Krebs to court under the arbitration clauses they had in their contracts. "Our fathers are lawyers, so that kind of stuff was second nature to us," said Burnstein. "And in arbitration we won. We got all the money that was coming to us."

"Each one of our acts had a key-man clause, which said that if we were no longer involved, they could leave. AC/DC soon left—they hated everyone," Mensch said. "But Def Leppard stayed with us. And the Scorpions—even though I moved there for them and Cliff signed them, they said no to us. They stayed with Leber and Krebs, and that blew my mind."

Burnstein and Mensch didn't take long to figure out their next move: Both wanted to be in business for themselves. Yet when Q Prime was formed in 1982—the name is a mathematical conceit on prime numbers—Def Leppard was their only act. It was a hard time psychologically. The company didn't earn a penny of income while Def Leppard recorded *Pyromania*. But the day *Pyromania* came out it exploded, following the success of a previous Def Leppard record that was selling five thousand copies a week with sudden MTV exposure. Eventually, *Pyromania* sold ten million copies worldwide.

All the same, Burnstein was still living like a student in an apartment in Brooklyn Heights. Each day he'd go into Manhattan and do as much business as he could. When he got home there would be thirty messages on the machine, which he'd dutifully answer late into the night. The money from Def Leppard didn't go into BMWs and silk suits. Instead, Burnstein hired an assistant in 1983 to sit in his apartment and answer his phone. A year later, he bought a house in Hoboken.

Q Prime's next breakthrough, in 1984, was signing Metallica—a group destined to become even bigger than Def Leppard. But Burnstein and Mensch weren't Metallica's first managers. In what would prove to be a pattern, Metallica came to Q Prime on the rebound, unhappy with its previous manager, Jon Zazula.

"Nobody wants to know us who never had a manager before. It takes a bad experience with somebody," said Burnstein. "We took Metallica over when the second Megaforce record came out. But they were hardly stars. And I was putting out a lot of fires. They had so many skeletons in the closet it was unbelievable. Zazula was supposed to hand over any agreements that would be a further obligation on Metallica, but as time went by all these people would come out of the woodwork. Every day I'd get a call. Somebody in Rochester would call saying, 'The band owes me two points because they used my studio.' Well, the papers were in order and we bought them out. A guy who used to live with Metallica said he was promised a point, and we ended up giving him half a point. And Lars [Ulrich] himself wasn't completely forthcoming about things."

Once all the fires were put out, Burnstein and Mensch set about breaking Metallica. Though the typical Metallica song clocked in at six to eight minutes and had a ferocity that barred it from ever getting on radio, Burnstein and Mensch never once asked the band to alter its vision.

"We realized Metallica was great, but they weren't going to get on the air next to Bon Jovi," said Burnstein. "So why should we beat ourselves to death trying to do something that's impossible? We just let the mystique continue to build. Then, when it got to a certain level, we were able to actually fight it out with the Bon Jovis."

"The first record we worked from scratch was Metallica," Mensch said. "And it's not that we didn't want to get them on MTV. We did. But nobody would let them on."

"The band's rise was extraordinary—outside the realm of normal media exposure," said Burnstein.

"They never opened for anyone of significance until they got to play on the Ozzy Osbourne tour. This was when *Master of Puppets* was out," said Mensch. "It helped a lot. It showed that it wasn't just a speed-metal thing. Here was Metallica playing with Ozzy Osbourne. They weren't slashing themselves with razors. The promoters were prepared for the worst, because Slayer would've just come through before, and every bathroom was destroyed, entire buildings trashed. They expected the same thing from Metallica, but they didn't get it."

It was taken as axiomatic that a band had to have great videos and get on MTV to reach huge audiences, but Metallica had sold more than seven million records before a video of the band ever appeared on MTV. And when the group did get on MTV, it was in a groundbreaking video.

"The first video we made, 'One,' took scenes from a movie that was the most jarring film I'd seen in a decade—*Johnny Got His Gun*," recalled Burnstein. The book, written by Dalton Trumbo, was about a World War I American soldier who wakes up to find he has no arms, no legs and no face. It was a horrific book, maybe the most powerful antiwar novel ever written. When the band told him they wanted to write a song about a guy who had no arms and no legs, Burnstein told them to read Trumbo's book. And when it came time to make the video, Burnstein suggested using actual footage from the film.

"Here we were mixing images of Metallica in the rehearsal room with scenes of a guy with no arms and no legs trapped on the hospital bed. They [MTV] never had a video like that," Burnstein said. "Plus with real dialogue from the movie."

"We had a surgeon talking about a guy shaking his head. And it was perfectly synced with Metallica, who shook their heads," said Mensch.

A week before "One" was aired on MTV, Metallica got an invitation to perform on the Grammys telecast. The two events couldn't have been timed more perfectly.

"MTV was afraid of playing 'One'—Metallica was heavier than anything the channel had ever played," said Burnstein. "But a day after they played it, it was number two requested. And then it was the number one requested video." Sales of Metallica's album ... *And Justice for All* soared, jumping a million in less than six months; the album eventually sold six million copies. But it was 1991's eponymous "black" record, which has sold more than eleven million copies, that pushed Metallica into superstardom.

"Cliff and Peter think ahead. They used Metallica's early work to lay the foundation for the latest album," said Mark Ryder, a onetime Epic marketing executive who left the label to do marketing for Q Prime. "By any other label's measure, ... *And Justice for All* was a huge success. But they constantly do things differently. When it came time to do a tour they asked, 'What can we do to make it more unique?' So they came up with the snake pit idea. Which was genius."

"That was Peter's idea," said Burnstein, "and it was brilliant. No one had ever done that before."

For the band's international tour, the Metallica stage was a giant triangle with an X-shaped catwalk above it. In the middle of the triangle was another little triangle, called the snake pit. Fifty kids were allowed into it every night with tape recorders and camcorders to do whatever they wanted.

"The kids were in the middle of the stage every night," said Ryder. "The band walked around these kids all night. It allowed for gigantic radio promotions, which allowed for gigantic airplay. And this was true to Metallica, because they're a fan's band."

Metallica had become so huge that Q Prime had to keep track of all the people and companies trying to exploit the band's music and fame. One afternoon, when I was spending the day with Burnstein and Mensch, one of their assistants walked in with a yellow plastic Metallica wall light. Burnstein took one look at the schlocky light, now plugged in, and shook his head.

"We're passing on this. This is the kind of stuff we get all the time. But I have a little sideline where I get money from people ripping off Metallica," Burnstein said with a mischievous smile. "There are constant requests for licensing the band's music. Well, we got a request from *The Jackie Thomas Show* to use the intro from Metallica's 'Enter Sandman' for their theme music. It came in at the end of last September and I was somewhat interested in it because the money was very good. It could've been a hundred thousand dollars a year for the guys as long as this is on the air. And the show would only be using the instrumental parts. But before I get a chance to reply to this, they withdraw the offer—literally over the weekend. Well, *The Jackie Thomas Show* comes on the air the next day and I get five hundred calls saying, 'Wow, they're using Metallica as the theme music.' We check it out and it's not Metallica they're using but a soundalike thing. So I chased them and we wound up getting some money out of them."

Burnstein had to do the same thing for the film *Army of Darkness*, whose producers had asked to use two Metallica songs for the trailer to the film. "So [Metallica drummer] Lars Ulrich is watching some movie one night and the fucking trailer comes up for *Army of Darkness*, and note for note it's our song. So I went after them and got some money. I do it myself—I don't want to spend legal fees. I call up the person in business affairs and tell them they have no rights to use the songs. And as soon as you tell them they have no rights, they get nervous. Then you make a deal with them."

By 1988, Q Prime's reputation was so strong that the Rolling Stones hired Burnstein and Mensch as consultants for the band's Steel Wheels tour. Though both managers soft-pedaled it at first, the experience had an enormous impact. As consultants, Q Prime did everything from suggesting the order of singles and video directors to commenting on the Stones' live show and working the records.

"We suggested songs they should drop. We made them meet and greet, which was the opposite of what they'd done the last tour," said Mensch. "The Stones wanted our record experience, and they wanted to make sure they were doing stuff right live. I dealt with them like they were these schmoes in a room. They listened to a certain degree. It was probably more a validation of what they wanted to do.

"We thought it would be good for the résumé, because Jagger and Richards are the smartest guys in the business," said Burnstein. "This was like going to school, except they were going to pay us."

"I now know the Stones tour is the biggest event of my musical life," said Mensch. "It'll never again be topped. The sheer magnitude of what they could accomplish because they were the Stones was amazing. Instead of playing one night at a stadium, they played three. They could've played five nights at Shea Stadium. It's like, you think you're rich and then you meet the sultan of Brunei and you see his jet, his mansion, his yacht. And if you care about that stuff, you see that you're just an ant on a hill."

Right before the actual stadium tour started, the Stones set up all of their gear in Nassau Coliseum, a twenty-thousand-seat arena on Long Island, and did a complete run-through of their songs.

"It was just the Stones going through their whole set," said Burnstein, who brought along his family. "They weren't trying to posture. We had been involved in picking their songs, and there it was, one song after another. And it was clear that without the big light show and the whole grandeur that would follow, the songs were absolutely brilliant—simplicity themselves. But suddenly you realized that seeing them here, they had written these elegant, simply timeless rock songs. I have never seen a better concert in my life—and this was not a concert, it was running through twenty-five songs. But it was a real revelation, because I described the experience to Metallica and they picked up on it. They suddenly realized that they could do that as well. They realized their songs didn't have to be needlessly complicated. If they could distill one element in each song, they could make a more powerful statement. And Metallica bought into that. And it's made them an even more amazing band."

"A lot of managers are shortsighted. They think of the quick buck," Lars Ulrich told me one day in August when I asked him to talk about being managed by Q Prime. "But ever since we started with these guys, there's always been one law: Do what's right for you long term, not what's going to put the most money in your bank account tomorrow. Honesty was beaten into our heads from the first time we met them. And that's rubbed off on us in all of our dealings."

In fact, Ulrich couldn't forget the first encounter with Q Prime. It was back in 1983 when Def Leppard's *Pyromania* was the biggest record in the universe.

"Me and [lead guitarist] Kirk Hammett were standing in a record store somewhere looking at the *Pyromania* record jacket and it said: 'Management, Q Prime Inc.' I remember this like it was this morning. And I remember saying to Kirk, 'Wow—Q Prime Inc. That sounds heavy.' I had some vision in my mind of a fucking boardroom up on the seventy-second floor of the Rockefeller Center with twelve guys in suits directing the biggest rock and roll band in the world and figuring out all the moves. Anyway, a year later, in the summer of 1984, we got a phone call from Mensch and Burnstein and we're fuckin' freakin'—doing backflips. We were out on the East Coast doing a show, and we were still managed by Jon Zazula, but we were going to secretly meet with Burnstein, because Mensch was then in London.

"Comes the day we were going to meet him, we got directions to his house, which was in Hoboken. But we didn't know anything about New York; Hoboken could've been New Jersey's Beverly Hills. So we were driving around in this skanky section of New Jersey, which looked like the rough areas of where we were living in Oakland. We thought we'd come to the nice streets, but when we found the street and the house, we thought we'd written the directions down wrong. We're parking our car and there's a Puerto Rican street gang looking like they're ready to jump us. And we thought, 'No, this is not right.'

"We rang the doorbell anyway, thinking that maybe one of the front guys for Q Prime would take us to where Burnstein really lived, but the door opens and there was this little scrawny guy, who looked like Rasputin's long-lost brother. He sticks out his wet, limp hand and says, "Hi, I'm Cliff Burnstein.' And I nearly fuckin' fell down the staircase I'd just walked up. That was one of the most shocking moments of my life."

Ulrich remembered Burnstein's Hoboken house/office as a dump. The minute he and Hammett walked in, the phone rang and Burnstein went to another room. When Ulrich and Hammett looked through a pile of nearby mail, they saw letters from Def Leppard.

"So this was the right place. But talk about shattering your illusions. We knew then that this was something different. There was never greed involved. So it became apparent early on that this was not about a quick buck. And that this was a place where Metallica belonged."

One night Burnstein invited me over to his house in Kew Gardens, a prosperous section of Queens with tree-lined neighborhoods, excellent schools and a large Indian population. The house was furnished sparsely with folk art. The den was lined with thousands of records and CDs, the shelves arranged alphabetically by genre—"I'm an anal-type guy," Burnstein said. There was music by everyone from soul singer Swamp Dogg and late-sixties funk great Arlester Christian to protorocker Del Shannon and country singer Kitty Wells. My eyes came to rest on Burnstein's extensive collection of records by Swamp Dogg, a gravelly-voiced soul singer who specialized in hilarious tales of bedding down women.

"I have a lot of Swamp Dogg. Someday I'd like Metallica to

do a Swamp Dogg song. That would fuck people up good," Burnstein said, offering me some home-cooked brownies. Soon, Hash, one of Q Prime's new bands, would arrive and Burnstein was going to play them some songs they might do as B sides on their Elektra debut. But as Burnstein rummaged through his CDs he answered a question I'd put to him the day before: Who were the performers that had amazed him?

"I saw everybody—once. I saw Jerry Lee Lewis in Chicago. There was sweat pouring out of his body. He was very thin, not an ounce of fat. It was a great performance, but he had this flunky manager. I have to say that era disabused me of hero worship. I got to work at a record company and got to meet these people who I had idolized, like Tom T. Hall, one of my all-time favorites. He wrote probably six dozen great songs, but when I met him he was going all to hell. He had a two-night stand. The first night I talked to him for half an hour. And the second night he didn't even recognize me. I remembered he knocked some drink into someone's electric piano. Plus he talked in clichés, like Rod McKuen.

"In the midseventies I was in Detroit and we visited *Creem* magazine and saw Lester Bangs. Well, Lester and I went to see Captain Beefheart that night, probably at the Fox Theatre. After the show we went up to talk to him. He was there with his wife. And I remember he'd ask her, 'How many poems did I write last week?' And his wife would go, 'Seventeen, Don.'[5] And he'd ask, 'How many landscape paintings did I do?' And she'd go, 'Twenty-seven, Don,'—like she was responsible for stating his output. He kept us there, talking for hours. He was desperate. Finally we had to go and Beefheart was out in the hall with us. We were walking through the garage and he was in the hotel's garage with us. He couldn't let go. He was so desperate. It was sad."

Just then the doorbell rang and it was Hash. Burnstein offered the four young musicians brownies and led everyone

[5] Beefheart's real name is Don Van Vliet.

into the den, where he immediately sifted through a stack of CDs he'd pulled. Without telling anyone the names of the groups or the songs, Burnstein began what turned into a two-hour listening party. He played a bubblegum garage-pop ditty called "The Little Black Egg" by the Nightcrawlers, followed by Sopwith Camel's "Hello Hello." But no one in Hash seemed to respond to either song, so Burnstein pulled some more CDs. He put on "Potato Chip" by the Shadows of Knight and followed it with the Del-Vetts' "Last Time Around." But when neither cut made a deep impression, Burnstein put on a Del Shannon CD.

"This guy died a tragic death, but this is a good illustration of his twisted mind. He had the most deep-set eyes I've ever seen."

"He sounds like Neil Young," Aaron Collins, Hash's bassist, said midway through Shannon's "Sister Isabelle."

"We want something funky," said Seth Abelson, the group's singer.

"OK, you want funky, we'll get you something funky. This guy is known as Dyke—Dyke and the Blazers. His real name is Arlester Christian and he died a tragic death. A gunshot wound."

"What's this about playing us music by guys who all died tragic deaths?" asked Abelson. But Burnstein didn't answer—he was busy putting the CD in the player.

"All right, here we go—the funkiest guy of all time," he said.

As the band listened to "We Got More Soul," a raw slice of gutbucket soul, I noticed Collins and Abelson rolling their eyes. But Burnstein was tapping his feet, lost in the groove.

"Dyke wrote 'Funky Broadway,'" Burnstein said when the song was finished.

Dyke was funky, but *too* funky, as it turned out. "I think you should only do drug songs," Burnstein said with a wink and a smile, putting on "Some Kind of Wonderful," a shot of Stax/Volt-era soul by the Soul Brothers Six.

"This is *savage*. This fuckin' *stomps*," he said, looser now than he'd been all day, happy to be riffling through his collection with a bunch of kids who weren't even born when the music was recorded. When "Some Kind of Wonderful" ended, Abelson smiled and said: "That's *too* black."

"Hey, Grand Funk Railroad did that—and they're white," Burnstein said. "You've got to expand your horizons."

"OK, here's another song. This is the original, but it was also done by a white group—the Human Beinz—and now it's on every commercial on TV. And if it's on a commercial, you know it's fuckin' good." Out of the speakers came the sanctified soul of the Isley Brothers' "Nobody but Me," Ronnie Isley's wild tenor cutting through a bed of lean, mean funk. It was getting late and I had to meet someone. I left as Burnstein was putting on Curtis Mayfield's "Pusherman."

The next morning, when I showed up at Q Prime, Burnstein had a big grin. "After you left I played Hash 'Trouble Man' [by Marvin Gaye], but they liked 'Pusherman' more. Then at the end of the night I pulled out my Blowfly collection and they were just boogying. They ended up picking 'Secret Love,' a single by Doris Day from the movie *Calamity Jane,* to do as a B side.

"See, Seth knows all these musicals because he sang them in high school. But he said, 'I'm gonna really have to sit down and work on this one because it's all jazz chords with weird changes.' The backups are 'Pusherman' and Spencer Davis Group's 'I'm a Man.' I played them all this midsixties garageband pop and Seth said, 'We need something that sounds black. When we do it it sounds white. But if we start white, it's no good.' "

Even though he'd been fired by him, Mensch considered David Krebs one of his gurus. It was Krebs who had told him the mark of a great manager: "He said that if you get one act that becomes a headliner it's luck, but if you got a second one, just maybe it was skill."

All the same, Burnstein and Mensch learned more what *not* to do at Leber-Krebs than vice versa. "They handled a lot of money themselves; they had their own accounting office. But that was something we never wanted to do," Burnstein said one day when we were talking about the art of managing. "They always wound up getting sued. We wanted to keep our acts' moneys separate. They tried to do too much. And they put too much money into some of their bands. They had a club and threw money into that. And they had sixteen employees—way too many people. People were worried about getting their paychecks all the time. But Leber and Krebs were sitting there on Long Island with nice houses, big money and lots in the bank. As soon as the money would come in they would pull it out and everything would be run on a heart-attack basis."

Krebs and Leber had separate offices and handled their own acts, but Burnstein and Mensch vowed never to do that. "That's why Peter and I operate out of two couches in the same office," said Mensch. "We each know what the other one is doing."

Most managers served as agents. Their bands screamed at them from the road. But Q Prime actually managed its bands. And if Burnstein and Mensch had a reputation for running things on the cheap, it was probably because both had seen musicians' lives destroyed because of big-spending managers who never thought past the next few months.

"You've got to think what it cost to keep the whole enterprise afloat over a period of years while you're on your way up," Burnstein said, excited now. "What does it take to house one band?"

"You can't tell them to live at home with their parents. They'll say, 'My parents live in Kentucky,' " Mensch said.

"So, after taxes, what's the minimum a band will take home?" Burnstein said. "Twenty thousand dollars a year, which is twelve thousand a year after taxes. So that's twenty thousand dollars gross. For a five-member band that's a hundred thousand dollars a year. Where does it come from? People are making a record every two years, so over a two-year cycle it's two hundred thousand dollars just to keep everybody in peanuts."

"And record companies don't want to give any money," said Mensch, who happened to be then working on renegotiating Metallica's deal. "They give you two hundred thousand dollars to make the record. What do you do the rest of the eight months of the year? It's your problem? Sometimes if you're powerful, you can convince record companies to house and feed the bands so they're not huddling underneath an overpass."

"Some managers will put out the money themselves, say, two hundred thousand dollars. But if they're inexperienced, at a certain point the burn rate on their money is so severe they have to give up," said Burnstein. "If it's the guy who got lucky, who decided to have several people in his office and five acts at a hundred thousand dollars each, that guy's going to go out of business. One of the ways he goes out of business, as he starts burning the money on everyone else, is by going to his big act and saying, 'What you guys need to do is play summer festivals.' Or: 'There's a perfume you could sponsor—' "

"So he's whoring on his own act," Mensch said.

"And before long the act doesn't bring in the income it used to."

"That happened with Journey's manager. The group's record stopped selling, and Cliff and I always remembered the day we went to their offices and announced who we were. Well, the woman went through a two-column list of people and extensions. The only success they *had* was Journey, but they had maybe forty people working for them—ridiculous. And within two years of Journey's *Raised on Radio* record they were history—down to six people."

The annals of rock were full of managers and performers who had attained dizzying heights only to fall far and hard. I mentioned the rapper M.C. Hammer, whose debut had sold more than fifteen million copies, making him a superstar with lots of disposable cash—until he decided to spend it in splashy ways.

"I feel sorry for M.C. Hammer," Burnstein said. "If Hammer had come in here two years ago and said, 'Hey, my record is selling ten million copies. What should I do?,' we'd say,

'Don't start your own record company. Don't invest in the fuckin' racehorses. The money comes and goes, but you could lose it all tomorrow, so take it easy. If it turns out you're absolutely brilliant, you can spend the money in five years. But don't spend it *now*, before you have the first five years locked up.' Most artists start in their late teens—it's not as if they've gone to business school. They're at everyone's mercy. Sting just lost his ass—his accountant allegedly just stole five million pounds[6] from him. Pink Floyd went through that. Creedence Clearwater went through that. It's fraud. It's scary. I feel sorry for Hammer. He got lucky, he got huge and now he's pissed it all away. And he'll never have another chance."

The day before I left New York, a slow day for Burnstein and Mensch, we decided to take in a Yankees game. It was a hot, muggy afternoon and the tabloids all had screaming headlines about a local serial killer named Joel Rifkin who'd been picked up by police. Less than ten yards away from the entrance to Q Prime a three-card monte player was hustling rubes out of twenty-dollar bills with the help of three or four shills who won each time they played.

"I can't believe there's someone left in New York who could fall for that," Burnstein said as he handed me a subway token from the bag of them he carried.

Yankee Stadium was jammed when we got there. The Yankees were on an incredible winning streak and were tied for second place with the Detroit Tigers, so a mob of fans had turned out to cheer on the Bronx Bombers. Our seats were less than thirty feet from the dugout, closer to home than first base.

"Great seats," said Mark Ryder, who'd come along, too.

---

[6] The British press set the amount at six million dollars, but Sting said the figure was much higher than that, according to a May 27, 1993, piece in *Rolling Stone*.

"Yeah," said Mensch, who was wearing a specially commissioned T-shirt, done by Pushead, of Mets pitcher and Metallica fan Sid Fernandez.

When the Yankees came out the crowd exploded, but Mensch and Burnstein weren't moved. Each was busy preparing his scorecard.

"We hate the Yankees," Burnstein said a moment later, with withering sarcasm. "Peter's a Mets fan and I'm a White Sox fan. The Yankees are fat cats. We're just here because we're in one of these rotisserie leagues."

Each spring, Burnstein, Mensch and their two other "team owners" went down to Florida for four days to scout out players. Typically, they would take in eight games—a day game and a night game each day—eat ribs and bond. "We do it like it's a rock tour," Burnstein said, "but when we get back I'm the guy that crunches in all the numbers."

When Yankee relief pitcher Steve Howe was announced, Mensch laughed. Howe had been in and out of numerous drug-treatment programs for cocaine addiction. There had even been an attempt to kick him out of the league at one point. But he was still pitching.

"He just got out of another clinic," Mensch said. "I don't think any of our players are on drugs."

"And we wouldn't want to get a guy who's coming off of drugs," said Burnstein, "because if he was doing drugs before and he was doing well, it's very possible that taking his drugs away will harm his performance. The same thing with the bands. A studio musician told me that behind every great song is a great drug."

The Yankees came out swinging hard and quickly took a commanding lead, but none of Burnstein's or Mensch's drafted players were doing particularly well. Wade Boggs was up at the plate.

"He's a good hitter, but he doesn't hit home runs. The only way you get points in our league is when you hit home runs."

Ryder, who was talking to the office on a portable phone he'd brought along, handed it to Burnstein.

"Bruce Hornsby is freaking out. His single is having a tough week," Burnstein said after hanging up. "But I want to have time to talk to him and this just isn't the place."

When there was a lull in the action, Mensch went off to get hot dogs and Cokes. I asked Burnstein about Primosphere.

"The government has come up with a new frequency band. Essentially what this means is that one day we'll have radios with AM, FM and the satellite band, so you'll be able to hear the same station everywhere in the United States. You'll be able to shove a number of stations into these frequencies, so you'll have a system where you wouldn't have to worry about small audiences for specific stations. You wouldn't be competing with yourself. Just like cable TV was able to make big money on slivers of audience, we should be able to do the same with radio."

Called Digital Audio Radio Service, satellite radio would operate at a frequency band between 2310 and 2360 megahertz. Burnstein still couldn't believe that only four groups had applied by the December cutoff date.

"I just read about it—it was public information, but the FCC was very low-key about it. And the government is a real bureaucracy. Most people didn't get it. Even today, most people I talk to think of it as cable. But it's not cable. It's satellite broadcast. I think it'll take two years to get it licensed, and it'll take a minimum of three years to build and launch the satellite. It'll cost four hundred to five hundred million dollars for any one system. Right now it's a big chess game. But I'd like to program some of the channels and have a say in it."

Q Prime was so serious about Primosphere that it had hired a public-relations firm to generate publicity. "We've done some interviews. There's going to be a piece in *Newsday*. And people came out of the woodwork. We got calls from venture capitalists. Radio is a low-tech business, but this is a high-tech way of delivering it. A lot of radio listening is mobile. That's the market I want. And if you can listen to it in a car and on a Walkman, why not have it at home? The idea is to be consistent on each station. If somebody gets tired of listening to jazz, encourage them to listen to the classical station or the soul station. You don't care if they move around, just as long as they stay within your system, which could have twenty stations. In Peoria, they don't have a classical station. They don't have a jazz station. No one can afford to buy a station in a local market and put on advertising that will only appeal to one percent of the population. You can't charge enough for your spots. But if you get a small share of a national market, you can do great. MTV has a .5 share. Give me a .5 share and I'll make a lot of money, too."

Burnstein's interest wasn't merely financial. Both he and Mensch loved radio. "I grew up on AM radio," Burnstein said. "In Chicago I could hear everything at night. I could hear WBZ from Boston, WLAC from Nashville, KAAY from Little Rock, WABC from New York. I heard CKLW from Detroit, KYW from Cleveland, KWK from St. Louis and WKBW from Buffalo. I was listening to soul and rock and blues. That's why my record collection is the way it is."

The purchases of the three California radio stations were the beginning of a long-range plan Burnstein and Mensch had. The Bakersfield station, which played rock, had cost $1.5 million. Q Prime had financed the Fresno station, which played classical music, from scratch, investing about $1.25 million in it. And the San Luis Obispo station, which played soft adult contemporary music, had cost just over $1 million.

"We bought it too high—it's probably worth seven hundred fifty thousand dollars. We're not making any money on any of these stations because of the recession in California. But we're in this for the long haul."

Just then, Mike Stanley hit a grand-slam home run, giving the Yankees a huge lead. Even Mensch and Burnstein cheered.

"It would be nice if we could do something like this," Burnstein said. "We're putting a lot of money into Primosphere. If everything works it'll revolutionize the way people hear music in America, and I'd like to be in on that. If you like music, who wouldn't like a hand in saying what people will listen to and how they'll listen to it? As a manager you're commissioned; you don't own anything. But with this we could be a builder. And that would mean something."

CHAPTER 8

Living in Exile

Benny Medina

J ust because you were raised on black fundamentalist teachings doesn't necessarily mean you grew up in some rocking Pentecostal church where folks fell to the floor and started gurgling in tongues.

"I was a Jehovah's Witness, and that didn't imbue much musical spirit into you," Benny Medina, the head of black music at Warner Bros. Records, told me one night when we were eating dinner at an upscale health food restaurant in West Hollywood called Nowhere. "This was a *fear* religion. I grew up with Armageddon pending. I know that at one point there was an attempt to possess me. I could *feel* it—and I was paralyzed with fear. The Jehovah's Witnesses based itself on the fact that the world was coming to an end. And I remembered the world was supposed to be coming to an end in 1975, which was when I was supposed to graduate from high school."

Medina smiled and took a sip of chardonnay, his gaze bearing down on me. He had mocha-colored skin, wide sideburns and a lean, angular face that sometimes gave him the fierce look of a wolverine and at other times, when he laughed, made him seem like a mischievous child. He was fresh from a two-hour workout; his muscles rippled underneath his shirt. But it was his eyes that held me: a burning stare that both sized you up and, if you could meet it head on, accepted you—without necessarily granting any trust.

"We were doing Bible studies every Saturday. There I was, getting the word in a way that scared the hell out of me—that made me *fear* demonic possession. You were promised the chance for everlasting *life*, but before that was to occur there was going to be everlasting *damnation*. The hands of God were going to come up from the Earth"—Medina pushed his palms up—"and drag the world down. The only survivors were going to be the ones who were good. That scared me to death. And I'm *still* too young to challenge it. I *do* see the world in a state of deterioration. But this was like the nuclear holocaust—without the bomb. I'm sure this is the reason I retreated early and didn't want to talk to many people."

His aunt Erma was the one who exposed him to the Jehovah's Witness teachings. She and her husband, an artist by the name of Rozzell Sykes, took custody of the Medina kids, five brothers and sisters, after their mother died suddenly in 1961.

"When I went to court to get the kids," Rozzell Sykes said, remembering the trip to McLaren Hall, a juvenile detention center in Los Angeles, "their father didn't offer no fight. He was incarcerated. He was a musician—played his ass off. Played with Sonny Stitt and Harold Land. Played right here. But he messed with that *horse.* He couldn't leave that horse alone."

"Life started for me at seven and came close to ending at eight" was the way Medina put it. "That's when my mom died. But she used to encourage our creativity. We used to have talent shows. I'd sing Gene Chandler songs—'Get my hat, I'm checking out/Because you and my friends really hurt my pride." I knew that song and [Marvin Gaye's] 'Hitch Hike.' I'd do lip-syncing onstage. And I loved the Lloyd Thaxton show. It was a TV show out here, a local show, like *American Bandstand,* and they had a great lip-syncing segment. Lloyd was a white guy who used to have soul musicians.

"I was around five kids who were really talented. My older brother was a really, really good singer. My older sister was a really good singer and my younger sister was a guitar player. They all had more talent than me. Mom must've told them they all were special. She had to have. But there was so much shit that happened between the ages of eight and fourteen—and I don't know all of it. I'm afraid to talk about it, but I have to. I know that if my mother had lived, everything would've been great. I know that."

Children who are abandoned and abused react in different ways. Some become victims for life, violent, needy, self-destructive. Others, forced to become premature adults, anesthetize themselves, emotionally shutting down, constructing their own fragmented memories, obliterating what's too painful. When you ask Medina about his childhood, he talks about being dragged away to McLaren Hall, separated from his brothers and sisters, and then bouncing around from one foster home to the next before the Sykeses took the children to their house. But Bonita Medina, Benny's older sister, clearly remembered what happened to all of them, and her account of their early years differs in many ways from Benny's.

"I was six and Benny was three when my mother died in 1961. Benny doesn't remember that, but we had been living in a house in St. Elmo Village[1] with my parents—though it wasn't called that then. Rozzell and Erma were living in a back house. My father was never around—he wasn't a good person—so after my mom died we were left in the house alone. I was six years old and responsible for all of them, and I remember we didn't always have food. We used to eat cornflakes and lettuce sandwiches. But in the evening time we'd walk to my aunt and uncle's house and eat dinner and come back to where we were staying.

"One night we were having dinner at Erma and Rozzell's house and two detectives knocked on the door and said we had to be taken to McLaren Hall. All five of us went and we were all separated because of our ages. Benny thinks we were there for months, but he was mentally and emotionally detached from

---

[1] The Sykeses' house and nine neighboring bungalows would be christened St. Elmo Village in 1969. They represented an attempt to create a community amid the marginalized black ghettos of Los Angeles.

the situation. We were there less than twenty-four hours. That's when Rozzell and Erma came to have us live with them."

Rozzell Sykes had come from St. Louis with a dream of founding an arts colony in Southern California. He soon located ten ramshackle cottages a few blocks East of La Brea Avenue and south of Venice Boulevard, rented one of them and lived out his vision of the artist's life. He sold paintings on the street and anywhere else he could, hustling to keep the wolf away from the door.

"We sold paintings in Hollywood, in South Central, in midcity—wherever we could," recalled Roderick Sykes, Rozzell's nephew, who started living on St. Elmo Street around 1964 and still lives there as a painter, photographer and muralist. "Wherever there was a wall going up, we'd hang out paintings."

It was Rozzell's vision of the bungalows as an art colony, fused with Roderick's vision of them as a community center, that led to St. Elmo Village, named after the street on which the bungalows were located. Almost immediately, the village took on an aura of hipness.

"In the late sixties and seventies we were the place to be," said Roderick Sykes. "At first it was tokenism. But when people came here, they found it was *real.*"

For the African-American community, the village stood as a shining example of black empowerment—a place where underprivileged kids could get away from crime and poverty and possibly become artists or musicians. But it wasn't just black people who went there. TV and record producers, jazz musicians, actors and politicians would show up regularly. Jeff Bridges and Christie Brinkley went to paint there; Tom Bradley, who would become mayor of Los Angeles, and A&M Records cofounder Herb Alpert were St. Elmo regulars. The community's annual street festivals drew thousands of celebrants and got written up in the newspapers.

A mostly self-taught artist, Sykes was given to speaking in aphorisms. In Los Angeles, a city where blacks lived isolated, marooned in vast, tawdry ghettos, his messianic vision won the respect of community leaders as well as the media. But Medina remembered his uncle in a different way—as a kind of wild-eyed fanatic and strict disciplinarian.

"I never remember getting spanked with anything other than an extension cord, an ironing cord or a telephone cord. And I'm talking about getting whipped with that just *walking* into the room. In the dark I got whipped. He'd sit up and wait for me and then I'd hear this whoosh, and the next thing I knew something would be wrapping around my face and my legs. The next day I was supposed to go to school but my legs were mangled. Gone. And I'd fail physical education, which was another reason for him to hurt me.

"If one of us did something and didn't confess to it he would line up all five of us buck naked and whip us all at the same time. I felt like nobody was there for me. I was all alone. And my brothers and sisters were all scared, too."

"We all got whipped—that's when black families really disciplined their children," Bonita said when I asked her about life with the Sykeses. "Nowadays you can't do that. We can all say we were definitely abused. It was a scary time."

"I *had* to beat their ass if they didn't hear me. I *had* to. I had to *paint*, and in this house there were seven of us. *Seven* of us. So there had to be order," Sykes said when I went to visit him one afternoon at St. Elmo Village. It was hard to imagine seven people living in the tiny three-room cottage, whose walls were plastered with photographs and paintings.

"There *had* to be or there would be *chaos*. Benny was adventurous, but I had to curb some of that because his sisters and brothers wanted to follow him—and they *couldn't* do that."

A tall man with a full head of salt-and-pepper hair, Sykes spoke in a booming baritone that gave everything he said the portentous feel of a sermon. If you made the mistake of asking a question out of sequence, he impatiently reprimanded you. It was easy to see him as a younger man, wielding absolute authority in his house.

"When [Benny] out-and-out defied me—that's what *enraged* me. Like coming in when he thought *he* wanted to. He couldn't do that. One day I was sitting in this chair and I said to myself, 'I'm just gonna see what time he's gonna come in tonight.' And about four o'clock in the morning he came. A broom used to be sitting right *here*"—Sykes pointed to a corner right near the door of his three-room cottage. "Well, Benny eased in the door. I let him close the door and I met him with that broom. *Crack*—it scared him more than hurt him. Because brooms don't hurt you. The broom broke. But it scared the *shit* out of him. I told him, 'Benny, this can't work.' You see, the kids of my day, they adhered to Mommy and Daddy or they got backhanded hard. You didn't come up talking about challenging mommies and daddies. The only time I gave my kids hell was when they pushed me to the edge. I told them, '*Stay* away from the tip. Don't get me there.' "

Sykes paused and leaned back in his chair, shaking his head. "As I look back upon it, I did none of them harm. I exposed them to my best. I was blessed by them—five wonderful souls."

But Medina saw little that was wonderful about Sykes or St. Elmo Village, a place where everybody seemed scared of everybody else. "There was so much doubt and so much fear. Man, you'd get your ass *whipped* with an extension cord for something someone *else* did—like not filling up the water pitcher. Now Rozzell's softer and mellowed. But he *knows* I know. I always look people in the eye, and I looked him in the eye back then—and I think that's what he hated.

"I know what he tried to give my brothers and sisters in terms of a home, but I know what he robbed them of in terms of an identity. I just know that they're different people. They're all smarter and more talented than I am, but none of them really used it. I got a message today that I'm frightened of: A guy who's a second engineer called and said, 'Your brother Michael is in big trouble.' I don't even know what kind of trouble. I called my brother, but he wasn't there."

Medina knew about drugs as a child. From the age of twelve, even while he was living with Erma and Rozzell, he had another life, with a bunch of fast friends, as a small-time dope dealer.

"It was fun. We were selling Red Devils [downers] and marijuana cigarettes. And that didn't even seem like a problem. We had Red Light rum punch parties and we had seniors in high school drive us around and take us downtown. We had it all—the beautiful women, the best dope. We were able to pull in things that the seniors came all the way from L.A. High for. They were working for *us*. We were getting our suits tailor-made, buying the fabric and having the Hispanics make them. We had crepe suits, triple-stitching—we were so dope. We had our names monogrammed over the pockets. None of the guys I was hanging with were the guys who smoked the cigarettes, took the reds and drank the whiskey.

"We were block kids and that was our universe. We were industrious and we ruled that universe. But we didn't have guns—that's the difference. When I did get a gun, when I was fifteen, I remember thinking, 'Shit, I don't want it.' But it was available. It wasn't to protect myself. I was twelve when all this started. We were a crew. We didn't call ourselves any particular name, but we all had our personal identities. There was Sonny and there was Louis, Sharkie, Blue and Chin.[2] But only two of them are alive now. And the last time I saw Sonny it was a nightmarish experience.

"That was a couple of years ago, and he'd graduated into being a full-time big man—a dope dealer, scared for his life. I saw him driving down Sunset Boulevard in a Rolls-Royce Corniche. He was heading to the same club I was heading into—a place they didn't even park cars. But they parked *his* car. A place they didn't even have seats to sit at—but Sonny had a booth. He walked in there and he ruled the joint. I thought, '*Damn*, I thought I had it made. I'm in the record business. I know these people.' Well, I got a call the next night from someone saying I should not be hanging out with Sonny. And that night Sonny told me about how he had killed somebody who'd fucked him over in a deal."

---

[2] The names have been changed.

Medina told the story without much emotion. But when he talked about the death of his thirty-eight-year-old brother Gary, his eyes registered some deep pain he'd barely acknowledged. By all accounts, Gary Medina was outgoing and warm—but he was also a heavy drug user. When Benny learned of Gary's death[3] shortly before his own thirty-fifth birthday, he was stunned. Benny had never been close to his brother or the rest of his family, but he went to the funeral.

"There were a lot of people who had not seen Benny in a long time," Erma Sykes would tell me later. "Gary had died January sixteenth, but we had the service a week later. And because Benny's birthday was the next day, we also had a cake for Benny. After the funeral it was like a celebration. It wasn't planned that way—it just happened. But it was a lot for Benny to deal with. He hadn't seen his brother or his family in a long time. It was very overwhelming."

"I saw my family members crying—and I cried because of the pain around me," Medina said. "But I didn't cry because of the death itself. Because that's final. I cried because I saw so many other people crying. And it didn't make me feel any closer. We're not that close because how we were brought up didn't breed any kind of closeness. I know for a fact that I wasn't the one who got on well with the other kids. After my mom died, I was pretty isolated. I was into my poetry writing and my music—until I made some friends on the street."

Medina speared a vegetarian spring roll, took a bite and then took a sip of wine.

"When my mom died my world fell apart, and to this day it's never been put back together. She's the only friend I ever had. The only real consistent form of encouragement and love came from her. I'd still like to have a friend like my mom."

---

[3] The official cause of death was listed as heart failure, but all of the Medinas acknowledged that Gary's death was probably attributable to his use of drugs.

＊　　＊　　＊

I'd first met Medina in the spring of 1993. The Jungle Brothers, one of his rap acts, were in town—they'd just finished doing their new record—and Medina and I were sitting in his Warner Bros. office, talking about his life in music.

"My first really clear memories of idolizing a star was of Marvin Gaye in a sharkskin suit. You'd look at those peg-legged pants—that bug, that flash, that whole thing got me really early," he said. "The records that changed my life were Stevie Wonder's *Innervisions*, Marvin Gaye's *What's Going On*, Earth, Wind and Fire's *That's the Way of the World*, Miles Davis's *Sketches of Spain*. I loved the Beatles and the lyrical content of the Bible.

"All I'd really like to do is get enough time where I can get a Winnebago or some recreational vehicle and drive all around this country. Because I know there'll be somebody playing a harmonica or a guitar on a porch somewhere that everyone in town thinks is the greatest but nobody in L.A. or New York or Atlanta has heard of, which pretty much means nobody's fucked him or her over yet. So there's a certain purity that you might actually get.

"I want to find the young Booker T's and Stevie Wonders and Steve Croppers. Another Muscle Shoals rhythm section. To me, the greatest A&R man—the guy who found the most amazing number of African-American geniuses—was John Hammond, a white man from a wealthy family who was digging around in Harlem. He was not the guy who should've been hanging in Harlem. But look what he pulled out: Billie Holiday and Bessie Smith. Those records are timeless. He went driving around the country and found people like Count Basie."

Medina's dream of being the Charles Kuralt of A&R got a cold reception among Warner's top brass, to whom the idea of actually scouting the country for talent à la John Hammond seemed perhaps quaint and ludicrous, given the fact that thousands of demo tapes rolled in each week.

"I pursued the Winnebago idea for a while and Warner Bros. said they didn't want to do it. I've talked to the highest people at Time Warner. I wanted to call it the Warnerbago. I'd equip it with video and recording equipment and be able to set up anywhere. You could ask [Warner Bros. president] Lenny Waronker or [Warner Bros. chairman] Mo Ostin about this. The entertainment business has been missing a real big slice of Americana. It's up to us to get out of Burbank and find it. We should've figured out how to have little satellite companies all around the United States. By the time it gets to certain managers and certain producers, the music's already been fucked with, and somebody starts to tell you you're great, but you need to write a hit. What determined that used to be originality, but now what defines it is mathematics. Record ads.

"What I asked Lenny Waronker was 'How can we as a record company still give people a chance to be themselves?' Why are there no great R&B bands now? Where would they play? The chitlin circuit? You know how small that's gotten. We should pray for an expansion of the chitlin circuit. We're probably not going to find the great ones half as dressed up as John Hammond did. You know what I mean? They're going to be even rawer. Like I said, they're going to be at a church or a porch or some town hall somewhere or at the local talent show. And you're gonna sit through some of the worst moments you will have ever heard."

All around Medina's office were photos of great African-American musicians—reminders of a time when art and entertainment were largely synonymous. On the back wall was a giant picture of Charlie Parker with the singer Sweet Pea, taken at the time of the legendary saxophonist's seminal Dial sessions. Another wall had a photo of Jimi Hendrix, and another had a picture of Miles Davis.

"That's one of the only pictures of Miles smiling," Medina said, grinning. "Usually he's got a scowl."

There were other heroes, too, of a different order: a photo of Mahatma Gandhi and one of Albert Einstein. Underneath the latter was a quote: "Great spirits have always encountered violent opposition from mediocre minds."

"All this is for inspiration—integrity checks," Medina said, in a tone of voice that suggested it was all too easy to forget about art and genius when chasing hit records in Burbank.

"You've got to play it for the love of music and sing it because it *matters*. But the musicians we're seeing now are really good marketing guys. They can go into meetings and tell you how to promote their shit because they figured it all out. They're now all marketing people, calculating this or that. A lot of them are already signed, and they happen to be the people most respected."

I asked Medina what he thought of rap, the latest incarnation of African-American rhythm and poetry.

"Country and R&B are the reflections of two different people's souls. Country is doing OK, but black people's souls are being repressed. The only form it's coming out in is hip-hop, and that's become highly manipulated and highly calculated lately. Record companies are putting out a lot of really jive shit, so there's a total misrepresentation of us. There are so many people in the African-American culture right now who just feel completely misrepresented."

As Medina spoke, his voice got louder, more passionate. His feet came off the sofa and he leaned forward now.

"Take that film *CB4*," Medina said, referring to a just-released movie that was a send-up of the whole rap genre. "I just think it's making a parody a little too soon—as opposed to making fun of *something*. It's one thing to make fun of yourself in an artistic way, and it's another thing to dismiss something as a total joke. That's a fine line, between laughing *at* me and laughing *with* me."

The film had only a few minutes in which rap music was taken seriously. The rest of it treated rap as *This Is Spinal Tap* treated heavy metal: as a joke.

"How many films came along before *The Player* that made fun of Hollywood? Not many. You better be solidly entrenched before you start doing that stuff. Otherwise, it gives people an excuse to say, 'That wasn't *shit* anyway.' And people are lining up to say that about rap already."

Just then the Jungle Brothers arrived, with Peter Edge, the New York–based Warner Bros. A&R man who had signed the group. Pharoah Afrika Baby Bambaataa was wearing wild-colored shorts and a flowered shirt; Michael Small had jeans and long, flowing dreadlocks.

"Yo, where are we gonna eat?" Afrika said.

"You wanna go to the Roxbury? They got an interesting atmosphere," Medina said.

"What do they have there?" Michael asked, grinning.

"Liquor and pussy," Medina said, and everybody laughed.

"I could definitely go for a phat turkey burger," said Afrika.

Someone suggested barbecue and Medina shook his head and smiled. For the past few months he'd been religiously working out, running five miles a day, pumping iron, eating healthy foods, no grease, no hard liquor, losing thirty pounds. But talk of barbecue and soul food and wine was enough to make his mouth water and his will weaken.

"I'm on a healthy thing until someone says, 'Let's go drink some liquor and eat popcorn shrimp,' " Medina said.

"Roxbury is the place," said Steve, one of Medina's two assistants. "They've got a table waiting for you."

"Now you got me all excited," said Medina, as we headed for his black Bronco.

The Roxbury was full of models, actors and scenesters from the entertainment industry. There were beautiful young women in tight leather miniskirts or leggings, with velvet chokers around their necks, and guys decked out in jeans and blazers or biker outfits: a roomful of beautiful phonies. As we sat down to dinner, Medina ordered some bottles of the best chardonnay and platters of popcorn shrimp, which soon arrived steaming hot and plenty greasy.

When the subject of Prince came up—the shows were a few weeks away then—Medina immediately dove into the conversation. Over the last few years, the two had become closer.

Medina talked frequently to Prince and sometimes had long, draining conversations, reassuring the star when the critics didn't understand him or completely misinterpreted his music or image. Medina had tried to serve as some sort of editor occasionally, but Prince trusted almost nobody but himself.

Like so many geniuses, Prince could be his own worst enemy. Lenny Waronker, the president of Warner Bros. Records and an acclaimed producer, had once tried to give Prince some advice, but His Purpleness had reportedly sneered. "How can I take advice," he told Waronker, "from a guy who wears jeans and white socks to work?"

Maybe Waronker wasn't the one to be a mentor; maybe nobody could fill that role. But part of Prince's problem was that he'd isolated himself artistically.

"Do you want to edit people that have so much potential?" Medina asked. "Or do you want to start to look at people who have a body of work? Who's to say what we're supposed to do with that kind of person who has so much talent? Is he that insulated? Or is he that original? Are *we* that original? It ain't like the record industry is making a whole lot of great records. . . . The few times that Prince does listen—man, I got him writing up music for a Jim Brooks musical—a forty-million-dollar film. I don't know whether it's going to work or not. But I think he's written some shit that's like George Gershwin.

"Prince needs the slack. But he's got to get rid of that N.P.G. shit," said Afrika, who'd been listening the whole time even as he was checking out some fly chicks over at the next table. The N.P.G., or New Power Generation, was Prince's flashy new band. "I want to see Prince *without* the N.P.G."

"Prince is just trying too hard," said Edge, who grew up in Great Britain but lived in New York.

"I think this is the last time you'll see Prince with this band," Medina said. "Prince knows I don't like this band. He knows I don't like [rapper] Tony M. I love Rosie Gaines. Prince is most comfortable onstage. He doesn't like parties. . . . How many geniuses are we gonna sit around and talk about? How many people are on a genius level? Prince is one of those. I mean, look at Michael Jackson. He has to go on TV and spend more time talking about his cosmetic surgery and his father than about the music he is writing."

"It takes away from the whole art," said Afrika, "having to watch that Michael Jackson–Oprah shit."

"You ever seen Michael Jackson sit down at the piano and play something?" Medina asked.

"Michael can't play jack shit," said Afrika, finishing off his glass of wine, pouring a refill and checking out some almond-eyed beauties at the next table.

"I'm more concerned today that a guy like Prince has to worry about charts and the media instead of just making music," Medina said. "People think his shows make a whole lot of money, but they don't. You think with the shows at Radio City Music Hall and the Apollo next week—you think that he's making money? He's not. So who are we to edit him? Buy one record, and if you don't like it, it's OK. But be careful how you edit, because you don't know what you might miss."

"From a Gemini to a Gemini," Afrika said, "I'm saying, 'Prince, I'm just as *lost* as you. I *forgive* you for this video.'[4] Cause when I look at him, I'm thinking, 'Gemini, we will get *through* this. We will get *through* this. Because these are some very hard times for creative people. I pity him because I'm going through the same shit. But that N.P.G. shit is too fucking childish. And that rapper? He's a joke."

"I don't think Prince should ever do rap," Medina said. "I don't think he should ever be doing rap like he's got it on this record. I told him, 'You picked some whacked-ass rap mother-fucker who you done dressed in a silk outfit, all pomped up and pimp tipped.' But when I listened to the tracks he put up underneath them, I asked him, 'Why couldn't you write a song to that? You're an amazing lyricist and melodist. Are you getting lazy about this sort of thing? Are you trying to pander to these other art forms?' "

---

[4] Afrika is referring to the video for the song "My Name Is Prince."

"Prince is trying too hard," Edge said.

The waiter came by with dinner, and the conversation went on pause for a minute. Medina ate some fried chicken and popcorn shrimp. But Prince was still on his mind.

"Everyone else is picking from each other's brain. There's no originality. Everything they listen to is something somebody else did. They're just trying to kick ass. How many record company people you know who write anything? They're all basing their opinions on something they heard that somebody told them is really cool. And their opinion could be changed tomorrow by their girlfriend or their wife, or by their boyfriend. How many creative people do you ever really deal with? You have to ask yourself. On a given day, how many people are starting something visionary from beginning to end? Most people are surrounding the artists and trying to facilitate the process. In a way it's pathetic, because a lot of the artists become victims of the facilitators. I wish more artists could hang with more artists."

"Can't we make aesthetic judgments on Prince?" Edge asked. He and Medina were used to playing devil's advocate for each other.

"Does Prince put out too much stuff? Yeah. Could it be condensed? Maybe. But we're here to put that out, as far as I'm concerned. Because nobody knows what's going to work. And I don't know any artists who don't have periods they go through where people question what they do—the greatest painters, the greatest dancers, the greatest musicians. It's how they come out of it, like any indulgence. And if they're not indulgent, they're not artists. They're probably marketing people. Who knows what it's like to really be on top, to have been the number-one-box-office-gross, Elvis-type motherfucker?"

"Eighty-five percent of music today is working the machines," said Afrika. "And this nigger is going out with his *hands*. He's one of the few people left from the old school."

"Personally, I think it takes a lot of courage to walk around with that hairstyle and those clothes," Medina said.

"Especially if you ain't doing drugs," said Michael, and everyone howled.

"Most of the great ones who've reached Prince's age are already over," Medina said when the laughter died down. "Think about it: James Brown, George Clinton, Sly Stone. Hendrix was dead by this time. Little Richard and Robert Johnson."[5]

"And Michael Jackson is not really alive," said Michael. "They killed Michael Jackson a few years ago. Imagine if we find out Prince is a white boy in disguise."

In a way, Medina was a good match for Prince. Both were loners and both had a wide appreciation of everything from rock and Delta blues to soul and funk. A few weeks later, I went with Medina to see Prince, who was playing three sold-out shows at the Universal Amphitheatre.

"Prince *does* push everything to the edge, and I know how lonely that feels," Medina said a few minutes before the show started. "We had a five-hour meeting about that today, and Prince asked me, 'How can I compete with an industry now where everyone wants to copy each other? If there's no room left for originality, then what time am I living in?' He asked the right questions."

The concert kicked off with florid chords and a prissy woman news reporter's voice: "Prince, it's been a long time since you've done an interview. Where have you been the past five years?"

"I been at your mama's house," Prince's offstage voice said, and the audience convulsed in raucous, bawdy laughter. The concert, fashioned around a silly story involving an erotically repressed princess named Mayte, had gotten panned a few days earlier by a *Los Angeles Times* critic who seemed to judge all music by how political and socially conscious it was. Prince had written powerful political songs—"Sign 'O' the Times" had

---

[5] Actually, Medina wasn't quite accurate about James Brown and George Clinton. Even in their late thirties, they were making important music.

proven that. But he wasn't Woody Guthrie or Bob Dylan. Musically he was a spiritual descendant of James Brown, George Clinton, Jimi Hendrix and Sly Stone: a revolutionary who worked within a tradition even as he broke all the rules and pushed everything else to the edge. A lot of people raised on the formulaic bilge that black R&B had become didn't have the patience for him; others got turned off by Prince's weird persona and eccentricities.[6] But once you got past all that, the show was protoplasmically funky.

Medina hadn't signed Prince, but he had helped steer the singer back to the top of the charts. *Diamonds and Pearls*, a slick R&B album that had spawned a big hit ("Cream"), had positioned Prince as a mainstream, silky-voiced heartthrob. But on his latest CD Prince was mostly back to his hard-funk roots, making music that was both bold and intelligent. Not that he didn't make bizarre judgments that drove Medina crazy—like the inclusion of "My Name Is Prince," a silly rap song. With slick, lame rapping, the song proved that Prince, on some fundamental level, didn't understand the basic street attitude of hip-hop culture.

"Even though *Diamonds and Pearls* was a hit, I told him, 'Prince, I can't believe you ain't funky,'" Medina said, shaking his head. "On this record, we got into some huge fights. He wanted 'My Name Is Prince' on the album and I wanted it off. He wanted it as a first single, but I knew this record wasn't finished yet. 'It's not time yet,' I told him. 'Take some time. Take some *time*, man.' But who am I to sit there and tell this artist what to do? Prince thinks that whatever he writes is something being sent through him, and that as he plays he needs to put it out—because he's done *now*. Whoever gets this will get this and receive it in the way *he* wanted, and whoever doesn't, *won't*. Prince told me, 'I'm not trying to sell records like Michael

---

[6] Critics loved to ridicule Prince's name change to ♀, a symbol combining male and female. But owning up to one's androgynous nature could be seen as a daring move in a Western world where men repressed the feminine aspects of their psyches.

Jackson. Look what selling records has done to Michael Jackson. I can still *play*. But Michael can't play *nothin'* I can. Not as *good* as I can. *Ever, ever, ever*.' Maybe that's his ego talking, but I've seen Prince play and I know it's also reality. By your standards or mine. Prince will get back to the place where he figures out what he needs to do. Prince told me, 'This music is something I created and I need to get it out there, because as soon as I get it out I got something *else* to do.' You need to indulge those artists."

Medina listened carefully to the next few songs, which included "7," one of Prince's best new compositions, and some jungle funk that saw the Minneapolis star working the audience like a backyard barbecue. Medina grinned and leaned into my ear.

"That's what I *love* about him. Most pop stars aspire to play stadiums; Prince aspires to play clubs. Contact, you know? At Radio City Music Hall he played three nights in a row and he had them in his hands. He took New York by storm. Every night after he did Radio City Music Hall he went to some other club and played for hours. One night, he went to the USA club and played 'til four thirty in the morning. Another night I hooked up with him and Lenny Kravitz and he took Lenny on stage with him at the Apollo. Lenny laid in the back—he was smart. He was blown away."

With each successive song, Prince seemed to be loosening up. Midway through "Get Satisfied," a tune he'd written for George Clinton, Prince led the crowd in a call-and-response sequence. I noticed Medina boogying hard, hands jabbed in the air, rocking to what had become a butt-shaking meltdown. "C'mon, I can't hear you!" Prince yelled as the New Power Generation nailed down a slow-grinding groove and the crowd chanted, "Let's get satisfied!"

"See, what Prince does is weave ideas of tunes that he's working on for other artists into his show," Medina said after the song shuddered to a stop. "It's an interesting way to make audiences identify with it before they've even heard it. Prince doesn't separate music. The whole thing is his universe: what he's working on today, what he's working on in the studio, what he's doing for other artists."

At the intermission, Medina handed me a backstage pass and took off without a word, moving like a shark through water. Already a huge crowd had gathered and fans were pushing their way toward two bouncers who guarded the gates into a buzzing hive of Hollywood scenesters. There were music executives and film producers, models and actors. But no one was more famous than Magic Johnson, who was standing in the center, towering above everyone, surrounded by bodyguards. Medina saw him, but was busy for the moment talking to the president of Paisley Park Records, Prince's label. It was only later, when Johnson had had his fill of signing autographs, that Medina went up to him and said a few words in private.

"I wrote an episode for him on *The Fresh Prince*," Medina said right afterward, referring to the TV show based on his own life story. "That's what we were talking about."

At thirty-five, Benny Medina was one of the most powerful blacks in entertainment, but after eight years at Warner Bros. he had yet to deliver on his promise. Some of the artists he'd signed—Tevin Campbell, Karyn White, Club Nouveau and Naughty by Nature—had had big records. And it was Medina who had set up the deal that linked the Cold Chillin' rap label, with Big Daddy Kane, Biz Markie and others, to Warner Bros. But he hadn't found any artists who were visionaries.

In fact, for all his talk about following in John Hammond's footsteps, most of Medina's signings played mainstream R&B and hip-hop, much of it junk. He might rhapsodize about discovering the next Billie Holiday or Robert Johnson, but his signings showed no evidence that he spent much time looking for raw genius in the various cultures of the African diaspora. What's more, Medina had come off a big slump.

"Luckily I work for a label that understands you go through cycles and doesn't put pressure on you to always deliver hits,"

Medina said—though just how long Warner Bros., a label that lately had trouble breaking *any* new band, would tolerate slumps was anyone's guess.

Medina's mentor had been Berry Gordy, the founder of Motown Records and one of the grand pooh-bahs of black entertainment royalty. In high school Medina and Gordy's son Kerry had sung in a group called Apollo, which was signed to Motown. The legendary Motown mogul immediately took a shine to Medina.[7]

"I always became the kid in the house. I was Berry's tennis buddy in the morning and chief bottle washer/flunky out here. This was atop the palatial Berry Gordy mansion in Bel Air. It was like being in the film *The Last Emperor.* I wished more people could've sat around with that guy. Berry was amazing. I'd see him sit around talking to Marvin Gaye about what he was writing. Berry was very playful, very childlike, but he was tough. He inevitably had a standard he wanted to uphold. That household was where I learned A&R. Berry knew what to save, what to eliminate, how to cast a song, how to get writers motivated. You were either applauded for your brilliance or insulted for your lack of genius."

Though Motown's glory days were behind, Berry's Bel Air mansion was still abuzz with famous musicians and actors. Diana Ross might float in in the morning and the Four Tops or the Temptations might drop by Gordy's mansion later on in the afternoon. At the parties you could talk to Sidney Poitier, Harry Belafonte and Sammy Davis, Jr.

"That's where I got to see black royalty. Everyone was family and Detroit was still in the air at Bel Air. We'd be at parties, doing the slide, eating soul food. Everyone who came there, even if it was Hugh Hefner, knew they were in *Gordy's* house."

Realizing that he wasn't in the same league with his idols, Medina opted to be a staff writer and producer—a job that had

---

[7] For a while Medina stayed at Gordy's mansion.

him assigned to work with some of the most gifted R&B artists in history.

"I got to produce Smokey Robinson—a lousy, lousy album. I wrote one of the songs, too—and that must've been a bad day for Smokey. Seeing soul on that level was amazing. I said to myself, 'Damn! I ain't ever been around this many black folks who have money.' They had a different food, a different style of dress, different everything."

After eight years at Motown, where he rose to become head of A&R, Medina jumped to Warner Bros. in 1985, where Mo Ostin saw potential—enough to give Medina one of the most complicated and impressive deals offered to any young executive who wasn't a label head. Aside from becoming a vice-president and head of A&R for all of Warner Bros.' black acts, a roster of talent that ranged from Prince to Quincy Jones, Medina was promised he could run his own Warner-owned label in the future. Meanwhile, together with producer Jeff Pollack, a longtime friend, Medina got a three-year deal that allowed him to produce films. What made the arrangement so unusual was that Medina was allowed to spend 25 percent of his time doing *anything* he wanted—as long as it wasn't competitive with Warner Bros. He could produce a TV show for, say, Fox and a film for Paramount. *Above the Rim*, an urban basketball film based on a story Medina came up with, was going to be his venture into films. But Medina had other scripts in development.

"His deal is unheard of," said Ken Hertz, the entertainment lawyer who negotiated the contract for him. "But the reason is Benny wanted it all. He forced the people around him to jump higher and swim faster and run harder. It didn't matter how good his deal was, he was never going to be happy with it. When Mo finally caved on the money and said to me, 'Is this gonna make him happy?' I said, 'Mo, you'll never make Benny feel overpaid.' Benny believes in his heart of hearts that no one is as good as him and he can do it better."

From Medina's standpoint, though, he wasn't half as

wealthy as his white counterparts who frequently did nothing to merit the deals they got. Medina might pull down a seven-figure salary and have a house with a pool in the Hollywood Hills, but the record business was still mostly run by whites—most of them Jews—who weren't willingly giving up much power.

"I don't think the Jews came over as the great oppressors. They tried to create a community for themselves. Have they given other people a break? No. They've kept what they've gotten very, very isolated, within their community. And the Jew does remain, in the entertainment business, the great oppressor—especially in terms of more opportunity. Has the Jewish brother earned it? I say he *has* earned it. But has he been giving it? I say no. Do we ever get power? Maybe when you get to be Quincy Jones. But there's a whole lot of pimping going on there.

"There is a possibility to build a company bigger than Warner Bros. We can have dreams like that. We can't let the fact that the Man has most of it right now stop us. And it's a *race* thing. Why does Allen Kovac have a label?[8] Why do [Rod Stewart's] managers, Arnold Stiefel and Randy Phillips, have labels? They're managers. Their claim to fame is having dinner with people. They haven't done anything."

I asked Medina if he had any problems with the divisive and incendiary racial teachings being spouted by many Afrocentric rap groups—beliefs that portrayed white people as blue-eyed devils and monsters.

"The rappers ain't screaming about shit that isn't *true*. You've got to *take* power. The Jews ain't gonna *give* it to you, but the brothers ain't necessarily gonna give it to you either. And the WASPs ain't gonna give it to you and the Japanese man ain't gonna give it to you. Nobody's giving up *shit* anymore. No one's charitable. Where are the Indians? At least they

---

[8] Medina is referring to Kovac's label, Impact Records. Kovac's company manages Meat Loaf, Richard Marx, Duran Duran and other groups.

have casinos, where they've created billion-dollar businesses because people like to gamble.

"I happen to believe that the white man is *really* evil—*inherently* evil. I think he's proven that. I think he's been horrible to his white women and horrible to his black brother. And that leaves everyone else in real lousy third or fourth positions. I'm not into the 'Five Percenter' theory[9] or being racially isolated. But I do speculate on what it would be like being in a place where I didn't have to question what I was proud of as far as heritage, where there would be some sense of community. What was done to rob us—Indians and African-Americans—of community was incredible. And if I sound crazy when I say that the white man is the enemy, it's only because I have not seen the white man treating the white man well. And he certainly doesn't treat his *woman* well. For a long time, white women might as well have been *niggers*—the rights that they had. That alone shows me that guy stands for green—that he's a capitalist pig, bent on dominating others. I just say, 'Do me a favor and stop *lying*. Admit you're a fucking *pig* and I'll know how to deal with you.' "

Even before he was a music power broker, Medina had done stints acting. He'd been in TV commercials, had sung on the Dinah Shore show (with his group Apollo) and had done bit parts in films.

"I had the great fortune of playing the stable boy in *Black Beauty*—one of the great ethnic parts," Medina said mockingly, sitting in his living room late one evening. Located above the Chateau Marmont hotel, the house had a big view of the city. "And I was in *The Greatest*. And I did walk-ons on the Bob Newhart and Mary Tyler Moore shows."

But the show Medina was known for was the one he conceived and pitched, with the help of Quincy Jones, to NBC

---

[9] A radical offshoot of the Nation of Islam, the Five Percenters are separatists who hold that white people are inherently evil—devils who aeons ago intentionally corrupted the black race through miscegenation.

entertainment chief Brandon Tartikoff. Supposedly, it took Medina and Jones just eight minutes to convince Tartikoff that Medina's story of a streetwise kid who moves in with his rich cousins in Bel Air would be a hit sitcom. Not that the show, produced by Medina (with Jones as executive producer), was completely true to life. In reality, the teenage Medina moved in with a wealthy white, not a black, family: Jack Elliott, a TV composer/musician/conductor; his wife, Bobbi; and their children. It was at St. Elmo Village that Medina ran into the Elliotts.

"I latched onto his son. [Jack] never took a shine to me—to this day—but his wife Bobbi did. I feel like I just intruded on their lives, if you want to know the truth. I literally forced myself on them. I told them, 'I have to get away from my uncle.'"

At the time, Medina was still hanging out with his crew from South Central L.A., dealing weed and Red Devils. But that world, he knew, would only lead to trouble and possibly an early grave. For a while, Medina rode his bike every day from St. Elmo Village to Beverly Hills High School. He worked at a florist's shop near Venice and La Brea to make money. He lived in different worlds—one black and poor, the other wealthy and white. And since his fast friends weren't welcome at the village, that was yet another world. Meanwhile, Medina tried to avoid Rozzell's beatings while living up to one of his frequent sayings: "Be the best you can be."

"I was trying to be in drama, trying to be in football, trying to be in high-school politics. I had to keep up my grades and I did. I had to get out of there, because one more ass-kicking and I didn't know what I was going to do."

Of course, Rozzell tells his own version of why Medina left St. Elmo behind, never to come back.

"I remember Benny came to me when he wasn't getting the *food* he needed at Mount Vernon Junior High School," Rozzell told me when I asked him about Benny's time with the Elliott family. By *food* he meant mental stimulation. "I thought Benny was in trouble. But when I walked in the school, I saw what he meant. The atmosphere wasn't *conducive* to learning. Well, Benny had met Jack Elliott and his sons and he wanted to go to Beverly High School. So I took him out there. They rejected me because I didn't have any gas bills to prove I lived there. So I took him from there to Jack Elliott's house. And Jack took us to the school.

"Now, at Beverly High, Benny wanted to stay there. I told him, 'You can't drive a Mercedes, but you'll be messing with people that do have 'em. You're gonna have to discipline yourself.' That's where he and I clashed. He wanted to stay out 'til three or four A.M. in the morning, and I said he had to get back by two A.M. I told Benny, 'If you ain't in their pants by two A.M.'—meaning girls—'you ain't gonna get it.' So I had to *tell* him that. I gave him play, but I told him he had responsibilities, too. I *had* to be a tough disciplinarian. I wouldn't *be* here if I hadn't. I had to be that way with myself in order to maintain this order."

One day, when he was sixteen, Medina made a fateful decision.

"I was riding my bike from Jack and Bobbi's house, and I just said, 'I'm not going back.' It was morning, and I had my book bag on. I knew it. If I had to sleep in a Volkswagen, which I did for a year with Berry Gordy's son, I wasn't going back. I was tired of fighting Rozzell. I thought I might kill him if I stayed. And I didn't like how he was treating anybody.

"Well, that day I went to Jack and Bobbi and I said I needed to live with them. But Jack didn't want me to live with them. So for a while I was half in his garage, half at friends' houses. I never lived in [the Elliotts'] *house*—even when I moved in I fixed up their *garage*. I didn't even want to be in the house. Besides, he had three kids already. The Elliotts never knew what was happening to me. When I finally sat down and told [Bobbi] how life was with Rozzell, she couldn't believe it, because she always thought he was so great. But I never showed them my scars. I just told them I would work hard, keep up my grades and keep out of their way. There were not many believers. But I forced myself on people who had doubts."

The transition from a black ghetto high school to a white, superaffluent high school was a shock that no episode of *The Fresh Prince* could ever capture. Medina can still remember the first day he entered Beverly Hills High School.

"The class I walked into that day was cinema arts, nine A.M. in the morning. They give you your own camera, film, you watch Fellini. I didn't even know who Fellini was, but this was interesting. And they gave me an eight-millimeter camera with film? C'mon. Even Beverly High doesn't have that program anymore, which shows how times have changed economically for all schools. None of this stuff was available at the high school I'd just left—Mount Vernon Junior High School. But at Beverly they had a media-arts center. The first video that I ever made—and one of the first videos that Motown added—was a video I made at that high school."

Once he got registered at Beverly Hills High School and began living with the Elliotts, Medina's life forever changed. Suddenly he was thrust into widening circles of power, exposed to another level of culture—wealthy, white Jewish culture swirling around the epicenter of Hollywood's entertainment empire.

"I had grits and gravy and matzo balls and kreplach—you know what I'm saying? And I loved that. I went through high school wearing a *chai* around my neck and a Star of David."

What would've happened if the Elliotts hadn't taken him in—if he'd stayed at St. Elmo? No one can say. But the crew he hung with outside that compound all went on to lives of crime.

"I'll tell you straight up, all of my other friends became full-time dealers and pimps. The last time I saw my boy Sonny, he looked a lot richer than I was, only he didn't have any credit cards. He had a ranch somewhere, but he felt that at any moment he was going to be busted or shot dead. And you want to know what he kept asking me? 'What did you *do*? How did *you* get out?' And I remembered the day I left. I was walking home with Sonny and I told him, 'I think I'm gonna have to figure out something else to do, someplace else to go.' And that's still the way I am. As soon as I get tired of a place—a company, a person, a bar—I'll leave. I'll just say, 'Could you pull over?'

Because then I'm no good to anybody, you know? And I don't like to get angry."

"Whatever Benny tells you, for him to have survived and be doing what he is doing is amazing," said Roderick Sykes. "Rozzell was a control freak—he had to have his way. And for Benny to survive his power trip and get out of the community and do what he did took a strong will. But even as a little kid, Benny was always confident. He had a clear vision. He was always organizing things, and kids looked up to him."

"When he was five or six years old, Benny used to throw change away, and we'd all be scrappin' and scavenging for it," Bonita Medina recalled. "And Benny used to say, 'When I grow up I'm going to be a millionaire.' That's all he ever talked about. And I told him, 'That's the reason you were successful— because you started at a young age. Your determination to get out of the situation kept you going'."

When their mother died from cancer she went quickly. Benny Medina still remembers her: a beautiful woman who infused him with a sense of having some special destiny.

"My mother once told me that there's something I was meant to do. She saw something special in me. And I have to believe that she saw that in my brothers and sisters too. I saw that in them." But if you ask him about his father, who now lives in Dallas, he tenses immediately.

"He was gone, on the road. When he came back to the house it was always to test it, flex his muscle. He was a hardcore womanizer. He played with Miles and other famous cats. He was a club musician. Supposedly he was really smooth and good-looking."

Over the years, his father has called him from time to time, trying to make contact. But Medina's never called him back. He's never wanted to hear the apologies and the explanations.

"My dad didn't even get her a tombstone. She's buried somewhere in Plano, Texas. I haven't seen him since my mom died," Medina said, his eyes suddenly darkening. "Times he's called me I know I didn't want to talk. He did what he wanted to. I just hope that he's happy, because he made a choice. It wasn't *my* choice. He had five kids and some beautiful people he should have hung around with. But I'm not angry. I don't have enough emotional connection to be angry."

Of course, the icy chill in his voice said that he *was* enraged—beyond words. Medina had banished his father, written him off, but in punishing him, he'd forever bound himself to anger. And that anger, when he didn't stuff it down, ate away at his soul.

Before his brother Gary died, Medina drank heavily, got high and lived the fast life, disorganized and unpredictable. But the day his brother was buried, Medina started working out. He hired a personal trainer, ran every day and transformed his body into lean muscle and sinew. It was as if the fierce discipline and weight training might restore some sense of stability in a life that never had any. But no amount of discipline could make Medina feel close to his family.

"I'm not close to anybody. I'm probably one of the biggest loners you'll ever meet," he said one night when I met him down at the West Side gym where he worked out. "I don't think I'm the most friendly person anyway. A lot of people don't think I'm that friendly. All I can remember being concerned about when I was young was my career. I was trying to get out of the situation I was in, which was a different home every week. I never thought of anything as being stable."

"I feel really sorry for Benny, because he separated himself so much from things that he actually separated himself from his brothers and sisters," Bonita Medina said. "Regardless of what happened, we always had each other. But I understand, because that was true of myself. I told him that's the reason we survived. We didn't dwell on the negative. We focused on a better way. Whereas with some of my other brothers and sisters, they couldn't come out from under it."

"Benny wants to be loved, and desperately loved. He says he's a loner, but meanwhile he can't be away from people," said

Ken Hertz. "If he goes to a party, he has to be in the biggest limousine. Benny goes through times where he looks great, feels great, but then he gets to a place where he's not eating well, puts on weight, gets into a funk, gets depressed. And the reason is he sees how far he can push it. He flirts with disaster."

If life at St. Elmo Village wasn't enough to drive a wedge between the brothers and sisters, Medina's success was. He kept in touch with Bonita over the years and made some effort to be there for his brothers, but he felt he was either resented or rejected.

"My younger brother Michael asked me for some money a while back and I loaned him some," Medina recalled. "He said he was going to pay it. And months later I called him and said, 'What's up? You going to pay me this money? You need some more time?' And he started asking me who the fuck I thought I was. I just wanted to know if he needed more *time*. I was trying to see, out of this really haphazard life that we had, if we couldn't establish some consistency ourselves. The terrible thing is that every one of my brothers and sisters is smarter than me. I was motivated by *their* intelligence and *their* drive.

"They vent a lot of hostility at me—particularly when I try to help. They either don't want it or take the help and then admonish me for giving it. I can't win. If I do nothing I'm a jerk, and if I do something I'm the jerk who did something. It would be up to me to get close."

Yet that would be scary. Though the door back to his family is open day and night—every one of Medina's relatives told me that—to go through that doorway would be to enter the deep waters of grief. For only by grieving—and then forgiving—could he let go of the rage and heal the wounds.

"I would like to get close to Benny—I really would," Erma Sykes told me one winter night. "He's got a lot going on inside that he has to release, and the only way he's going to do it is to get close to his family. No matter how far you go in life, you know that someone brought you here. You didn't enter this life yourself. . . . Benny has a loving family. Benny has nieces and nephews that would like to be part of his life also. Because

Benny loves kids. But he won't let them in. He hangs on to those old feelings. And you have to let that go. If you don't, you'll be this way for the rest of your life. For what? And you'll pass it on to your kids."

One night, when we were up at his house, Medina told me a story about the late Warner Communications chairman, Steve Ross, whom he counts as a hero.

"Did you ever hear of an organization called the Hundred Black Men? Well, it's huge now. It started in the 1800s. It's a group of prominent businessmen who want to do more for the community. Well, Steve took me with him to New York to give a talk to them. He and Mayor Dinkins were being honored and for some reason Steve asked me to be with him.

"Well, Steve ran around making sure I got to meet the mayor and Jesse Jackson. And he had this story he told about why he had accomplished what he had accomplished. It was a story about this group of people that he felt you should always want to be a part of. He started with the dreamer, a story his father had told him, about a guy who wakes up and dreams all day. And then he talked about the worker, who wakes up, gets dressed and works all day. Those are two groups. But Steve said, 'What you want to be is a dreamer who dreams for a little bit and then gets out there and makes it work. Because if you can ever get in *that* club, you'll find there's very few members there.' I'm paraphrasing, but what he was trying to say was that you want to be in that club because there's very little competition."

Ross eventually got Medina an introduction to Jesse Jackson. There's a photograph in Medina's Burbank office of Steve Ross introducing him to Jackson. It hangs between photos of Martin Luther King and Malcolm X.

"Steve went to great pains to find Jesse and bring him over to me. But—and I'll never forget this—when I shook Jesse's hand he never looked me in the eye. It was completely consistent with my feelings about him, because Jesse Jackson was always too busy looking somewhere else to even recognize an opportunity right in front of his face."

The meeting confirmed what Medina has felt all along: that there had been a falloff in black leadership after the death of Martin Luther King, Jr., and Malcolm X, and no black leaders have come along to fill that void.

"I remember watching the TV when Martin Luther King died. I was never so devastated in my life. I was ten years old and I couldn't believe it. First JFK. Then Martin. There was no reason for it. Didn't we reconcile this? One of my teachers, Mrs. Bernard, had reinforced the Dream in my mind. She'd made it real to me. I definitely think I was a product of that Dream theory."

When I asked who had impressed him the most in his life, it took him only a moment to answer: Maya Angelou, the great black poet. "Because of how she makes me feel and what she's had to say and where she comes from. I've read all of her books. She did a reading the night I met her. And *I Know Why the Caged Bird Sings* was one of the great books. Her depiction of blackness—of how consistently proud she is of being black, from the gesture to the smell, from the walk to the touch—was extraordinary. She's not let any of it go. If there is a queen of African-American culture it would have to be Maya Angelou. She knows the black person, she knows herself and she knows me. She's articulate and intelligent and speaks five languages. She can wine and dine with presidents and kings and still hang with regular people."

I asked Medina about the volunteer work he did with violent youths at McLaren Hall each Saturday. But Medina's eyes darkened.

"I'm trying to give something back, but they *scare* me. I go there and I'm looking in the eyes of teenaged *killers*. Their anger is specifically focused and nobody gives a *fuck* about them. They know that for sure. You try doing stuff, but you have to have the time, and I don't have enough time. I still think it's more important to make a living, even though it's

Jory Farr

probably not, because what's a living if we're all going down a rat hole? I'm both idealist and victim.

"The ones who are pathetic are the ones who can't enjoy. I don't understand dying with a lot of money. Why does Mr. Wal-Mart want to die with three billion dollars? Couldn't he have helped some more kids? How many gates you gonna build? I'm just the opposite.

"I wanted to do that until I realized how much time and energy that takes and how much of your soul it robs. The few geniuses I've been around have a different level of integrity. I'm drawn to the people who create the substance of what all of these corporations are. I love the people who wrote the book, wrote the song, know the chord changes. And I'm sorry that doesn't seem to have as much of a place as it used to."

Index

Index

Index